The Spirit-Controlled Life

by
Bob Yandian

BOB YANDIAN
MINISTRIES

bobyandian.com

THE SPIRIT-CONTROLLED LIFE

To contact the author:
Bob Yandian Ministries
9610 S. Garnett Rd.
Broken Arrow, OK 74012
phone: 1.800.284.0595 •
e-mail: bym@gracetulsa.com
web site: www.bobyandian.com

ISBN: 0-885600-22-4
Printed in the United States of America
© 1985 by Bob Yandian

Library of Congress Cataloging-in-Publication Data

Yandian, Bob.
   The Spirit-controlled life / by Bob Yandian.
      p. cm.
   ISBN 0-885600-22-4 (pbk.)
   1. Bible. N.T. Galatians—Commentaries. I. Title.
   BS2685.53 .Y36 2002
   227'.4077—dc21   2002005019

Contents

Introduction

Galatians is an exciting book. In it, the apostle Paul laid down a foundation that every Christian needs to guard against. It's the most subtle trap believers can fall into, the trap of legalism.

Now when legalism is mentioned, most Christians automatically think of the Ten Commandments or the Mosaic Law. But legalism involves much more than these two obvious examples. It is much subtler than that, much less evident and therefore much more dangerous.

To the Jews of Paul's day, legalism was primarily an overemphasis on the observance of Jewish Law that blinded their eyes to the Gospel of salvation by grace. To the modern-day Christian, legalism is more an attitude than an act, which makes it all the more difficult to detect and avoid. We may not even be aware that we are guilty of it. Because it is so insidious, we have unsuspectingly allowed this attitude to creep into virtually every facet of our daily Christian lives. In this study we will be defining legalism and examining its effect upon us as Christians. We will see how it has come to exert an influence upon everything in our church life from water baptism to personal witnessing. We will consider the dangers of legalism and discuss ways to overcome this most subtle of Satan's attack upon the church of Jesus Christ.

In essence, the book of Galatians is a declaration of faith and faith alone. Faith for salvation and faith for spirituality. This faith is not based on any effort or action or observance on our part, but is founded solely and entirely upon the grace of God. In fact, Galatians could be called the Manifesto of Grace.

Before we actually begin our study of this powerful book, let's review a moment. Exactly who were the Galatians to whom Paul addressed this letter? If you are familiar with New Testament history, you will remember that Galatia was an area northwest of Israel that had been settled by the Gauls in the third century and that became a Roman province in 25 B.C., some years before Paul began his missionary journeys to the region. The Galatians were descendants of barbaric tribes that had infiltrated the Roman Empire. These tribes were all branches of the Celts who later settled Ireland, Scotland, and Wales. The Galatians are distant cousins of the modern-day Irish.

In his opening salutation, Paul directed his remarks to the churches of Galatia. Notice, this word is plural. Galatians is the only one of Paul's epistles directed to more than one church. Ephesians was written to the church in Ephesus. Philippians was addressed to the church in Philippi. However, Galatians was sent to the churches of Galatia, because Galatia is not a city, but a province. There were four major cities in the province of Galatia: Antioch, Iconium, Derbe, and Lystra. The city of Lystra should be familiar to us because that's where, on his first missionary journey, Paul was nearly stoned to death. But God restored him, and he was able to go back into the city to preach to the people. (You can read about this event in Acts 14.)

In the book of Galatians we will be considering several basic themes: the Abrahamic covenant, the blessing of Abraham, redemption from the curse of the Law, the fruit of the Spirit versus works of the flesh, and several others. As we study, we will be referring back to the Old Testament where we will learn about Abraham, Sarah, Hagar, Isaac, and Ishmael. From there we will go to the New Testament to follow Paul's missionary journey to

Galatia. We will talk about Paul's thorn in the flesh and consider what it might have been. We will see how his message was always the same: faith for salvation, faith for spirituality. We will see how, because of his message, everywhere he went Paul was hounded and harassed by the legalistic Judaizers with their insistence that organized religion was the only means to salvation. Through all this, our attention will be fixed upon one central truth: the grace of God poured out at Calvary, freeing us from all self-striving so we may live truly Spirit-filled, fruitful lives of freedom and joy.

In chapter 1 of Galatians, we will read Paul's testimony of his call to the ministry. We will see how he stressed that it was the Lord Himself who called, commissioned, and ordained him to carry the Good News of salvation by grace to the Gentiles. We will see that Paul's knowledge of this truth came not from man or from men, but directly from God through personal revelation.

Later on, in chapter 2 of Galatians, we will see how Paul met some of his enemies among the religious people of his day and how he dealt with them, utterly defeating them with the message of faith. But we will also see how, although they were afraid to oppose him face-to-face, these enemies of the Gospel would work against what Paul was doing by sneaking in behind him to undermine what he had begun in the establishment of new churches. They would plant seeds of doubt in Paul's followers, insinuating that he was not a true apostle of the Lord Jesus Christ, casting aspersions upon his character and his message, laying heavy legalistic burdens upon the new believers, upon those who were not even Jews and thus never subject to Jewish Law.

Also in chapter 2 Paul recounted two stories: the first story will be that of the Jerusalem incident in which he gave us an example of an attempt to receive salvation by works; the second story is that of the Antioch incident, which illustrates the false concept of spirituality by works. The end of the chapter deals with his famous confrontation before the whole church at Antioch in which he openly rebuked Peter for becoming involved in legalism.

Then in chapter 3, we will see how Paul used these two incidents to set up the Galatians for the rebuke he levels against them for falling into legalism because of their lack of understanding of grace.

In chapter 4 Paul took the example of Abraham and his offspring to illustrate this faith principle, which he further developed in chapter 5 using Abraham's two wives and sons to contrast works of the flesh with the fruit of the Spirit.

Finally, in chapter 6 we will see how Paul concluded his remarks by examining the question of how a person can become spiritual again after having been carnally minded for so long.

In its overall outline, the book of Galatians is parallel with the book of Ephesians. Both address the subject of grace versus legalism. But where Ephesians emphasizes the positive side, Galatians stresses the negative aspect of this conflict, not that the book itself is negative. However, in Ephesians Paul laid more emphasis on how wonderful it is to understand grace, whereas in Galatians he points out the stupidity of falling for legalism.

As we approach this book, we must remember that Paul learned through written letters what had been happening in the churches in Galatia during his absence following his first missionary journey there. He was so disturbed about these events he was moved to write this letter. Note that Paul was not coming to Galatia in person to straighten things out. He was simply writing to these churches to confront them with their foolishness in turning back to "dead works" after having once received the glorious Gospel of grace. In our study we will see that this is not a sweet letter. Paul was obviously angry with these people and made no attempt to hide his anger. We get the distinct impression that he must have been pounding on the table as he wrote these words of rebuke. He did not mince words with the Galatians whom he referred to as "foolish." (A more accurate term would be "stupid"! We will examine some translations other than the King James Version to show that this was indeed the tone of Paul's message to these people.)

We will see that the primary problem was the Galatians, who had entered their spiritual walk by faith, were now attempting to complete that walk by adhering to Jewish Law. This happened because they had begun to listen to the legalistic Judaizers, many of whom were truly born again, but yet insisted that compliance with the strict codes of Judaism applied equally to Gentile Christians as well as to Jews. The Galatians who had embraced the message of Christ were now trying to combine the message of grace with the observance of Jewish Law. In essence, they were trying to straddle the fence between legalism and grace, to live by the precepts of the New Testament while adhering to the rules and regulations of the Old. Paul made it abundantly clear that such a walk is not only impossible, it is a denial of the atonement and an abomination in the sight of God.

The Galatians simply did not have a proper understanding of the Old and New Testaments. They did not realize that the old covenant was not abolished, but rather that it was fulfilled by the birth, death, and resurrection of the Messiah. The old covenant is still to be studied and taught, but it is not to be observed. The Old Testament merely points to the coming of the Lord Jesus Christ who perfectly and completely fulfilled all the righteous demands of the Law for all those who will accept that fulfillment by faith. Once Christ made the supreme sacrifice for sin, no other sacrifice is necessary.

Old things passed away; all things became new. The shadow gave way to the reality.

This led to questions like circumcision, which is one of the major topics of the book of Galatians because it represents the whole gamut of rules and regulations embodied in the old covenant. In this book Paul stressed to the Galatians that while circumcision is fine for health reasons, it no longer has any spiritual value.

This letter was delivered to Galatia where it was to be passed around among the four churches in Antioch, Iconium, Derbe, and Lystra. Let's begin our study of this, the most scathing accusation ever leveled against religion, allowing it to set us free from the law of sin and death, that we may discover in it the fullness of life in the Spirit.

1
Apostleship
Galatians 1:1

Paul, an Apostle

Galatians 1:1

Paul, an apostle, (not of men, neither by man, but by Jesus Christ, and God the Father, who raised him from the dead).

"Paul." In this opening verse Paul immediately identifies himself as the author of this book. The word *Paul* in Greek is *Paulus*, meaning "little." This seems to be descriptive of the man because tradition has it that Paul was not a man of great physical stature. He was short. In the natural realm, Paul considered himself small. But we know that if a person is small in his own eyes, God considers him great in the spiritual realm.

So many Christians today are boasting of how they are the righteousness of God in Christ Jesus, which is scripturally true, but it is also nothing to get puffed up in pride about. Unless a person realizes he is nothing in the natural realm, he will be nothing in the spiritual realm either. God looks upon the heart, and no heart is great that boasts of its greatness. It is the inner man that is important, not the exterior man. I like the expression,

"I'm bigger on the inside than I am on the outside." That's true. Since Jesus lives inside us, we believers are bigger within than without. Even when this outer shell has crumbled into dust, the inner man will keep on living with the Lord Jesus forever and ever.

"An apostle." Here Paul made his strongest claim to his calling, noting that he was an apostle "not of men" (plural), "neither by man" (singular), "but by Jesus Christ, and God the Father, who raised him from the dead."

Paul was actually saying: "I am an apostle. No group of men chose me, and no individual man chose me: I was ordained to this position by Jesus Christ and by God the Father." Paul stressed two negative aspects of his calling, and one positive aspect of it. He was not appointed by men, not by a man, but by the Lord Himself.

This raises the question: What is an apostle? The English word *apostle* is actually a transliteration of the Greek word *apostolos*, just as the English word *baptize* is a transliteration of the Greek word *baptizo*, meaning *to immerse or dip in water*. Since we had no word in English for this concept, the original translators simply adopted the Greek word into English. So it was with apostle. Since English had no real equivalent of the word *apostolos*, the translators transliterated it almost letter for letter into our language.

What does the word *apostle* actually mean? Strong defines it as "a delegate; spec. an ambassador of the Gospel; officially a commissioner of Christ ['apostle'] (with miraculous powers): apostle, messenger, he that is sent."[1]

Ephesians 4:11 lists the office of apostle as one of the five-fold ministry gifts given to the church by the Lord Jesus Christ and God the Father. To understand this office more fully, seven different aspects of the word *apostle* will be considered.

Seven Points about Apostleship

1. Apostleship was the First Office Placed into the Church of Jesus Christ.

As we have seen, the Greek word *apostolos* means *"a sent one."* If we trace the word back even further into history, we learn it came from the ancient Phoenician language in which it referred to the highest ranking officer in the Phoenician navy (the equivalent of our English word *admiral*). Does this have any significance for us today? Although the apostle does not outrank other ministers on a scale of authority, rank does have significance in the modern church. In 1 Corinthians 12:28 Paul writes: "And God hath set some in the church, first apostles, secondarily prophets, thirdly teachers, after that miracles, then gifts of healings, helps, governments, diversities of tongues." Notice that phrase, "first apostles."

Although an apostle may have authority over a church he established and possibly left, "first apostles" does not indicate rank over other ministry gifts; it indicates when the office of the apostle was placed in the body of Christ. After the Day of Pentecost, the first office given to the church was apostle. Through the remainder of the book of Acts, the other offices came into being as evangelism took place and local churches were raised up. The next office given after the apostle was the prophet, the third was the teacher, and so on with the remaining ministries.

This can be seen in the first area of conflict within the church in Acts 6. The problem associated with the neglect of widows was brought before the twelve. The church leadership consisted of apostles only, those who followed Jesus Himself. By the time we come to the sending out of the apostles to evangelize in Acts 13, they are brought before the church leadership made up of prophets and teachers (13:1). In Acts 14, the first churches were

3

established and pastors were ordained, called elders (14:23).

It is still the same today. Apostles may be the first to enter a city where there is little or no spiritual activity. They evangelize and disciple believers until a church is established. They then help raise up church leadership and finally leave to begin the process again in another city or country.

2. Apostleship is a Spiritual Ministry Gift Given by Jesus Christ and God the Father.

In 1 Corinthians 12:28, notice who sets these offices in the church: "And God hath set some in the church" (emphasis added). Bob Yandian did not set Bob Yandian in the office of pastor. God the Father placed him there. If you have a calling on your life to one of the five-fold ministry offices, no man placed that calling on you, God placed it. If God has called you, He will surely see to it that you have ample opportunity to fulfill that calling. All you have to do is stand firm and allow Him to fulfill it through you. Your part is to pray and stay in the Word. God will develop the gift. It's not up to you to promote yourself; your task is simply to prove yourself faithful. God will see to the rest.

In Ephesians 4:11 we find this statement: "And he gave some, apostles; and some, prophets; and some, evangelists; and some, pastors and teachers." Who "gave some"? Jesus Christ. How do we know this? Four verses back we read these words: "But unto every one of us is given grace according to the measure of the gift of Christ" (v. 7, emphasis added). The apostle is a gift given to (set in) the church through the cooperation of Jesus Christ and God the Father.

When Paul asserted he was an apostle (one of highest rank), chosen and commissioned to ministry; not by men, nor by man, but by Jesus Christ and God the Father, he

4

was claiming divine ordination (which is the case of every true apostle, prophet, evangelist, pastor, and teacher). When Paul made reference to the fact that he was divinely ordained rather than ordained by men, he was probably referring to the Jewish council in Jerusalem. The reason he stressed this point was because his credentials and his authority to minister as an apostle of Jesus Christ were called into question by the legalistic Judaizers. They wanted to know, "Who is this Paul?"

They were quick to point out he had no papers showing he had been certified as an apostle by the Jerusalem council. This, of course, was true, because Paul argued apostleship is not of men, but of God. These detractors would also say Peter or one of the other disciples had not laid hands on Paul and commissioned him as an apostle. This was also true, because Paul insisted apostleship is not conferred by any individual man, but by the Lord.

This is an important truth that deserves our attention. No group of men and no one individual passes on the spiritual gifts of the five-fold ministry. These come directly from God. There are other offices in the Word of God that can be given by men by the laying on of hands. (See Acts 14:23; Titus 1:5.) No one can make himself an apostle, prophet, evangelist, pastor, or teacher, and no one can choose and appoint another person to any one of these offices. The right and power of appointment to the five-fold ministry rests solely and exclusively with God the Father and Jesus Christ.

Neither can these ministry gifts be received by faith. Now I am a strong believer in the power of personal faith. I believe in it wholeheartedly. However, there are some things that simply cannot be received by faith, by simply believing and confessing you have them. One of these things is appointment to the five-fold ministry. No one can become a minister of the Gospel of Jesus Christ by simply proclaiming, "By faith I believe I am an apostle (prophet, evangelist, pastor, teacher)." That will not work. This appointment is a gift divinely and sovereignly conferred upon a person by God the Father and the Lord Jesus Christ.

Not only is apostleship not conferred by human hands or received through personal faith, it is also not determined by talent; rather, it is strictly a matter of grace, God's grace. A talent is a natural human ability innate within the individual who possesses it. In other words, talent is something you are born with. All of us have one or more inborn natural talents. Some of us are musically gifted, others have great artistic or creative talent, and others are endowed with a natural ability to learn languages easily. But none of these natural gifts has anything to do with the ministry gifts. These are bestowed upon individuals by God without regard to human ability.

Some people think just because they can play a guitar, they are called into the music ministry. Others think because they have some speaking ability, they are called to be a pastor or an evangelist. Still others mistake intellectual capacity as a call to become a teacher of the Word of God. That is a mistake. Apostleship, as well as any other ministry office, is not a matter of talent, but of divine appointment.

3. Apostleship Under the Earthly Ministry of Jesus is not the Same as Apostleship to the Church.

Apostles to the church were not appointed until after the resurrection of the Lord Jesus Christ. This is a vitally important point.

In Ephesians 4:7–11 we read:

> *But unto every one of us is given grace according to the measure of the gift of Christ. Wherefore he saith, When he ascended up on high, he led captivity captive, and gave*

gifts unto men. (Now that he ascended, what is it but that he also descended first into the lower parts of the earth?He that descended is the same also that ascended up far above all heavens, that he might fill all things.) And he gave some, apostles; and some, prophets; and some, evangelists; and some, pastors and teachers.

Since this passage makes it clear that Christ ordained and established the five-fold ministry after His resurrection from the dead and His ascension into heaven, it is obvious there is a difference between the "apostles" chosen and appointed in the four gospels (Matthew, Mark, Luke, and John) before Christ's ascension, and those true apostles given to the church after He had returned to sit at the right hand of His Father in heaven. This is even more evident when we consider that the church of Jesus Christ did not even come into existence until after the resurrection and ascension of our Lord. The five-fold ministry was initiated with the beginning of the Church age, which did not begin with the gospel of Matthew but rather in the book of Acts.

Let's consider this point for a moment. In Matthew 10:1–6 we read about Jesus' commissioning His disciples for ministry:

And when he had called unto him his twelve disciples, he gave them power against unclean spirits, to cast them out, and to heal all manner of sickness and all manner of disease. Now the names of the twelve apostles are these; the first, Simon, who is called Peter, and Andrew his brother; James the son of Zebedee, and John his brother; Philip, and Bartholomew; Thomas, and Matthew the publican; James the son of Alphaeus, and Lebbaeus, whose surname was Thaddaeus; Simon the Canaanite, and Judas Iscariot, who also betrayed him. These twelve Jesus sent forth, and commanded them, saying, Go not into the way of the Gentiles, and into any city of the

Samaritans enter ye not: but go rather to the lost sheep of the house of Israel.

Notice, in verse 1 these twelve men are referred to as *disciples*, whereas in verse 2 they are called *apostles*. Were these apostles the same as the apostles we read about in the epistles of Paul? In verses 5 and 6 we see that Jesus sent these men only to the Jews. They were specifically commanded not to minister to Gentiles or Samaritans. That brings up an interesting question: Is the church of Jesus Christ made up only of Jews? No, of course not. It's made up of both Jews and Gentiles.

It seems quite clear there is a difference between those called apostles in the four gospels and those divinely appointed as apostles after the establishment of the church of Jesus Christ. It is important we understand that difference. Although most of the twelve disciples did go on to become true apostles after the resurrection of the Lord Jesus, their ministry totally changed after the Day of Pentecost when the church came into existence. God was no longer dealing through one nation. He now dealt with all nations through the church, which is the body of Christ.

When Paul talked in Ephesians about the apostleship, he was not referring to the ministry of the twelve disciples, or to that of the seventy sent out in Luke 10. He was speaking specifically of those chosen and ordained by God the Father and the Lord Jesus Christ to go and minister the Gospel throughout the whole world. He was speaking of those divinely appointed to the five-fold ministry of the church.

4. Apostleship Still Exists Today.

Some people claim "the day of miracles" has ceased because "the day of the apostles" has passed. Is that true? No, not in either sense. Miracles have not ceased because the day of the apostle has not passed.

"Do you mean to say there are apostles today?"

Yes, I do.

"But some churches preach that when the original apostles died, miracles and tongues and prophecy died with them. They say all that was given by Jesus to get the church started, but once it was begun those things were no longer needed and no longer provided."

First Corinthians 12:28 says, "And God hath set some in the church, first apostles, secondarily prophets, thirdly teachers, after that miracles, then gifts of healings, helps, governments, diversities of tongues" (emphasis added). Does the church still exist today? Well, if God has set some in the church to be apostles and the church is still alive and functioning, what makes us think these apostles are not still alive and functioning as well? If teaching and helps and government have not ceased (and what church do you know of that does not teach, help, and govern its members?), then why should we believe prophecy, miracles, healings, or tongues would have ceased? To the extent that any of these things have ceased, it is not because God has withdrawn them for lack of need, but only because churches are simply not practicing them!

How can we say apostles and prophets have disappeared when we still have evangelists, pastors and teachers in our churches? Where in the Bible does it say any of these have been taken out of the church? You won't find such a Scripture because it just doesn't exist. Apostleship is as much a part of the New Testament church today as it was at the time Paul wrote this letter to the churches in Galatia.

Some people tell me they don't know any apostles today, but they do. We just don't call them by that name. Today they are known as missionaries, the sent ones. These are the ones who go into all the world to preach the Good News, win new converts to the Lord Jesus

Christ, establish churches, train pastors to fill them, and then move on to the next place of service. That's why we should give our prayer and financial support to our missionaries. The call to the mission field is a high calling of God upon a person's life. Apostles are missionaries, but all missionaries are not apostles. Many are called to help win the lost or to aid in ministry on foreign fields, but not to establish churches throughout a country. The term *missionary* is a broad one we use to identify those called to foreign mission work. *Apostle* is a specific calling on an individual by God the Father and the Lord Jesus Christ.

Whether you and I are called to that high office or not, we can do our part in that ministry through our prayers and financial support of those who do go forth to fulfill God's high calling on their lives.

There are still apostles today. They are the missionaries, those (like the apostle Paul) whose lives are devoted to carrying the Gospel to every nation. The only difference between today's apostles and those of Paul's day is modern-day apostles do not write Scripture. Today the written Word of God is complete. With the recording of the Revelation of Jesus Christ given to John on the Isle of Patmos, the Word was completed, but the ministry gift of apostleship still continues today. It will go on until the return of our Lord Jesus to this earth to gather His own unto Himself at the end of the church age.

5. Apostleship is Always Accompanied by Spiritual Gifts.

The office of apostle carries with it spiritual gifts. The same holds true of any one of the other five-fold ministry. If a person is called to be a teacher of the Word of God, he has been endowed with spiritual gifts to accomplish that work. The same holds true for the apostle, evangelist, prophet, and pastor. Each one called to fulfill an office of the five-fold ministry receives the spiritual endowments necessary to equip him or her for that assigned task.

In Romans 11:29 we read: "For the gifts and calling of God are without repentance." Gifts and calling go hand in hand. If you have been called by God to a particular ministry, then you have been equipped by Him with the spiritual gifts necessary to carry out that ministry.

Notice the Source of the gifts: *God*. Notice also the Source of the callings: *God*. Therefore, if you know you are called by the Lord, don't worry about your ability (or lack of ability) to fulfill that call. The gifts to fulfill the office come with the call.

Some people say to me, "Yes, that's easy for you to say; you've been a pastor for a long time. But I'm just beginning to minister. I'm not sure the gifts will operate through me if I launch out in my ministry." I tell them, "Don't worry about it. If you have been called by God, you have the gifts within you. If you will just stay in faith, those gifts will begin to operate in God's time."

Although you have certain spiritual gifts, you can't pick and choose which gift or gifts you want to work through you. You can't say, "Well, I believe I'll allow the gift of miracles to work through me, but I don't want the gift of tongues." That won't work. Neither can you "believe for" any certain gift you think you might like to have. The Bible says the Holy Spirit divides "to every man severally as he will" (1 Corinthians 12:11). It does not say you can pick and choose which ones you would like to receive and refuse the others. The Lord gives you the gifts of the Spirit that will best enhance the office in which you stand. Just as God is sovereign in choosing the office for you, He is sovereign in choosing the gifts you will always operate in. The gifts and callings of God are without repentance.

"Doesn't the Word teach us to 'covet earnestly the best gifts' (1 Corinthians 12:31)?"

Yes, it does. However, you are not to choose the gifts, but to seek earnestly for the best gifts, which will cause your office to come to its maximum effectiveness. Seek only those gifts that will accomplish God's calling upon your life. You have every reason to desire them and every right to receive them. They come with the call.

6. Apostleship is Conferred by God, Not man.

As we have noted, in Galatians 1:1, Paul claimed he was appointed an apostle by God the Father and the Lord Jesus Christ, not by man or men. That statement always raises the question, "But what about Matthias?" To answer that question, let's look at the story as found in Acts 1.

Just prior to His ascension into heaven, the Lord Jesus spoke to His disciples who were gathered together with Him on the Mount of Olives. He instructed them to wait in Jerusalem until they had received the gift He would pour out on them, the gift of the Holy Spirit. He told them with that gift of the Holy Spirit they would "receive power" to be His witnesseses "both in Jerusalem, and in all Judaea, and in Samaria, and unto the uttermost part of the earth" (v. 8).

After speaking these things to them, the Lord was taken up out of their sight. While they were still standing there in amazement and wonder, two angels appeared to them and said to them: "Ye men of Galilee, why stand ye gazing up into heaven? this same Jesus, which is taken up from you into heaven, shall so come in like manner as ye have seen him go into heaven" (v. 11). The disciples returned to Jerusalem to wait for the promise of the coming Holy Spirit.

It was while they were praying and waiting for the Holy Spirit to be poured out upon them that Peter got the idea of filling the vacancy left by the betrayal and death of Judas Iscariot:

And in those days Peter stood up in the midst of the disciples, and said, (the number of names together were about an hundred and twenty,) Men and brethren, this scripture must needs have been fulfilled, which the Holy Ghost by the mouth of David spake before concerning Judas, which was guide to them that took Jesus. For he was numbered with us, and had obtained part of this ministry. Now this man purchased a field with the reward of iniquity; and falling headlong, he burst asunder in the midst, and all his bowels gushed out. And it was known unto all the dwellers at Jerusalem; insomuch as that field is called in their proper tongue, Aceldama, that is to say, The field of blood. For it is written in the book of Psalms, Let his habitation be desolate, and let no man dwell therein: and his bishopric let another take. Wherefore of these men which have companied with us all the time that the Lord Jesus went in and out among us, beginning from the baptism of John, unto that same day that he was taken up from us, must one be ordained to be a witness with us of his resurrection. And they appointed two, Joseph called Barsabas, who was surnamed Justus, and Matthias. And they prayed, and said, Thou, Lord, which knowest the hearts of all men, show whether of these two thou hast chosen, that he may take part of this ministry and apostleship, from which Judas by transgression fell, that he might go to his own place. And they gave forth their lots; and the lot fell upon Matthias; and he was numbered with the eleven apostles.

Acts 1:15–26

This event took place after these people had been praying a few days. We must remember the Holy Spirit had not yet been given, so their praying had to have been in their own native tongues. Without the presence and the power of the Holy Spirit, Peter took it upon himself to act as spokesman and to declare to the group they needed to choose a replacement for Judas. Now his appraisal of the situation was accurate, a replacement did need to be chosen. But neither the Lord nor the Scriptures ever indicated it was the eleven disciples who were to do the choosing. The choice should have been left to the Lord.

"Yes, but didn't they pray and leave it to God to indicate which of the two men He had chosen?"

Yes. But there is no indication they prayed before they nominated these two men. They gave the Lord a choice, but how could they be sure they had nominated the man of His choice to begin with? Peter had pointed out what he considered to be the ideal qualifications for the replacement apostle, but the Bible never laid down those particular qualifications. Those were the qualifications for an apostle to Israel. However, there is a difference between an apostle to Israel and an apostle of the church of Jesus Christ. The apostle to Israel was sent only to the lost sheep of Israel. All of the eleven disciples fulfilled those qualifications, as did Justus and Matthias, but the Day of Pentecost had not yet come. The Holy Spirit had not yet been poured out. The Church age had not yet been ushered in. When that happened, the ministry gift of apostle would be totally altered. No longer would a person be required to have been present from the ministry of John the Baptist until the time of the ascension in order to be an apostle.

Peter's assertion that the new apostle would have to be someone who was an eyewitness to the Resurrection is not entirely valid either. What he didn't foresee was a man named Saul of Tarsus could be a witness to that event on the road to Damascus when the resurrected Lord appeared to him personally.

The name Matthias is never mentioned again in any book of the New Testament. Historians never tell us what happened to him. Do you know why? God didn't choose Matthias. The disciples chose Matthias. Now I didn't say there was never a twelfth apostle. There was. His name was Paul, "an apostle, [chosen] (not of men, neither by man, but [chosen] by Jesus Christ, and God the Father, who raised him from the dead)" (Galatians 1:1). What proof do we have that Paul was chosen by God as an apostle? We have the Word of God as recorded by Luke in Acts 9:15 in which the Lord says to Ananias about Paul: "Go thy way: for he is a chosen vessel unto me, to bear my name before the Gentiles, and kings, and the children of Israel." Apostleship is not conferred by man or by men; it is conferred only by God.

7. Apostleship Can be Conferred Upon Others Besides the Original Twelve Disciples.

The seventh and final point we need to understand about apostleship is it can be conferred upon whomever the Lord desires; it is not limited to the original twelve disciples. There are several instances in the New Testament in which it is evident people other than the twelve were recognized as apostles. Luke, the physician, numbers Barnabas among the apostles: "Which when the apostles, Barnabas and Paul, heard of, they rent their clothes, and ran in among the people, crying out" (Acts 14:14). Paul himself mentions at least four others whom he identifies as apostles:

James

> *Then after three years I went up to Jerusalem to see Peter, and abode with him fifteen days. But other of the apostles saw I none, save James the Lord's brother.*
> *Galatians 1:18–19*

> *After that, he was seen of James; then of all the apostles.*
> *1 Corinthians 15:7*

Apollos

> *And these things, brethren, I have in a figure transferred*

15

to myself and to Apollos for your sakes; that ye might learn in us not to think of men above that which is written, that no one of you be puffed up for one against another. For who maketh thee to differ from another? and what hast thou that thou didst not receive? now if thou didst receive it, why dost thou glory, as if thou hadst not received it? Now ye are full, now ye are rich, ye have reigned as kings without us: and I would to God ye did reign, that we also might reign with you. For I think that God hath set forth us the apostles last.

1 Corinthians 4:6–9

Silas and Timothy

Paul, and Silvanus [Greek, Silas], and Timotheus [Greek, Timothy], unto the church of the Thessalonians which is in God the Father and in the Lord Jesus Christ: Grace be unto you, and peace, from God our Father, and the Lord Jesus Christ.

1 Thessalonians 1:1

Nor of men sought we glory, neither of you, nor yet of others, when we might have been burdensome, as the apostles of Christ.

1 Thessalonians 2:6

The reason I have stressed these seven points about apostleship is because the book of Galatians is the strongest defense Paul ever made of his ministry office. Nowhere else in his writings did he make a stronger declaration of his apostleship than in this book of Galatians. Throughout the book, he continually pointed out that from his mother's womb he had been chosen and set aside for the work God had for him to do. It was as though he wanted to make sure all credit for his ministry gift would go to God the Father and the Lord Jesus Christ, not to man or to men.

2
God the Source
Galatians 1:2-14

Grace Versus Legalism

Most books of the New Testament have one central theme. For example, the book of Ephesians deals with the church, and the book of Philippians has to do with joy. The theme of Galatians is grace versus legalism. It is a twofold theme: *salvation by grace* and *spirituality by grace*. Now when I use the term *legalism* I am referring to the idea that something must be added to the grace of God either to obtain salvation or to attain spirituality. This usually implies some kind of works.

The basic theme of Paul's letter to the churches in Galatia will have to do with their mistaken idea that salvation and spirituality are not dependent solely upon the grace of God, but some other ingredient must be added to grace either to receive it or to remain in it.

To many, that idea seems ridiculous. We pride ourselves in thinking we would never have been as foolish as these people to think we could ever do anything to merit God's favor. Yet there is a great lesson found in this book, because we often come much closer to this way of thinking than we realize.

We know salvation is by faith plus nothing. We quote Ephesians 2:8-9: "For by grace are ye saved through faith; and that not of yourselves: it is the gift of God: not of works, lest any man should boast."

We know full well salvation is not obtained through any self-effort; it is received as a free gift from God through faith in His Son Jesus Christ. We read it is "not by works of righteousness which we have done, but according to his mercy he saved us" (Titus 3:5). We readily accept the biblical truth that all our self-righteousness is as filthy rags in the sight of God (see Isaiah 64:6), and it is only by the washing of regeneration and renewing of the Holy Spirit that we are made clean. (See Titus 3:5.) All this and more we believe and confess.

Yet even knowing we have been saved by grace, through faith, we would never think for a moment we might lose our salvation. We know better than that. We know better than that. Often, deep down inside we still harbor a fear that we will somehow not be pleasing to God, we will "fall short of the glory" (Romans 3:23 NIV), that we will not measure up to "the stature of the fulness of Christ" (Ephesians 4:13).

In other words, although we know we are saved by grace, we can't help feeling to some extent, we have to work out our salvation, with the emphasis on *work*. Despite all our claims to total dependence upon the grace of God, we still feel obligated to *do* something. It's just difficult for us not to believe we don't have to be careful to keep all the do's and don'ts if we're going to be truly "spiritual."

As understandable as that attitude may be, it is still *legalism*, just like the belief that circumcision or observance of some other part of the Jewish Law is necessary for salvation or spirituality. We tend to be legalistic in our thinking, even if that legalism just involves doing good works, attending church services faithfully, paying tithes, teaching a Sunday school class, praising God, praying, or even reading our Bible. We should do these things because we love the Lord, not to gain His attention and approval.

What is wrong with legalism is it takes our eyes off others and centers them on ourselves. We become so concerned with *our* thoughts, *our* words, and *our* actions that we lose sight of the Lord and of others. We begin to do what we do out of a sense of obligation rather than out of a heart of love and concern. Even witnessing can become legalistic if we witness because we feel obligated to instead of being motivated by our love for people.

There is also the whole range of rules and regulations we hear in many churches that place great emphasis upon *holiness*. Dress length, sleeve length, whether or not it is proper to wear jewelry or makeup, whether a Christian should own a television set or go to the movies, or swim in mixed company, or swim at all, and on and on. Churches that major on laws soon lose their zeal for evangelism. They become so engrossed in themselves and their rules and codes, they cut themselves off from the very people they need to be meeting and witnessing to and winning. As a result, they eventually dry up from within.

Legalism gets our eyes off God and others and onto ourselves. And that's exactly what the devil wants us to do, to start looking either at our own self-righteousness or at our own shortcomings and failures. Once we start doing that, he has us trapped because we will no longer reach out to bless and win others.

Paul knew all this. That's why he wrote this strongly worded letter to the churches in Galatia. He was vitally concerned they not fall victim to legalism because he knew, as he told the Corinthians, the letter of the law "killeth, but the spirit giveth life" (2 Corinthians 3:6).

In order to fully understand and appreciate Paul's message to the Galatians, we need to back up a bit and lay the foundation of what had transpired before this letter was penned. Paul was not an apostle to the Jews. He was an apostle to the Gentiles. On his first missionary tour, he and Barnabas went to the area of Galatia where they saw many people born again, filled with the Spirit, healed, and blessed. They organized these people into churches, got them started on their Christian walk, and then left to minister in other areas.

However, as soon as Paul and Barnabas had departed, zealous Jews (those who had a hard time breaking away from the Law) came in to "investigate" Paul's ministry.

When they discovered the message Paul had preached was grace, salvation through simple faith in Jesus Christ, they immediately began to teach these Gentile converts about the Jewish Law. They had never heard about the Law. Paul hadn't taught them they were freed from the Law because they had never been under the Law. Naturally, as soon as the Jewish leaders came in and began to teach them about the Law, they began to try to observe it. They started trying to combine the Law and grace.

Suddenly confusion reigned. These people were trying to live in grace yet keep every jot and tittle of the Jewish Law that they knew nothing about. Paul had to write them to explain they were under no obligation to live by a set of rules and regulations Jesus Christ fulfilled for them at the Cross.

With that background in mind, let's continue now our study of Galatians beginning with verse 2 of chapter 1.

Authority Established

Galatians 1:2

And all the brethren which are with me, unto the churches of Galatia.

Paul continued to emphasize his qualification and authority as an apostle of Jesus Christ by pointing out he was not alone in this ministry, but was accompanied by other well-qualified and recognized leaders in the church.

He was well aware of what had happened in Galatia in his absence: *how the legalistic Judaizers had come in to refute Christ's message of grace and to cast doubt on his character and apostleship.* That was the reason he began this letter in verse 1 with a bold assertion that his ordination and authority as an apostle had come directly from God and not from any man or group of men.

In verse 2, he was quick to point out that although he was personally chosen, hand-picked by the Lord Himself, he did not stand alone — he operated with a team. There is a lesson here for us today. We have each been chosen and elected by God to minister in His name. Yet we too must realize none of us stands alone. Like individual members of a team, we must all work together in harmony and unified purpose if we are to accomplish what God has called us to do. As members of the body of Christ, none of us must think of himself as some great high and mighty person to whom others owe allegiance and servitude. Even our Lord said He came not to be ministered to, but to minister and give His life a ransom for many. He also made it abundantly clear that he who would be greatest in the kingdom of God must be servant to all. (See Mark 10:42-45.)

Even though we have been individually chosen and anointed by God, we are nothing special in ourselves. We must remember all believers have also been individually chosen and anointed for the work the Lord has set them apart to do. If any of us are to succeed in our assigned tasks, it will require joint effort, teamwork. We are all individual members of a supernatural team under the leadership of the Holy Spirit of God. Each must contribute to the overall goal of that team by fulfilling his own individual assignment and by assisting the other team members to fulfill theirs. God works with us as a team, not as "stars."

Even the great apostle Paul worked as a member of a team. The rest of the team was made up of Titus, Silas,

Luke, Timothy, Tychicus, and Trophimus. At the time of this writing, the other team members were not physically present with Paul. They were spread throughout the province of Asia, but they were one with him in purpose and goal. They were the ones to whom Paul was referring when he sent greetings to the churches in Galatia from those who were with him in the ministry.

Grace and Peace

Verse 3

Grace be to you and peace from God the Father, and from our Lord Jesus Christ.

Paul got right into the theme of this book: *the grace of God.* He pointed out from the beginning where grace comes from: "from God the Father, and from our Lord Jesus Christ." These people in Galatia had left grace and had gone into works. That is the basic problem Paul was addressing, even in his greeting.

If grace comes from God, then where do works come from? From man. "Grace be to you and peace from God," not from men. Men don't give grace and peace; they prescribe works. They set up religions. Someone has said that Christianity is what God has done for man in Christ, while religion is what man tries to do for God in his own strength. Religion is not founded on God's grace, the gift of God's unmerited favor, but on works, man's attempt to gain God's favor by his own efforts. That's why Paul was so hard on those who were foolish enough to turn from grace to works.

"Grace be to you and peace." Peace is the product of grace. If you will notice carefully, you will see whenever you leave the true message of God's grace and start trying to mix anything else in with it, the first thing you will begin to lose is peace. You will become frustrated. If you are trying to build your Christian life on human works, sooner or later you will experience frustration.

There is a simple principle involved here. You simply cannot please God by works. There is only one thing that pleases God. We find it spelled out for us in Hebrews 11:6: "But without faith it is impossible to please him." It's not difficult to please God by works, *it's impossible*. Nothing pleases God but faith in the finished work of Jesus Christ on the cross. Anything we add to that finished work displeases our heavenly Father and results in our loss of peace.

Am I saying then that works are wrong? No, not at all. Works are fine. We are supposed to work, just as our Lord worked: "But I have greater witness than that of John: for the works which the Father hath given me to finish, the same works that I do, bear witness of me, that the Father hath sent me" (John 5:36, emphasis added). Later in John 14:10 Jesus explained how those works were done: "Believest thou not that I am in the Father, and the Father in me? the words that I speak unto you I speak not of myself: but the Father that dwelleth in me, he doeth the works."

We remember our Lord told us he who believed in Him would do the same works He did and even greater works than His. (See John 14:12.) But how? He gave us that answer in John 15:5: "I am the vine, ye are the branches: He that abideth in me, and I in him, the same bringeth forth much fruit: for without me ye can do nothing." Fruit (good works) is produced through us not because of anything we are or do of ourselves, but because of the Word that abides in us. Works are produced by the same indwelling Spirit who did the works through Jesus. Works are evidence of God's favor upon us, not a means to obtain or retain that favor. We remain in God's favor by remaining in fellowship with Him and His Word, not by works of might.

So we do work, but not to please God. We work because He has blessed us so much in grace we just want to work for Him. It's not the works we do that please God; it's the *faith* we exercise in Him. It's not giving itself that pleases God; it's the *faith* in Him we demonstrate when we freely give out of hearts of thanksgiving and praise for all His blessings upon us. We don't give as an act of obedience or obligation or duty. We don't "owe" God His ten percent. What does He need with our measly ten percent when the whole universe belongs to Him? He managed just fine without our tithe before we came along, and He will continue to do just fine without it after we're gone.

It's not the ten percent that pleases God; it's the freedom and unselfishness we display by our giving. God doesn't look at the amount of the gift; He looks at the attitude of the giver. The Bible doesn't say the Lord loves a *big* giver, it says He loves a *"cheerful* giver" (2 Corinthians 9:7).

Then there is witnessing. Some church people make witnessing such a burden and a task they destroy the whole purpose and meaning behind it. Either they make it out to be a quota that every Christian must fill, thus producing all kinds of guilt in those who don't feel they have met the standard, or they make it out to be some kind of contest in which the one who gets the most converts wins the prize of God's favor and blessing. I have never understood any concept of witnessing that sees it as a means of "buttering up" God or winning "brownie points." Witnessing is not meant to be a chore or a contest. It is supposed to be the natural consequence of a heart so filled with joy and peace in the Lord, it cannot help but speak of the One who is the Source of that blessing.

Like works, witnessing is not wrong, but many times our concept of it is wrong. Witnessing is good if we witness for the right reason.

T. L. Osborn loved to tell about the old Methodist

preacher who used to ask his parishioners, "Has the Lord done anything so good for you that you just can't keep quiet about it?" When God so freely provides for you that you just want to do something for Him, that's witnessing! You want to work for Him. You want to clean the church carpet, sweep the floor, take up the offering, serve Communion, work in the nursery, teach a Sunday school class, visit the sick—tell others about Him. Not to get a gold star by your name on God's "bless-me" list, but simply because you want to bless others as you have been blessed. That's grace!

Once you understand grace, you begin to understand peace. When you can receive God's grace, then you are in a position to receive His peace.

When I was a youth, I was in a church camp with a girl who had been raised on the do's and don'ts. All her life she had tried to live by a strict religious code. At camp that year the leader taught on the theme of our being complete in Christ. He kept hammering away at the fact that if a person is complete, he can't get any "completer." The more he talked on that subject and the more the girl listened, the more she became aware of the truth of that message. For the first time in her life, she began to realize she didn't have to work for holiness (wholeness); she was already complete (whole) in her Savior. Finally she broke down in tears, weeping with joy and relief.

"I see it; it's all God's grace," she sobbed. "I feel as if a ten-ton weight has been lifted off my back. I don't have to try to please God anymore; He is already pleased with me. That puts a whole different light on it. Now I want to work for Him rather than *have to* work for Him."

The moment she understood grace, peace overwhelmed her. Oh, if only more Christians could come to that understanding. The faith life is not trying to please God by our action, even our great faith. It's just living by the principles of the Word He has already provided.

Salvation, peace, prosperity, success, health, joy, life in all its fullness and abundance, has already been provided for us by our loving heavenly Father. If that's so, then we don't need to try to obtain His blessings by winning His favor. We already have His favor, His grace. It was His grace that moved Him to do all this for us in the first place. We simply need to receive the blessings that accompany His favor.

Deliverance

Verse 4

Who gave himself for our sins, that he might deliver us from this present evil world, according to the will of God and our Father.

"Who gave himself for our sins." The Greek word translated in English as "for" actually means "in exchange for." Jesus Christ gave Himself in exchange for our sins.

You see, throughout the Word of God, we read Jesus took the curse of the Law upon Himself and gave us the blessing of God in its place. We received redemption, but what did He receive? Sin. We received righteousness. What did He receive? Unrighteousness. We received riches. He took poverty. We have healing. He became sickness. Don't you like that trade? Isn't it wonderful to know Jesus took all our sin, unrighteousness, poverty, and sickness upon Himself and in return gave us His holiness, righteousness, riches, and health? That's what happened at the cross of Calvary. That is the truth Paul wanted these people to understand right from the outset. Jesus gave Himself in exchange.

"That he might deliver us from this present evil world." The word translated *world* is actually the Greek word for *age*. The world itself is not evil; it's the age in which we live that is evil. The world, God's creation, is good; it has just been corrupted by the evil that is loose in it. It is this present evil age. That means it will not last forever; it is only temporary. Jesus is coming soon. It's also comforting to know in the midst of this present age of sin, sickness, poverty, and misery you and I can live in righteousness, health, riches, happiness, and joy. All this is because of that exchange that took place at Calvary.

Notice also this word *deliver*. Deliverance is potential, that "he might deliver us." If there are people in this evil age who are not delivered from it, it is not God's fault, it's their fault. Salvation, and all that goes with it, is potential. Jesus Christ has done everything He could do to remove sin and unrighteousness from people. He took it all upon Himself when He was nailed to the cross. In exchange, He gave us His righteousness, prosperity, and peace. He traded His salvation for our sin, but He will not force that exchange upon anyone. It must be accepted by each person individually. Each of us must ratify the agreement personally. Unless a person does that for himself, he cannot benefit from the exchange.

"According to the will of God and our Father." In the original Greek the word "and" does not appear. This phrase should read, "According to the will of God our Father." What is the will of our Father? The apostle Peter said God is "not willing that any should perish, but that all should come to repentance" (2 Peter 3:9). And from John we learn God's commandment is "that we should believe on the name of his Son Jesus Christ" (1 John 3:23). Jesus said He was sent to this earth by the Father so those who believe in Him might have life, "and that they might have it more abundantly" (John 10:10). It is obvious it is God's will for everyone to be born again and enjoy eternal and abundant life.

Eternal life does not begin when we die; it begins when we receive the Lord Jesus Christ. In the same way, abundant life is not something just laid up for us in heaven;

it, too, begins here and now. Grace doesn't end at salvation; it continues every day of our lives, now and forever.

In Psalm 103:2–5 we read these words written by David:

> *Bless the LORD, O my soul, and forget not all his benefits: who forgiveth all thine iniquities; who healeth all thy diseases; who redeemeth thy life from destruction; who crowneth thee with lovingkindness and tender mercies; who satisfieth thy mouth with good things; so that thy youth is renewed like the eagle's.*

If you are not enjoying all God's blessings of forgiveness, healing, redemption, loving-kindness, mercy, prosperity, and strength, then perhaps it is because you have simply forgotten all His benefits. In Jesus Christ, God has already done all He can do to bless you. The next move is up to you.

I picture the plan of salvation (deliverance) like a game of checkers. God has made His move; now it's our turn. He has done His part; now He's waiting for us to do ours. Our part is simply to receive what He has done for us at Calvary.

Some people say faith moves God. That's not true. Faith doesn't move God; God has already moved. Faith moves us into a position to *receive* what God has already done. The Bible is one long recitation of God's movement throughout history, culminating in the Cross where the Great Exchange took place. There God took our sins, laid them on His own Son, and then nailed them to the cross with Him, freeing us from them forever. In their place He gave us His righteousness. That exchange is completed. God has done His part. Now it's our move. That move is to accept what He has already done in Jesus Christ.

No one who goes to hell can ever blame the Lord for his condemnation. God made the first move. If the person refuses to accept what was done for him in Christ, that's his fault, not God's. The same can be said of the born-again believer who goes through life beaten down and defeated because he has not received the fullness of God's grace and love. If that is your situation, it's your fault, not God's. He has done His part. You now need to do yours. You receive the abundant life in the same way you received eternal life, by simple faith. Believe on the Lord Jesus Christ, and you will be saved (healed, prospered, restored, set free, delivered).

To Whom Be Glory

Verse 5

To whom be glory for ever and ever. Amen.

Notice the last word in this fifth verse, "Amen." Now we are accustomed to this word coming at the conclusion of a prayer or hymn or sermon. To us it marks the end of an utterance or thought, but here we find it inserted between the fifth and sixth verses of the very first chapter of this book. Why?

The reason is obvious. This word marks the conclusion of Paul's greeting or opening remarks. In three little verses (verses 3-5) Paul gave the entire plan of salvation, ending it with an amen. For all practical purposes he could have ended the letter right there. He has actually said everything he needs to say. It is regrettable that from verse 6 to the end of the book he has to talk about these people's problem. The solution is given in three verses, but the discussion of the problem takes an additional five and three-fourths chapters.

This brief opening section contains the whole plan of salvation. But is there anything mentioned in it about the Jewish Law? Any discussion of animal sacrifice? What about circumcision? Nothing said about dietary restrictions? No dress code? No lists of do's and don'ts? No "do this and live"?

None. The whole plan of salvation is summarized in one concept: *Jesus Christ went to the cross for our sins, so we might be delivered from this present evil age.* Amen.

Another Gospel

Verses 6-9

I marvel that ye are so soon removed from him that called you into the grace of Christ unto another gospel: which is not another; but there be some that trouble you, and would pervert the gospel of Christ. But though we, or an angel from heaven, preach any other gospel unto you than that which we have preached unto you, let him be accursed. As we said before, so say I now again, If any man preach any other gospel unto you than that ye have received, let him be accursed.

In these verses Paul nailed down the problem. In most of his books, Paul usually started out with a message of tremendous edification. In Ephesians, for example, he began by telling the believers in Ephesus about all God did for them in times past, how He had blessed them with all spiritual blessings, how they had been redeemed, and how wonderful the things of God are. But in Galatians he launched right into the problem at hand. He immediately levelled a scathing accusation against these people for being so foolish as to fall for "another gospel."

"I marvel that ye are so soon removed from him that called you into the grace of Christ unto another gospel" (v. 6). This expression "I marvel" could be translated, "I am astonished" or "I am shocked." "So soon" refers to the short time span of the few months in which Paul has been absent from these people. The word translated "removed" is actually a Greek military term meaning *to go AWOL* (absent without leave). Paul was saying, "I am shocked to hear that some of you who joined ranks with the Lord Jesus Christ have so quickly deserted!"

I'm sure those who read this letter said to themselves, "We haven't deserted!" But they had. To turn away from the grace of God by mixing anything in with it is to go AWOL. It is to climb over the fence and run away.

Notice in this verse Paul again referred to the grace of Christ. In verse 3 he prayed grace and peace would be theirs. Now here in verses 6 and 7 he told them they had removed themselves from the grace of Christ to follow "another gospel: which is not another." That may seem a little confusing, so let's look at this term "another gospel."

How could these people be following "another gospel: which is not another"? In the Greek there are two words for *another*. One is *heteros* and the other is *allos*. *Heteros* means *"another of a different kind." Allos* means *"another of the same kind."* In the King James Version both are translated by the same English word *another*, but they do not have exactly the same meaning. For example, if someone gave you an apple and then handed you an orange, they would both be pieces of fruit, but the second one would be *heteros, another of a different kind.* If, however, you had one apple and someone gave you a second apple, it would be *allos, another of the same kind.*

What Paul was saying is, "I am shocked that you have so soon deserted Him who called you into the grace of Christ to follow after another gospel of a different kind, which is not another of the same kind." In other words, Paul was telling these people the Jews were telling them their message was just another form of the Gospel, but it wasn't. It was "another gospel," but it was most definitely not the true Gospel of the Lord Jesus Christ. It was *heteros, another gospel of a different kind* than what Paul and Barnabas had preached in Galatia.

Is there such a thing as an *allos*, another Gospel of the same kind? Yes, there is. The Bible mentions the Gospel of grace, the Gospel of the kingdom, the Gospel of peace, and more. All these are Gospels of the same kind. They all refer to the same Gospel; they just emphasize different aspects of it. When something other than grace is mixed in with that Gospel message, it ceases to be a different form of the same Gospel and becomes a different "gospel" altogether. That's what Paul was telling these people about the new Jewish "gospel" they had been so quick to embrace.

"But there be some that trouble you, and would pervert the gospel of Christ" (v. 7). Perverting the Gospel of Christ refers to mixing something in with it. The Bible pronounces a curse on anyone who dares to add to or take away from the Gospel contained in it. (See Revelation 22:18-19.) To do so is to pervert it into "another gospel of a different kind." Later on in Galatians Paul pointed out that a little leaven leavens the whole loaf. Leaven refers to some foreign object added to dough to make it rise. It makes it appear bigger than it really is because it is puffed up. That's what foreign matter does to the Gospel; it "puffs it up" to make it appear to be something it is not.

Leaven also speeds up the manifestation. Many times people will try to "speed up" the manifestation of whatever it is they are praying and exercising faith to receive. For instance, they may be believing for an extra $500 for some need. It is always a temptation to "help God out" a little by letting rich Aunt Suzie know about the prayer request. Such an attempt to take matters into their own hands while supposedly trusting God is a good example of adding a little leaven to the lump. Even though people may try to justify their lack of faith by asking what harm it would do to just speed things along a bit, the answer is obvious. Either they are depending solely on God or they are not. There is no middle ground. To try to hedge faith is to deny it altogether.

"Yes, but sometimes it's quicker to sort of take things into your own hands than to wait around on God to move. Sometimes the faith way just takes so long!"

Yes, it does, but while you are waiting and exercising patience, your faith is being perfected. The next time you step out in faith, it won't take quite so long. You will have grown, matured. What you receive from God by faith is always like seed; it has the capacity of increasing again and again, nut not if you bail out before God's manifestation arrives. Such an action indicates a lack of patience to see faith through to its completion. You have perverted the Gospel by mixing self-effort with it. That's what Paul was berating the Galatians for.

"But though we, or an angel from heaven, preach any other gospel unto you than that which we have preached unto you, let him be accursed. As we said before, so say I now again, If any man preach any other gospel unto you than that ye have received, let him be accursed" (vv. 8-9). "*We...an angel...any man.*" These three terms cover just about any way a person could hear the Word of God. Paul was making it clear. If anyone, whoever he might be, preaches a "gospel" other than the true Gospel of Jesus Christ, that person is accursed and if any person preaches the true Gospel, he is blessed.

This is an important point. Paul was stressing it's not the messenger who matters; it's the message that is important. So often we get our eyes on the messenger and take them off the message. We become so enamored with the "great preachers," we don't hear what those closest to us have to say.

Why didn't we believe it when we heard it the first time? We didn't believe it because we put more emphasis on the messenger who delivered it than on the message itself. That is dangerous. God speaks to us in many ways and through many people, many times through those we least esteem. We need to recognize the message of the Lord as surely as we recognize the Lord Himself.

Paul was stressing that the message matters, not the

spokesman. The Gospel is most important.

Not to Please Man

Verse 10

For do I now persuade men, or God? or do I seek to please men? for if I yet pleased men, I should not be the servant of Christ.

"For do I now persuade men." By this expression Paul meant, "Am I trying to appeal to men?" If that were the case, then Paul would be going along with what these Jews were saying to the Galatians. Instead, he was standing firm against them and their "gospel." It seemed Paul was standing alone, but there was a team with him, though at times it seemed even they were against him. Oftentimes that's the way it is in the ministry. When you embark on the faith walk, you will soon discover not everybody is going to rally round you to support you in your every decision and stance. In fact, you will soon find where your faith really lies, in men or in God.

"For if I yet pleased men, I should not be the servant of Christ." Notice this word "yet." Paul used this word because at one time in his life all he sought for was to please men. When he was Saul of Tarsus, the zealous Pharisee, his whole existence was wrapped up in pleasing the "powers that be," so much so he hunted and persecuted the church so he could advance himself in the Jewish religion.

But no more. Now his whole life was devoted to pleasing God, even if it meant being persecuted himself, as he was, repeatedly, until the end of his days. That's the price of apostleship. Paul knew what so many of us have learned: *In order to be a servant of Christ, a person has to be prepared to suffer the opposition of man.* A servant pleases his master. If you seek to please men, they are your masters; you are a servant to men. Be a servant of Christ, and please Him.

Religion versus the Gospel

Verses 11–14

But I certify you, brethren, that the gospel which was preached of me is not after man. For I neither received it of man, neither was I taught it, but by the revelation of Jesus Christ. For ye have heard of my conversation in time past in the Jews' religion, how that beyond measure I persecuted the church of God, and wasted it: and profited in the Jews' religion above many my equals in mine own nation, being more exceedingly zealous of the traditions of my fathers.

Notice the contrast Paul made between the Gospel of Jesus Christ and the religion of the Jews to which he himself was at one time totally dedicated.

"But I certify you, brethren, that the gospel which was preached of me is not after man. For I neither received it of man, neither was I taught it, but by the revelation of Jesus Christ" (vv. 11–12). The first difference is religion comes from the minds of men and is passed on through their teachings, but the Gospel comes directly from Jesus Christ through personal revelation. Here again Paul was stressing that his apostleship came from the Lord and not from man or men.

"For ye have heard of my conversation in time past in the Jews' religion" (v. 13). Here Paul began to get into his former life. The word "conversation" means "way of life." "Time past" refers to that time before his conversion. Paul is describing his lifestyle before he met Jesus Christ face-to-face on the Damascus road.

Note carefully the next expression: "the Jews' religion." Judaism is a religion and religion is man's effort to achieve salvation through his own efforts. That's why Paul went on to stress how zealous he was when he was "religious." In Philippians 3:4-6 he described how devout he was, referring to himself as "a Hebrew of the Hebrews" (v. 5), and claiming that in matters of the Jewish Law he was "blameless" (v. 6). Yet he wrote to Timothy, "This is a faithful saying, and worthy of all acceptation, that Christ Jesus came into the world to save sinners; of whom I am chief" (1 Timothy 1:15). Paul had learned by personal experience that "by the works of the law shall no flesh be justified" (Galatians 2:16).

If personal works could save anyone, Saul of Tarsus would have been a shining example of salvation. If self-effort could save even one person, Jesus would not have had to die on the cross. Saul not only came face-to-face with Jesus on the road to Damascus, he also came face-to-face with himself, the chief of sinners.

"And profited in the Jews' religion...being more exceedingly zealous of the traditions of my fathers" (Gal. 1:14). Notice that word "traditions." That is a good definition of religion. Paul knew firsthand about religion. That's why he was so aware of the dangers of trusting in the traditions of men rather than in the grace of God. He knew religion is probably the worst thing that has ever happened since the fall of man. Of all the sins and evils we can think of, religion is by far the worst. Religion has caused more people to miss salvation than all the other sins and evil combined. Not only that, religion has been the worst persecutor of the church in the history of mankind.

No dictator or tyrant, no totalitarian regime in history has ever come anywhere close to causing damage to the church of Jesus Christ as religion. The sad part is all the persecution, misery, and suffering religion has caused has been done in the name of God!

Look at many Hindu nations today, filled with disease, famine, dissension, and hatred, where thousands of people are literally starving to death in the streets while food walks right past them. Yet they will not kill and eat the food available because according to their religion, cattle are sacred. They are taught that cow might be the reincarnated form of their own relative! That's what religion does to people. It blinds them to the truth while it destroys them physically, mentally, and spiritually.

Religion blinds people to the Gospel. Of all the people I have ever witnessed to about the Lord Jesus Christ, religious people are by far the most difficult to win. They are so proud of their traditions, rituals, and good deeds that it is almost impossible for them to receive salvation by simple faith. Consider the rich young ruler who came to Jesus seeking salvation. He was so devoted to his strict observance of the Law he could not let go of either his earthly possessions or his own self-righteousness. Religion, with its emphasis on self-examination and self-achievement, has robbed more sinners of their salvation (and more Christians of their joy and peace) than any evil under the sun. It is hard for people to receive when they are convinced they must achieve.

Paul was a prime example. When Paul stated he had "profited" in the Jews' religion, he meant he had advanced in it. He did that by persecuting the church of Jesus Christ. The more he advanced, the more determined he became to destroy every Christian he could find. The more Christians he destroyed, the faster he advanced. He was caught in a vicious cycle. Sooner or later something had to give. It was either the church or Saul of Tarsus.

When Jesus said the gates of hell would not prevail against His church (Matt. 16:18), He meant exactly what He said. Therefore, it was not the church that fell; it was Saul—on the road to Damascus. He fell to the ground at the feet of a risen Savior and arose a new creature. From that day, Saul of Tarsus became Paul, "an apostle, (not of men, neither by man, but by Jesus Christ, and God the Father)" (Galatians 1:1). Remember the meaning of the word apostle? Paul was instantly promoted from "chief of sinners" to "a sent one" in the church of Jesus Christ. That's the difference between what religion does to us and what the Gospel does for us.

3
Paul's Revelation
Galatians 1:15-2:10

Revelation Precedes Proclamation

Galatians 1:15-16

But when it pleased God, who separated me from my mother's womb, and called me by his grace, to reveal his Son in me, that I might preach him among the heathen; immediately I conferred not with flesh and blood.

"But when it pleased God, who separated me from my mother's womb" (v. 15). Paul said he was "separated" (set aside for service to God) before he was born. This can also be said of you and me, of every true believer in Jesus Christ. In Ephesians 1:3-4 Paul wrote to the believers in Ephesus, "Blessed be the God and Father of our Lord Jesus Christ, who hath blessed us with all spiritual blessings in heavenly places in Christ: according as he hath chosen us in him before the foundation of the world, that we should be holy and without blame before him in love."

"And called me by his grace" (v. 15). If God chose Paul before he was born, that must be grace, because how could Paul have worked for something bestowed upon him in his mother's womb? This choosing of Paul was not an isolated incident, as we have seen in Ephesians 1. Rather, each child of God was chosen "before the foundation of the world." It was not only Paul who was saved and sanctified by grace, but every believer, before we ever have opportunity to work for, earn, or deserve it. Salvation is not dependent upon anything a person does; it rests solely upon the grace of God.

Everything in the Christian life is grace. Like Paul, you and I were chosen before the foundation of the world to fulfill the particular ministry to which the Lord has called us. Many Christians think they have no ministry because they are not involved in full-time church work. But the truth is, in the New Testament church there is no distinction made between the clergy and the laity. Every member of the body of Christ is in full-time Christian service, whether he knows it or not, whether he fulfills it or not.

If you are a Christian, you are a minister of the Gospel of Jesus Christ. Like Paul, you were separated and called by God's grace to preach the Gospel to those to whom He will lead you, those whom no one else but you can reach.

"To reveal his Son in me, that I might preach him" (v. 16). Notice what Paul said about the purpose of God's revelation of His Son to him: "that I might preach." There is a sequence here. Revelation always precedes proclamation. No one can truly preach who has not first received revelation from God.

In my ministry I meet so many young people who seem to have the idea that since the return of the Lord Jesus to this earth is so imminent, they don't have time to fully prepare themselves for ministry. They are so afraid time will run out before they get on the field, they rush into the ministry without adequate training and instruction.

"Oh, I'd love to be able to go to Bible school or get my seminary degree, but there's no time. I've got to get started preaching right away!"

"No, you don't," I tell them. "You don't have anything to preach yet."

"Oh, but I've been called."

"I'm sure you have. But there is a sequence to be followed here. First comes the call, then the revelation, then the preaching. We are all called to preach the Gospel, but that doesn't mean we're ready to start preaching as soon as we are born again. Like every other one of God's blessings, ministry requires time and preparation."

"Oh, but what if Jesus comes back while I'm still in school?"

"Well, if He does, so be it. Personally, if Jesus came, I'd rather be in school preparing to preach than out there preaching with nothing to say."

If you are called to the ministry, get yourself in a place where God can teach you, where you can be instructed and prepared mentally and emotionally as well as spiritually. That's what Paul did.

"Among the heathen" (v. 16). Notice, not only did Paul receive a definite call to the apostleship, as a "sent one" he knew to whom he was sent to "the heathen." This word appears many times in the book of Galatians. So does the word *Gentiles*. These two words are the same word in Greek. It is the word *ethne*, from which we derive our English word *ethnic*, having to do with race or native origin. In this verse the word refers to the non-Jews. Peter was primarily called to minister the Gospel to the Hebrews and Paul was set aside as an apostle to the Gentiles. Later on these two groups will also be referred to as the *circumcision* and the *uncircumcision*. (See Galatians 2:7, Colossians 3:11.)

"Immediately I conferred not with flesh and blood" (v. 16). This is very important. After Paul received his call, his ordination as an apostle, not of men, neither by man, but by God the Father and the Lord Jesus Christ, he noted he did not confer with a man, with flesh and blood. Paul understood that revelation knowledge does not come from flesh and blood, but is always of divine origin. Do you remember what Jesus told Peter when he identified Him as the Christ, the Son of the Living God?

41

"Blessed art thou, Simon Barjona: for flesh and blood hath not revealed it unto thee, but my Father which is in heaven" (Matthew 16:17). Paul received his call to the ministry directly from God and was told to preach to the Gentiles, just as the Lord had told Ananias He was setting him aside to do. (See Acts 9:15.)

Into the Wilderness

Verse 17

Neither went I up to Jerusalem to them which were apostles before me; but I went into Arabia, and returned again unto Damascus.

"Neither went I up to Jerusalem." At this time Jerusalem was the center of religious activity of the day. It was the headquarters of the Jewish religion as well as the focal point of the Christian church.

"To them which were apostles before me." Paul was saying, once he received God's call upon his life, he did not immediately go to consult with the "leaders" of the church. He did not confer with men. He felt no obligation or need to run to James, the pastor of the church in Jerusalem, to seek counsel of him. Instead he went to God.

Paul did finally meet with James and Peter, but there is no indication he felt inferior to them in any way or that he tried to use his personal revelation from God to lord it over them. That should be a lesson to us. We are not subservient to church officials any more than we are to any other man. At the same time, we are not to feel or act superior to anyone because we have received revelation knowledge from God. If we have such knowledge, in due time people will come to recognize it and its source. Yet in this statement Paul did reveal he considered himself to be an apostle of equal rank with the others because he pointed out that he did not confer with those who were apostles "before him." I believe Paul was the twelfth apostle, the one chosen by the Lord Himself to take the place of Judas.

"But I went into Arabia." At the time this was written, the region called Arabia covered a huge area. How long Paul remained there we don't know. The interesting thing about this statement is the fact that Arabia was Gentile territory. It was there Paul received the full revelation from God that he would later share in his writings. Paul was thus the second graduate of Arabia. Moses was the first.

Moses spent forty years tending sheep in Midian where he received his call from the Lord to lead the children of Israel out of Egypt and into the Promised Land. When Jesus was anointed with the Holy Spirit upon His baptism by John the Baptist in the Jordan River, He, too, was led of the Spirit of God into the wilderness. It would seem there is always a time of solitary reflection and preparation that accompanies the call to ministry.

"And returned again unto Damascus." The word "again" indicates Paul left from Damascus (after his conversion on the road) to go into Arabia, and then returned after his time alone with the Lord. We read about this event in the ninth chapter of Acts, which describes Paul's conversion on the road to Damascus, Ananias praying for his eyes to be opened and that he be filled with the Holy Spirit, and finally, his baptism in water. (See verses 1–18.) Verses 19 through 22 tell us:

And when he had received meat, he was strengthened. Then was Saul certain days with the disciples which were at Damascus. And straightway he preached Christ in the synagogues, that he is the Son of God. But all that heard him were amazed, and said; Is not this he that destroyed

them which called on this name in Jerusalem, and came
hither for that intent, that he might bring them bound
unto the chief priests? But Saul increased the more
in strength, and confounded the Jews which dwelt at
Damascus, proving that this is very Christ.

"Straightway" means *immediately*. Immediately after
his conversion Paul began to preach Jesus Christ was the
Son of God, a basic salvation message. You can't preach
what you don't have. At that time Paul only knew the
Lord as his Savior based on his own personal experience.
Those called into the preaching ministry should not go
beyond what we know, beyond our own experience
because a witness is one who testifies of what he himself
has seen and heard. Paul didn't begin out by holding
great evangelistic crusades; he began by simply preaching
what he knew — that Jesus Christ is the Son of God.

However, it wasn't long before his field of personal
experience and knowledge began to grow. As his strength
increased, so did his powers of persuasion and influence.
So will ours, if we are faithful enough to preach only
what we know and patient enough to keep on preaching
it until we know more. As our knowledge increases, so
will our ministry.

Paul in Jerusalem

Verses 18–20

Then after three years I went up to Jerusalem to see Peter,
and abode with him fifteen days. But other of the apostles
saw I none, save James the Lord's brother. Now the things
which I write unto you, behold, before God, I lie not.

Verse 18 fits into the time frame between verses 22 and
23 of Acts 9:

And after that many days were fulfilled, the Jews took counsel to kill him: but their laying await was known of Saul. And they watched the gates day and night to kill him. Then the disciples took him by night, and let him down by the wall in a basket.

vv. 23-25

This expression "many days" refers to the period of three years Paul mentioned in Galatians 1:18. It was during this time Paul made his journey into Arabia where he received his New Testament revelation from God. How long that revelation lasted we don't know for sure, but we do know from Paul's other writings this was time well spent. Afterward Paul returned to Damascus where he began to preach and teach in the Jewish synagogue. His message so stirred up the Jews he had to flee for his life.

When he got to Jerusalem, he spent two weeks with Peter. Wouldn't you love to have been present to hear Paul share with Peter all the Lord had revealed to him? I'm sure it was good for Peter, because no one needed a good stable foundation more than Simon. We know he benefited from his association with Paul because later on in his own epistles he made reference to Paul's writings, noting they were far advanced and contained many things hard to understand, but needful to the body of Christ. (See 2 Peter 3:15-16.)

"I lie not" (v. 20). The reason Paul said this was because the legalistic Judaizers had come into Galatia behind him to stir up the people by casting doubt upon his message and his qualifications as an apostle. Paul had to defend his apostleship against these men whose purpose was to lead the uninformed and impressionable Galatians back into the bondage of the Law.

If you go into the ministry of the Word, it is likely your greatest opposition will also be from established religion.

Like Paul, you may find yourself the object of ridicule and scorn. If so, don't be surprised or overcome by it. Above all, don't give in to anger and retaliation. Be firm in your beliefs but operate in love both toward those who hear you gladly and those who oppose you and your message. Paul exercised his authority as an apostle, but he always did it in a spirit of love. So should we, for how can we ever convince the world (and the church) of God's love for them, if we don't demonstrate that love ourselves?

The Proving Time

Verses 21–24

Afterwards I came into the regions of Syria and Cilicia; and was unknown by face unto the churches of Judaea which were in Christ: but they had heard only, That he which persecuted us in times past now preacheth the faith which once he destroyed. And they glorified God in [because of] me.

"Afterwards I came into the regions of Syria and Cilicia; and was unknown by face unto the churches of Judaea which were in Christ" (vv. 21–22). After staying in Antioch for some time, Paul made his way into Syria and Cilicia, but he had never been seen by the "churches of Judaea," meaning the big established churches like the one in Jerusalem. This seems strange to us today. To our way of thinking, if Paul had wanted to be recognized anywhere it would have been in the "First Church" of the big city, the capital. Most young preachers today want to be known by "the powers that be," to become associated with and recognized by the "big names" in important places. Yet here was Paul who was personally ordained and commissioned by the Lord Jesus Himself, and he went about launching his ministry in an out-of-the-way place like Damascus, not even bothering to try to make himself known outside his small area of influence.

That's the way it should be done. God may call you to some great ministry some day, but if He does, more than likely He will start you out in that ministry in a small way. You may find yourself working for the Lord in some "backwater" area far away from where everything important seems to be happening. Why is that? It's part of God's "management trainee program." Before He gives you a great ministry, He will give you a small one. Once you have proven yourself in the small things, then you will be prepared for the larger. In our Father's business, there is always a proving time before promotion time.

If that happens to you, don't become discouraged. If you have what it takes, you'll get there. Advancement will come, but only when you're ready for it. Show yourself to be faithful and diligent where you are now, and when the time is right, God will reward that faithfulness and diligence by promoting you to a position of greater responsibility. The more responsible you prove yourself to be now, the more responsibility you will receive later on. Like it or not, that's just God's way: "And whosoever of you will be the chiefest, shall be servant of all" (Mark 10:44).

David tended sheep for years before he ever went out and slew Goliath. Do you know what he did after he had slain the giant? He went right back to tending sheep. You would have thought he would have been appointed governor of the land or at least captain of the armies of Israel. Of course, all that and more would come later. It wasn't this time. David wasn't elevated right away because he wasn't ready for it. He wasn't through growing yet.

The same is true of the prophet Elijah. We know nothing of Elijah's younger days. He just seemed to pop up on the scene when he was about thirty years old. Apparently he had spent those first thirty years of his life proving himself for the task that lay ahead of him. As is so often the case, it took Elijah years of preparation and effort to become an overnight success.

The same is true of Joseph. Joseph proved himself again and again: in his father's household, in the household of Potiphar, in the prison to which he had been wrongly sentenced. Whatever his circumstances, Joseph worked to show himself worthy of trust and responsibility, and he got them both, so much so that one day he was promoted to second in the land under Pharaoh himself. Another "overnight success."

Then there was our Lord Jesus Christ. God's own Son spent the first thirty of His thirty-three years of earthly life in obscurity, known only to a handful of people. But He was known to God. That's all that mattered, because in the fullness of time, when the time was just right, He was revealed for who He was. (See Matthew 3:17.)

Think about that for a moment. For the first thirty years of His life, few had ever heard of Jesus of Nazareth. Now how many millions of people down through the ages have heard of Him? In three short years Jesus went from the obscurity of a Galilean carpenter shop to become the very center of all human history.

So it will be with you if you are faithful. You will be revealed for who and what you are if you will stand behind the Word of God. Don't exalt yourself; exalt the Word: "Exalt her [wisdom], and she shall promote thee: she shall bring thee to honour, when thou dost embrace her" (Proverbs 4:8). If you want to be promoted, you must be worthy of promotion.

Many Christians are not prosperous today simply because they can't be trusted. God won't give them more money because they aren't faithful with what they have now. If the Lord can't trust a person with a hundred dollars, why would He give him a thousand? He would only squander it, waste it on his own pleasures and lusts.

God entrusts His finest blessings to those who know how to handle them: "For whosoever hath, to him shall be given; and whosoever hath not, from him shall be taken even that which he seemeth to have" (Luke 8:18). The same principle that applies to possessions also applies to power and position: Responsibility begets responsibility.

"And they glorified God in me" (v. 24). The New American Standard Bible translation of this verse reads: "And they were glorifying God because of me." Paul did not seek after glory or fame or power or riches. He just preached the Gospel to everyone he could, right where he was. As a result, in time his message spread throughout the Jewish world so even those in Jerusalem and the other great cities who did not know him by face knew him by report. Wherever he went, Paul's reputation preceded him. Why did that happen? Not because he was so handsome or intelligent or such a gifted preacher. It was not because he had such a dynamic personality. It happened because Paul put Jesus Christ at the center of his ministry: "For I determined not to know any thing among you, save Jesus Christ, and him crucified" (1 Corinthians 2.2).

Paul brought glory to God, and for that reason God saw to it that glory came to Paul. That's the way it will be in your ministry as well. Just be faithful to preach the Word, and sooner or later you will come to be known by name and face just as Paul was.

The Jerusalem Incident (Salvation by Grace)

Galatians 2:1-10

Then fourteen years after I went up again to Jerusalem with Barnabas, and took Titus with me also. And I went up by revelation, and communicated unto them that gospel which I preach among the Gentiles, but privately to them which were of reputation, lest by any means I should run, or had run, in vain. But neither Titus, who was with me, being a Greek, was compelled to be circumcised: and that because of false brethren unawares brought in, who came in privily to spy out our liberty which we have in Christ Jesus, that they might bring us into bondage: to whom we gave place by subjection, no, not for an hour; that the truth of the gospel might continue with you. But of these who seemed to be somewhat, (whatsoever they were, it maketh no matter to me: God accepteth no man's person:) for they who seemed to be somewhat in conference added nothing to me: but contrariwise, when they saw that the gospel of the uncircumcision was committed unto me, as the gospel of the circumcision was unto Peter; (for he that wrought effectually in Peter to the apostleship of the circumcision, the same was mighty in me toward the Gentiles:) and when James, Cephas, and John, who seemed to be pillars, perceived the grace that was given unto me, they gave to me and Barnabas the right hands of fellowship; that we should go unto the heathen, and they unto the circumcision. Only they would that we should remember the poor; the same which I also was forward to do.

As we have said, the book of Galatians has a dual theme: 1) *salvation by the grace of God versus salvation by works,* and 2) *spirituality by grace versus spirituality by works.* Both of these two themes will be brought out in chapter 2 of Galatians. The first of these is illustrated by this incident in Jerusalem that Paul related to the churches in Galatia.

"Then fourteen years after [later] I went up again to Jerusalem" (v. 1). In this verse Paul revealed this was his second trip to Jerusalem after his conversion. The first was three years after that event when he went to see Peter and spent two weeks with him, during which time he also saw James the brother of Jesus, but none of the other apostles. Now this second trip comes fourteen years after the first. In this passage, Paul revealed to us the reason for this second journey.

"With Barnabas, and took Titus with me also" (v. 1). This statement is significant because Titus is the key person in this story, which we also find in the fifteenth chapter of Acts in which Paul and Barnabas defend their ministry before the church in Jerusalem. "And I went up by revelation, and communicated unto them [the church in Jerusalem] that gospel which I preach among the Gentiles" (v. 2).

Now we begin to get an understanding of Paul's reason for going back to Jerusalem. He told us he went there purposely to explain to them the Gospel message he had been preaching to the Gentiles. Why, after all these years, did he suddenly decide he needed to go to Jerusalem to explain and defend his ministry? The answer has to do with what Paul perceived as a growing menace to the Gospel of grace that he was defending to the Galatians in this chapter.

With the passage of time, the church in Jerusalem had begun to become very legalistic. It had originally come into being as a result of the thousands who came to the Lord through the preaching of the disciples on and after the day of Pentecost. Jerusalem had become the center of Christian missionary activity as evangelists were sent out in all directions to carry the Good News. But as the site of the Jewish temple and the center of Hebrew culture, Jerusalem was also a hotbed of Judaism, which had infiltrated the church there through the years. Just as this situation came to a head, Paul received word by revelation of the Lord to make a journey back to the Jerusalem church. The timing of that revelation was no accident.

For over fourteen years Paul had never gone to the Jerusalem church to tell them face-to-face of his ministry and message. What the believers in Jerusalem knew of him and his ministry had come back to them as hearsay.

Only James and Peter had ever even talked to Paul firsthand. (See Galatians 1:18-19.) Now he was to arrive on the scene at a crucial moment, bringing with him one of his Gentile converts—an action that was bound to bring matters to a head, as Paul no doubt knew full well. As a result of this confrontation, Judaism was set back for a time in the capital city, though it later resurfaced as it did from time to time and as legalism has always done throughout the centuries.

"And took Titus with me also" (v. 1). I believe it was at the time of his sojourn in Arabia that the Lord revealed to Paul His marvelous plan of salvation he wrote about from then on until the end of his life on earth. If that is true, Paul's remarks to the Galatians underline his motive for taking Barnabas, and especially Titus, with him on his return trip to Jerusalem to share his revelation with the church there. As a Gentile convert to Christ, being uncircumcized, Titus would be a living example (as well as a test case) of the doctrine of salvation by grace rather than by keeping of the Jewish Law. So Titus' presence with Paul was not at all incidental; it was the real crux of his visit to the Jerusalem church. If Titus was accepted by the brothers in Jerusalem, it would stand as irrefutable evidence of the validity of Paul's apostleship and of his message of salvation by grace alone.

"And I went up by revelation, and communicated unto them that gospel which I preach among the Gentiles" (v. 2). Paul's visit to Jerusalem was not mere happenstance; it was divinely planned and timed. At just the right moment the Lord spoke to Paul and told him what to do to bring his message of grace to the home church.

"But privately to them which were of reputation" (v. 2). "Them which were of reputation" were Peter, James, and John, the leaders in the Jerusalem church. Paul was very diplomatic and wise. Prior to taking his message before the entire church body, he arranged a private meeting with the church leaders to communicate to them what he had been preaching to the Gentiles and the results of that message.

"Lest by any means I should run, or had run, in vain" (v. 2). By this expression Paul was simply saying, "I was aware if I didn't handle this situation very carefully, I could destroy everything I was doing and had already done up to that time." That, too, is a lesson for us, especially those of us in the ministry.

It is highly important how you and I handle ourselves when dealing with others, both in the church and without. We might have the right message, the right words from God, but if we don't present them in the right manner, we could destroy our ministry. While I appreciate the implied integrity of those who continually boast of how they always preach "the uncompromised Word," I must point out that there is a real danger in that attitude, the danger of spiritual pride.

Pride will destroy our witness faster than compromise any day. Nowhere is humility, tact, diplomacy, discretion, and wisdom needed more than when presenting the glorious Gospel of the Lord Jesus Christ.

We must always be on our guard against the dogmatism that so easily slips in to twist our message of love, grace, and forgiveness into one of ridicule and judgment of those who do not see things as we do. Although we cherish the right to preach the truth as we believe God has revealed it to us, we must never abuse that privilege by mistaking it as a license to impose our beliefs and convictions on others. We do well to always remember that none of us has an exclusive franchise on truth.

"But neither Titus, who was with me, being a Greek, was compelled to be circumcised" (v. 3). Paul's meeting with the three leaders of the church was a success. By receiving his Gentile convert without requiring him to submit to the demands of Jewish circumcision, they were in essence endorsing Paul's message and ministry. This point is of vital importance, which is why Paul pointed it out to the believers in Galatia, themselves Gentiles, who therefore could identify with Titus.

"And that because of false brethren unawares brought in, who came in privily to spy out our liberty which we have in Christ Jesus, that they might bring us into bondage" (v. 4). The New International Version says, "This matter arose because some false brothers had infiltrated our ranks to spy on the freedom we have in Christ Jesus and to make us slaves."

Paul's victory was not to be won easily. Somehow "false brethren,"legalistic Judaizers, heard of Paul's meeting with the church leaders and came in to challenge him before the elders. Paul used Titus to convince all who were present that salvation and spirituality were by faith alone. Since they could not beat Paul in conference, face-to-face, Paul's opponents began to follow his ministry and to undermine him privately after he had left the city so he could not be there to defend himself or his message. This was exactly what had happened in Galatia.

What was their ultimate purpose? "To make us slaves." That is the way legalism works. It always tries to bring into bondage those who have been set free by the Gospel.

"To whom we gave place by subjection, no, not for an hour; that the truth of the gospel might continue with you" (v. 5). The New American Standard Bible clarifies Paul's meaning in this verse, which it translates: "But we did not yield in subjection to them for even an hour, so that the truth of the gospel might remain with you." Paul was not fooled by these people for a minute, nor was he intimidated by them. He stood his ground against them and their attempts to bring him and his followers into subjection to legalism. Paul did this openly before all the church leaders of Jerusalem.

But of these who seemed to be somewhat, (whatsoever they were, it maketh no matter to me: God accepteth no man's person:) for they who seemed to be somewhat in conference added nothing to me: but contrariwise, when they saw that the gospel of the uncircumcision was committed unto me, as the gospel of the circumcision was unto Peter; (for he that wrought effectually in Peter to the apostleship of the circumcision, the same was mighty in me toward the Gentiles:) and when James, Cephas, and John, who seemed to be pillars, perceived the grace that was given unto me, they gave to me and Barnabas the right hands of fellowship; that we should go unto the heathen, and they unto the circumcision. Only they would that we should remember the poor; the same which I also was forward to do.

vv. 6–10

Since this passage is rather hard to decipher in the King James Version, let's read it in the New International Version to be sure we get Paul's message to the Galatians:

As for those who seemed to be important – whatever they were makes no difference to me; God does not judge by external appearance – those men added nothing to my message. On the contrary, they saw that I had been entrusted with the task of preaching the gospel to the Gentiles, just as Peter had been to the Jews. For God, who was at work in the ministry of Peter as an apostle to the Jews, was also at work in my ministry as an apostle to the Gentiles. James, Peter and John, those reputed to be pillars, gave me and Barnabas the right hand of fellowship when they recognized the grace given to me. They agreed that we should go to the Gentiles, and they to the Jews. All they asked was that we should continue to remember the poor, the very thing I was eager to do.

So Paul was fully recognized and accepted as an apostle by the church in Jerusalem, which also endorsed his message of salvation by grace. They made no attempt to impose any restrictions whatsoever on Paul or his ministry or upon his Gentile convert, though it was fully known that Titus was an uncircumcised Greek. Thus, Paul related this Jerusalem incident to the believers in Galatia to impress upon them his full and complete vindication before the church fathers in Jerusalem and to emphasize to these people the completeness of their salvation by grace through simple faith in Jesus Christ and His finished work at Calvary.

The Jerusalem incident (vv. 1–10) illustrates Paul's theme of salvation by grace. In the remaining half of this chapter (vv. 11–17), his second theme, spirituality by grace, will be emphasized.

4

The Law

Galatians 2:11–17

Thus far in our study of Galatians we have seen that the book was written by Paul to the churches in Galatia to warn them about the legalistic Judaizers who had come into their midst to try to get them bound up in a system of law to which they as Gentiles had never been subject. This seems to have been a continual problem with which Paul had to contend throughout his ministry. Wherever he went, his greatest opposition was not from the paganistic Romans or the hedonistic Greeks, but from the legalistic Jews—his own countrymen. Even though they were born again, they still could not free themselves (and would not free others) from what they perceived to be the righteous demands of the Law.

Incidentally, this constant aggravation and harassment is what I believe to be Paul's "thorn in the flesh" (2 Corinthians 12:7). No physical infirmity or affliction could have possibly dogged Paul's steps and caused him more torment than this religious "spirit" that plagued him at every turn for the rest of his earthly life and ministry.

We have said a great deal thus far about the Law, but what exactly is it? And why did it pose such a hindrance and obstacle to the message of grace Paul preached wherever he went? There are five basic aspects of the Mosaic Law we will consider here before continuing our study of the second chapter of Galatians. We are going to consider the Mosaic Law carefully because it has had such a profound effect upon our own religious thinking even today. Whether most Christians realize it or not, our New Testament viewpoint and attitude (and thus our actions) are to a very real degree determined by an Old Testament legal system that was fulfilled and put away at the cross of Calvary, thus setting us free to live a whole new way of life.

Five Points about the Law

1. The Content of the Mosaic Law is Found in the First Five Books of the Bible.

The entire content of what was referred to by the ancient Hebrews as "the Law" was contained in only five books of the Old Testament: *Genesis, Exodus, Leviticus, Numbers,* and *Deuteronomy.* The Ten Commandments are not the entire Jewish Law, but neither is the whole of the Old Testament part of that Law. When the Lord commanded Joshua in Joshua 1:8 that this "book of the law" was not to depart out of his mouth, He was referring only to the first five books of the Old Testament. This was all of the Bible that had been written up to that time.

In Matthew 5:17 when the Lord Jesus indicated that He had come not "to destroy the law, or the prophets... but to fulfil" them, He was referring to the entire Old Testament: the Law being the first five books of that body of holy writings, and the prophets, the major and minor prophets, comprising the rest of it. We need to remember that distinction in our consideration of the old covenant, which our Savior came to fulfill on our behalf. Jesus fulfilled every law and prophecy of the Old Testament written about Him.

The Law is divided into three categories:

A. The Moral Law

The moral law is comprised of the Ten Commandments. This body of rules and regulations was never intended as a means of salvation or spirituality for God's people. Then what was its purpose? Paul told us this in Romans 3:19-22:

> *Now we know that what things soever the law saith, it saith to them who are under the law: that every mouth may be stopped, and all the world may become guilty before God. Therefore by the deeds of the law there shall no flesh be justified in his sight: for by the law is the knowledge of sin. But now the righteousness of God without the law is manifested, being witnessed by the law and the prophets; even the righteousness of God which is by faith of Jesus Christ unto all and upon all them that believe.*

The purpose of the moral law was to show man he is a sinner and in need of a Savior. It was given as an unattainable standard of absolute perfection so men would realize their need of accepting God's free gift of righteousness through faith. That's why legalism is so damnable. By striving for perfection through self-effort, it attempts to circumvent the very plan of salvation that God Himself established from the beginning — which was salvation by grace and not by works.

Even in the Old Testament, salvation, God's righteousness, came "without the law." Faith has always been the means of salvation and spirituality. This was "manifested" and "witnessed by the law and the prophets." The Law taught salvation by grace. Every sacrifice pointed to Jesus and away from man. Every prophet taught salvation by grace and told of the coming of the Lord Jesus, the only One who could redeem mankind.

No one, no matter how pure or devout he may be, can ever attain salvation through self-effort. The only way to attain salvation is to be born again. Spirituality afterward comes as we live by the Spirit. Not only does the moral law not lead to salvation, it doesn't even lead to spirituality. It is impossible to live the Ten Commandments in the natural. The only way to keep the commandments is in the supernatural. A person must be born again to even fulfill the moral code.

Can you see then why no one up until the time of Jesus could keep the Law? The Law could not be kept before the resurrection of Jesus Christ from the dead because no one had yet been born again. No one had ever had the Holy Spirit imparted into their human spirit to re-create them and fill them with supernatural power. Can you also see why after the Day of Pentecost the Law was put away forever?

You and I are no longer under the Law. Jesus Christ fulfilled the Law for us. We are under a new dispensation called *grace* because we live, not by a set of rules and regulations carved in stone, but by the supernatural infilling presence and power of God's own Holy Spirit. Therefore as we walk in that Spirit, we keep the Law. The Spirit leads us in love, and we keep all God's laws whether we realize it or not. Love is the fulfilling of the Law. (See Galatians 5:14.)

B. Shadow Christology

This second part of the Law included the sacrifices, temple furniture, feast days, and ritual of Jewish ceremonial worship. Its purpose was to symbolize the fulfillment of the moral law. That fulfillment was Christ.

First the Jewish Law presented the problem: *no one could be saved by the Law because no one could keep it.* The Law was like a chain with ten links in it. To break any one of those links was to break the entire chain. (See James 2:10.) That's why the people had to constantly bring sacrifices to the temple to atone for their sin in breaking the Law. Life under the old system was a vicious cycle of breaking the Law and making sacrifice for being a lawbreaker.

> *For the law having a shadow of good things to come, and not the very image of the things, can never with those sacrifices which they offered year by year continually make the comers thereunto perfect. For then would they not have ceased to be offered? because that the worshippers once purged should have had no more conscience of sins. But in those sacrifices there is a remembrance again made of sins every year. For it is not possible that the blood of bulls and of goats should take away sins.*
>
> Hebrews 10:1–4

As the writer of Hebrews pointed out, this continual process did not permanently remove sin or the sin nature or sin consciousness. On the contrary, it served only as a constant reminder to the people of their sinfulness. That was what it was designed to do, to make the people aware they were sinners in constant need of redemption and unable to redeem themselves.

Second, the Law presented the solution to that problem: there would one day come a Savior who would fulfill the righteous requirements of the Law for all those who would put their faith in Him.

> *But Christ being come an high priest of good things to come, by a greater and more perfect tabernacle, not made with hands, that is to say, not of this building; neither by the blood of goats and calves, but by his own blood he entered in once into the holy place, having obtained eternal redemption for us.*
>
> Hebrews 9:11–12

Under the old system, every time the people made sacrifice for their sin, it pointed to the coming of the

Lord Jesus who would one day put away that Law forever (because it was imperfect, being conditioned and dependent on man who was himself imperfect and fallible). This system was just a shadow of the real sacrifice yet to come. The ritualistic elements of Jewish worship all had a meaning. They symbolized the death, burial, and resurrection of the promised Messiah, the Savior of Israel, the Lord Jesus Christ.

Whether the worship ritual involved a grain offering, an offering of wine or oil, the bringing of the firstfruits to the altar, or the blood sacrifice of a dove, lamb, or oxen, it always portrayed one thing: the Atonement, the sacrifice of the life of the Savior for His people. Thus the whole ceremonial system evolved around and centered on blood. Why? To continually remind the people of the blood of the Anointed One that would be shed for the remission of their sin.

C. The Social Law

The third part of the Law had to do with dietary regulations, rules of sanitation, and instructions on the proper care of land and crops. Like the first part, this was also fulfilled by part two, the coming of the Messiah. He fulfilled the moral law and the social law by His perfect life, but He fulfilled the shadow Christology by His death, resurrection, and ascension into heaven to sit at the right hand of God the Father.

2. The Law was Given to Israel Only.

And Moses went up unto God, and the LORD called unto him out of the mountain, saying, Thus shalt thou say to the house of Jacob, and tell the children of Israel.
Exodus 19:3
These are the statutes and judgments and laws, which the LORD made between him and the children of Israel

in mount Sinai by the hand of Moses.

Leviticus 26:46

Now we know that what things soever the law saith, it saith to them who are under the law.

Romans 3:19

Who are Israelites; to whom pertaineth the adoption, and the glory, and the covenants, and the giving of the law.

Romans 9:4

If it was to the house of Jacob, the children of Israel, to whom Moses gave the statutes and judgments and laws, then it stands to reason that these statutes and judgments and laws were not given to Gentiles:

For what nation is there so great, who hath God so nigh unto them, as the LORD our God is in all things that we call upon him for?

Deuteronomy 4:7

For as many as have sinned without law shall also perish without law: and as many as have sinned in the law shall be judged by the law; (for not the hearers of the law are just before God, but the doers of the law shall be justified. For when the Gentiles, which have not the law, do by nature the things contained in the law, these, having not the law, are a law unto themselves).

Romans 2:12-14

3. Christians are not Under the Mosaic Law.

For sin shall not have dominion over you: for ye are not under the law, but under grace.

Romans 6:14

For I through the law am dead to the law, that I might live unto God.

Galatians 2:19

Since we Christians are Gentiles and not Jews, we are not under the Jewish Law. Jesus Christ fulfilled that Law for us two thousand years before our birth. Why then should we be bound by it today? We aren't. That's the good news of the Gospel, that Jesus Christ fulfilled all the Law. When He said on the cross, "It is finished," He was not referring to the plan of salvation because that would not be completed until He had ascended to the Father. He was referring to the Mosaic Law He had come to fulfill (Matthew 5:17). Now because that Law is completely fulfilled, you and I are under a higher law, "the law of the Spirit of life in Christ Jesus," which has made us free from "the law of sin and death" (Romans 8:2).

Since Jesus Christ fulfilled the Law for us long ago, the only way you and I can fulfill the Law today is to believe in Him and have His perfect life, His righteousness, imputed to us. We did that when we accepted Him into our life. We received everything He did on the cross. He did all the work for us. He earned the righteousness, He won the salvation, and He merited the grace, for us. We did nothing but receive it all by faith.

The Law tried to produce life from the outside in, but the weakness of the Law was in the flesh. The reason the Law could never succeed is because all men have the nature of flesh, and that carnal nature can never please God: "So then they that are in the flesh cannot please God" (Romans 8:8). The way Jesus Christ produced life was from the inside out. He recreated our human spirits. When a person listens to the dictates of the human spirit guided by the Holy Spirit, which he has received through Christ, the flesh must line up and the Law is kept in him by the power of the Holy Spirit.

Some people, hearing me preach this message, say to me: "You're teaching Christians are not supposed to keep the Law."

"Well, yes and no," I tell them. "No, we don't have to go back and try to keep the Law. But yes, we do keep it."

As a Christian, I don't break the Law. Do you know why not? I walk after the Spirit, and according to Paul, those who walk after the Spirit fulfill the Law (Romans 8:1).

"Yes," these people say, "but if God put the Ten Commandments in the Bible, I think we ought to try to keep them."

"Well, if you think the Ten Commandments are so important," I say to them, "then quote them to me." Naturally they can't. They might get a few, but very seldom all of them, and almost never in order. "I don't understand that," I say. "You think you ought to be keeping something you don't even know well enough to quote correctly."

I follow the Ten Commandments. I live up to virtually all of them all the time, but I never learned to quote them. And I don't really care that I can't. I walk in the Spirit, not by Law. Because I walk in the Spirit, I find myself doing those things that please the Spirit. I walk in love, and according to our Lord, love is the fulfillment of all the Law. (See Matthew 22:37-40.)

Although we Christians are not under the Law, we do keep it. We keep it the same way Jesus did. Can you imagine our Lord walking along beside the Sea of Galilee worrying about whether He had broken any of the commandments that day? No, I don't think He ever did that. He didn't strive to keep the Law. He just walked in the Spirit, and therefore did not fulfill the lust of the flesh. By not fulfilling the lust of the flesh, He kept the Law. That's the way you and I keep it. By following the Holy Spirit who is in us.

Walking in the Spirit produces life from the inside out. It

produces the fruit of the Spirit: "love, joy, peace, longsuffering, gentleness, goodness, faith, meekness, temperance: against such there is no law" (Galatians 5:23–24).

4. Today the Law Applies Only to the Unbeliever.

Knowing this, that the law is not made for a righteous man, but for the lawless and disobedient, for the ungodly and for sinners, for unholy and profane, for murderers of fathers and murderers of mothers, for manslayers, for whoremongers, for them that defile themselves with mankind, for menstealers, for liars, for perjured persons, and if there be any other thing that is contrary to sound doctrine.

1 Timothy 1:9–10

Does the Law have any significance today? Only to the unbeliever, the unregenerate person. He is the only one affected by it. The Law is still there to do for him what it did for those under it, to serve to point out the need for a Savior. For us who have already received that Savior, we are no longer under the Law, but under grace. One day all the unregenerate will be judged by the Law, according to their works. (See Matthew 25:31–46; Revelation 20:12–15.) But to those of us who are in Christ Jesus, there is no condemnation, no judgment. We have already passed from death unto life. (See Romans 8:1; 1 John 3:14.)

5. The Law has Limitations.

In the book of Galatians, Paul pointed out four limitations of the Law:

A. It Cannot Justify.

Knowing that a man is not justified by the works of the law, but by the faith of Jesus Christ, even we have believed in Jesus Christ, that we might be justified by the faith of Christ, and not by the works of the law: for by the works of the law shall no flesh be justified.
Galatians 2:16

B. It Cannot Give Life.

Is the law then against the promises of God? God forbid: for if there had been a law given which could have given life, verily righteousness should have been by the law.
Galatians 3:21

C. It Cannot Provide the Holy Spirit.

This only would I learn of you, Received ye the Spirit by the works of the law, or by the hearing of faith?
Galatians 3:2

D. It Cannot Produce Miracles.

He therefore that ministereth to you the Spirit, and worketh miracles among you, doeth he it by the works of the law, or by the hearing of faith?
Galatians 3:5

This last point is very important: *The Law cannot produce miracles.* Think about that for a moment. If you have been in Pentecostal circles for very many years, you can recall when meetings were marked by numerous and tremendous miracles. Yet today such miracles seem to happen less and less in many churches. Why is that? What has happened to stifle the flow of God's power? Very simply, what we are seeing today is the result of legalism.

At first ministers were preaching only from God's Word, and God responded by pouring out His Spirit and by confirming the Word preached with signs following. However, somewhere along the line the classical Pentecostals began to turn away from the preaching of the Word to the preaching of rules, regulations, and codes of dress and speech and behavior. They got all caught up in deciding things like sleeve length and dress length. They turned their attention from proclaiming the Gospel of freedom to denouncing card playing, lipstick wearing, and moviegoing. So the power of God was cut off.

Today there is a new revival of miracles and healings in these latter days. Do you know why? We've gotten away from preaching all the do's and don'ts and started preaching the Word again. The miracles and signs and wonders have begun to occur once again, but do you know the amazing thing about all this? Spirit-filled people still dress and speak and behave modestly. The Word in their life sets the standard.

Some preachers seem to be afraid that if they don't constantly remind their people of all these rules and regulations, they will get completely out of hand and start doing anything they want to. My answer to them is, "Preach the Word and let your people make up their own minds. You'll be amazed at what the liberating Gospel of Jesus Christ does to people. Once they learn they are truly free to do what they want to, they seem to realize what they want to do is follow the Spirit of the Lord."

That is precisely why the Lord wants that Gospel preached. He wants His children to obey out of hearts of love and appreciation for all He has done for them in Christ, not because they're browbeaten and coerced into doing right, or because they're afraid not to behave. Preach the Gospel and people will receive the Spirit. Then when the Spirit moves, people will follow Him, not out of a sense of duty or obligation or guilt, but willingly and joyfully because where the Spirit is, there is joy and peace and liberty.

With that understanding of the Law, let's now look at the second of the two incidents Paul described in chapter 2 of his letter to the Galatians. Keep in mind he was writing to emphasize to them the sufficiency of God's grace to save to the uttermost those who come to Him not by the Law but through Jesus Christ His Son. (See Hebrews 7:25.)

The Antioch Incident (Spirituality by Grace)

Galatians 2:11-17

But when Peter was come to Antioch, I withstood him to the face, because he was to be blamed. For before that certain came from James, he did eat with the Gentiles: but when they were come, he withdrew and separated himself, fearing them which were of the circumcision. And the other Jews dissembled likewise with him; insomuch that Barnabas also was carried away with their dissimulation. But when I saw that they walked not uprightly according to the truth of the gospel, I said unto Peter before them all, If thou, being a Jew, livest after the manner of Gentiles, and not as do the Jews, why compellest thou the Gentiles to live as do the Jews? We who are Jews by nature, and not sinners of the Gentiles, knowing that a man is not justified by the works of the law, but by the faith of Jesus Christ, even we have believed in Jesus Christ, that we might be justified by the faith of Christ, and not by the works of the law: for by the works of the law shall no flesh be justified. But if, while we seek to be justified by Christ, we ourselves also are found sinners, is therefore Christ the minister of sin? God forbid.

Before we get into this story in detail, let's back up

a little and set the stage for what is happening in these verses. As stated previously, some time after its initial beginnings on the Day of Pentecost, the church in Jerusalem had begun to go downhill, as churches do when they start to become legalistic. The Spirit of the Lord had simply begun to move away from Jerusalem to find another place in which He could minister freely. He found that place in Antioch where He raised up a new church that was not preaching the do's and don'ts.

Most of the members of the church were Gentiles and knew nothing of the Jewish Law. Therefore, these people were free to preach the Gospel and worship God in spirit and truth. All they knew was the Word of the Lord brought to them by Paul on one of his missionary journeys. Since all they had to go by was the New Testament teaching of salvation by grace, this church was able to flourish and missionaries went out everywhere to spread the Good News of Jesus Christ.

In time, the church in Jerusalem, which by now considered itself the headquarters of Christianity, heard about what was happening in Antioch and immediately became jealous of its apparent success. Because the church in Antioch was made up of Gentiles and had been established by Paul (whom most of them had never met and were suspicious of anyway), naturally the Jews in Jerusalem were not at all sure about its orthodoxy. After all, it had never received their seal of approval. In light of the situation, they decided they had better send a representative to Antioch to investigate the church there and report back to them his findings.

Since Peter was one of the founders of the Jerusalem church and a devout Jew of good standing, they chose him as their envoy to Antioch. He made his way there where he soon became involved in the affairs of the local church, so involved, in fact, he remained longer than necessary. The church in Jerusalem became concerned enough to send others to find out exactly what was going on. This time they sent a team of legalistic Jews. It was the arrival of this group of Jewish believers from Jerusalem that sparked the incident in Antioch described by Paul in this passage.

"But when Peter was come to Antioch, I withstood him to the face" (v. 11). This word translated "withstood" is from a Greek word meaning "to resist" or "to oppose." So this very Paul whom the home church in Jerusalem knew so little about and generally mistrusted had the nerve to speak out publicly against the great apostle Peter (whom many Christians today look upon as the first leader of the church). Why did Paul oppose Peter?

"Because he was to be blamed" (v. 11). Paul opposed Peter because he was doing wrong.

"For before that certain [Jews] came from James, he did eat with the Gentiles: but when they were come, he withdrew and separated himself" (v. 12). While in Antioch, Peter ate and drank with the Gentiles there, which was expressly forbidden to devout Jews under the Law. What do you think Peter ate with the Gentiles? Surely their menu contained many foods that were forbidden to a Jew under the Law, but Peter knew he was no longer under the Law. He knew it because the Lord had revealed it to him through the vision He gave him when He sent him to preach the Gospel to Cornelius and his family who were Gentiles:

> And he said unto them, Ye know how that it is an unlawful thing for a man that is a Jew to keep company, or come unto one of another nation; but God hath showed me that I should not call any man common or unclean.
> *Acts 10:28*

Peter knew better than to separate himself from non-Jews. Then why did he do it? "Fearing them which were of the circumcision" (Galatians 2:12). Peter withdrew from his

71

freedom as a Christian and subjected himself to the dictates of the Jewish Law for only one reason, fear. As long as he was alone with the Gentiles, he ate and drank and fellowshipped with them freely. But as soon as the group sent by James from the Jerusalem church arrived on the scene, Peter became worried about what they would think of his actions.

This is curious because Peter had already settled this issue of consorting with Gentiles in the very Jerusalem church from which these men had been sent. When news about Peter's trip to preach to Cornelius and his family got back to the church in Jerusalem, they called Peter in to explain what he was doing in going to the Gentiles. We read about this incident and Peter's response in Acts 11:1–18:

> *And the apostles and brethren that were in Judaea heard that the Gentiles had also received the word of God. And when Peter was come up to Jerusalem, they that were of the circumcision contended with him, saying, Thou wentest in to men uncircumcised, and didst eat with them. But Peter rehearsed the matter from the beginning, and expounded it by order unto them...When they heard these things, they held their peace, and glorified God, saying, Then hath God also to the Gentiles granted repentance unto life.*
>
> vv.1–4,18

Notice who it was who contended with Peter about his dealings with Gentiles: "they that were of the circumcision" (Acts 11:2). Now notice who had just arrived in Antioch to investigate matters there, the ones Paul said Peter was afraid of: "them which were of the circumcision."

Isn't it strange this same apostle Peter who stood before the whole church in Jerusalem to defend his actions in going in and eating with Gentiles should now be afraid to be seen doing the same thing by these very same people? That's one reason Paul became so angry with Peter. Peter knew better than to do what he was doing. Paul also knew Peter was leading others astray by his wrong attitude and actions.

"And the other Jews dissembled likewise with him; insomuch that Barnabas also was carried away with their dissimulation" (v. 13). That one little act of legalism split the whole church at Antioch right down the middle. One bit of leaven will leaven the whole lump. This word translated *dissembled* is from a Greek word meaning *"to act hypocritically in concert with"* someone. 1

Who was it who acted hypocritically here in this situation? The Jews. Who was the someone they acted hypocritically in concert with? It was Peter, the great apostle, the very one who should have been taking the lead in promoting unity in the church (as he had done in the case of Cornelius and his family) instead of causing divisions in it.

Again, there is a lesson for us here. Just because we are not in total agreement with the doctrines or practices of other Christian churches does not mean we are to withdraw and separate ourselves from them. The biblical call to "come out...and be ye separate" (2 Corinthians 6:17) does not refer to separation from our brothers and sisters in Christ, regardless of their sectarian affiliation. Nothing is needed more in our society today than a united church of Jesus Christ. We need more and more churches (and individual Christians) coming together in a spirit of harmony and brotherhood.

How are we ever going to reach the world with our message of God's love and acceptance if we Christians don't love and accept each other? Unity in Christ is part of the message of grace. To separate ourselves into little self-centered cliques is to dissemble, to act the hypocrite. God forbid that we Christians should ever join these self-righteous Jews in their dissimulation.

Notice, Paul emphasized that even Barnabas was influenced by Peter's actions. Why is it so important that

Barnabas joined in with this dissimulation? Barnabas was the pastor of the church in Antioch. The pastor is supposed to be a bridge between the various elements of his church, not a cause of division. Any time a pastor gets personally involved in a church division, that church is destined to split. Paul stressed the importance of unity among the brethren by condemning the prime cause of division: *an attitude of exclusiveness.*

"But when I saw that they walked not uprightly according to the truth of the gospel, I said unto Peter before them all, If thou, being a Jew, livest after the manner of Gentiles, and not as do the Jews, why compellest thou the Gentiles to live as do the Jews?" (v. 14). "Them all" refers to the members of the church in Antioch. Whereas Paul had met privately with the church leaders in Jerusalem before presenting his case before the church there, he showed no such discretion in this case. On the contrary, he stood up in front of the whole church body to denounce Peter for his wrongdoing.

This is not the way I would recommend handling problems in the church, but obviously Paul thought this case called for drastic measures. He took Peter to task openly, knowing that his remarks to him pertained to all the Jews in that crowd who had joined him in his wrongdoing. In this letter to the Galatians, he used that incident as an object lesson to drive home his point of justification by grace and not by the keeping of the Jewish Law.

Let's look at Paul's logic in his argument for justification by grace without regard to the Law. He is saying to Peter, "You are a Jew, yet you have been living like a Gentile, just as though the Jewish Law had no jurisdiction over you. If you, a Jew, are not subject to the Jewish Law, then why are you trying to force the Gentiles to live by it?"

"We who are Jews by nature, and not sinners of the Gentiles" (v. 15). Here Paul included himself in his argument. *By nature* means *"by birth."* And "not sinners of the Gentiles" is part of the expression of the old Jewish attitude that there were only two kinds of people in the world: *Jews* and *sinners.* (To the ancient Jews the word *Gentile* meant *a heathen, one without God, a "sinner."*)

Paul used this age-old Hebrew phrase to lead up to the point he made in chapter 3: *being born a Jew does not make a person the seed of Abraham and heir to the promises of God.* He will show the seed of Abraham is not a physical race, but a spiritual race. Therefore, the true Jew is not one who is circumcised physically, but one whose heart has been circumcised through the New Birth. And the Law is not that which is written on tablets of stone, but that which God has written on the hearts of those who have exercised the faith of Abraham. These are the true Jews.

"Knowing that a man is not justified by the works of the law, but by the faith of Jesus Christ, even we have believed in Jesus Christ, that we might be justified by the faith of Christ, and not by the works of the law: for by the works of the law shall no flesh be justified" (v. 16). What did we say was the purpose of the Law? To show man he was a sinner and incapable of attaining righteousness and salvation by his own efforts. The Law was given to convince men of their need of a Savior. Its purpose was to bring man face-to-face with his own lack of righteousness so he would turn to God and receive the gift of His righteousness freely given through His Son Jesus Christ.

"But if, while we seek to be justified by Christ, we ourselves also are found sinners, is therefore Christ the minister of sin? God forbid" (v. 17). Paul used his debater's technique in this verse to finally put a noose around Peter's neck. What Paul was saying to Peter here is this: "Peter, if you and I are trying to live a spiritual life before God by keeping the Law, then we are saying it is the Law that makes us spiritual after we are saved by grace. By your actions you are saying a person is saved by grace but in order to be spiritual he must go back and

75

keep the Law.

"But what did the Law do, Peter? Didn't it reveal you were a sinner? You were born again by faith in Christ Jesus. Now you are going back to the Law that declares you to be a sinner! Do you know what that means? It means that Jesus Christ saved you to turn you into a sinner! You are telling these people that Jesus Christ is a minister of sin.That's blasphemy!"

Paul made it clear that the Law is not the way to become spiritual. If a person is made worthy by faith in Jesus Christ, then it is by faith in Jesus Christ he is made spiritual. If he couldn't save himself by his own efforts, he cannot sanctify himself by his own efforts. Spirituality, like salvation, is a gift of God, not the result of works. This is the message Paul would have the Galatians learn. It is also the lesson he would have us learn today.

5
Grace versus Works
Galatians 2:18–3:5

The Word of Reconciliation

In our previous study we noted that Paul recounted two incidents to the Galatians. The first incident, which took place in Jerusalem, served to point out to them the difference between the false concept of salvation by works and the Gospel message of salvation by grace. The second of these two incidents, in Antioch, emphasized that spirituality, like salvation, is also a product of faith, "not of works, lest any man should boast" (Ephesians 2:9). No one is ever saved or justified by works of the Law because the Law is nothing more than a mirror to reflect a person's own unrighteousness and to convince him of his need to receive God's free gift of redemption and righteousness.

No Christian ever has to work to become righteous; he is declared righteous by God. That's how he got saved. This is the basic concept Paul was trying to teach the Galatians so they would never again be deceived into trying to attain something by their own efforts that God had already given them by His grace.

This message is what Paul referred to in his second letter to the Corinthians as "the ministry of reconciliation; to wit, that God was in Christ, reconciling the world unto himself, not imputing their trespasses unto them"

(2 Corinthians 5:18–19). The New International Version translates verse 19: "God was reconciling the world to himself in Christ, not counting men's sins against them." It is this "word of reconciliation" (v. 19) that Paul was now sharing with these people in the churches of Galatia.

With that thought in mind, let's continue our study in the second chapter of his letter.

Crucified with Christ

Galatians 2:18–21

For if I build again the things which I destroyed, I make myself a transgressor. For I through the law am dead to the law, that I might live unto God. I am crucified with Christ: nevertheless I live; yet not I, but Christ liveth in me: and the life which I now live in the flesh I live by the faith of the Son of God, who loved me, and gave himself for me. I do not frustrate the grace of God: for if righteousness come by the law, then Christ is dead in vain.

"For if I build again the things which I destroyed, I make myself a transgressor" (v. 18). When Paul spoke of building again the things that he destroyed, he was referring to going back to the Law to seek justification. He said this because he knew when a person is born again, the Law is destroyed in his life; it will never again be valid to him. As far as that person is concerned, the Law is dead. To go back and try to resurrect it is to make himself a transgressor.

God never makes any person a transgressor. People do that to themselves. They do so by choosing the dead Law over the living Lord, which is self-deception. It is bad enough for a person to allow someone else to deceive him; it's even worse to deceive himself.

"For I through the law am dead to the law, that I might live unto God" (v. 19). The Law was not designed to give life; it was designed to kill. To attempt to achieve eternal life through the Law is to commit suicide.

In 2 Corinthians 3:6 Paul wrote, "For the letter [of the Law] killeth, but the spirit giveth life." The Law kills. No one knew the truth of this statement better than Paul. Until his conversion on the road to Damascus, he had been a Pharisee, a Hebrew of the Hebrews, "touching the righteousness which is in the law, blameless" (Philippians 3:6). He knew what he was talking about when he said the Law kills.

Once a person realizes he is dead, there is hope that he will turn to the Lord who alone can give him life. One purpose of the Law is to kill so God can resurrect to eternal life. Paul recognized this truth.

"I am crucified with Christ: nevertheless I live; yet not I, but Christ liveth in me: and the life which I now live in the flesh I live by the faith of the Son of God, who loved me, and gave himself for me" (v. 20). This verse is not translated correctly in the King James Version. The phrase "I am crucified" should read "I *have been* crucified." The Greek verb tense indicates that this is a past work that has already been completed. You and I are not in the state of being crucified, nor are we in a perpetual state of crucifixion. Like Christ, we were crucified once and for all time the moment we identified ourselves with His crucifixion and were born again of the Spirit of God. We died on the cross with our Lord. We were buried with Him in death. We were resurrected with Him to newness of life. We ascended with Him and now we are seated with Him in heavenly places. (See Ephesians 2:5–6.)

Aren't you glad Jesus is not still on the cross? Neither are you and I. We don't have to go around daily crucifying our old man. He's dead. He was nailed to the cross. We have become brand new creatures: "Therefore if any man be in Christ, he is a new creature: old things are passed away;

behold, all things are become new" (2 Corinthians 5:17). Just as Jesus never has to go to the cross to be crucified again, neither do we have to die again and again: "For the law of the Spirit of life in Christ Jesus hath made me [us] free from the law of sin and death" (Romans 8:2).

The expression "yet not I" is not found in the original Greek version of Galatians 2:20. This Scripture could better be translated: "I have been crucified with Christ, and I no longer live; but Christ lives in me."

Paul is saying the Law killed him. What happens when a person dies? When someone dies, he is not annihilated. Death is never annihilation. Physical death is the separation of the inward man from the outward man. The inward man, the real man, goes on either to be with the Lord in heaven or to be with the devil in hell — one of the two. The outward shell of the person remains here on the earth with nothing in it.

That's what happened when you and I were born again. Our old natures inside us, that once belonged to Satan, moved out, and the Spirit of Jesus Christ came to live in our physical bodies. Our bodies didn't change. It wasn't the outward man that changed; it was the inward man who was born again. It is not so much our "old [spiritual] man" we must contend with now that we are new creatures in Christ Jesus. It's the flesh that gives us so much trouble, and Satan who is at large in the earth. However, this is really no problem because greater is He who lives in us than he who is in the world (1 John 4:4). Therefore we can still overcome him by the blood of Jesus and the word of our testimony (Revelation 12:11).

"And the life which I now live (after the New Birth) I live by faith in the Son of God, who loved me, and gave Himself for me." This translation brings out better the twofold theme of the whole book of Galatians: *salvation by faith, spirituality by faith.* Paul stressed the fact he was dead, crucified with Christ, then resurrected, born again

80

by faith, and the life he now lived, after his salvation experience was also by faith. The life he lived in this fleshly body was not of the Law; it was full of grace.

Our salvation is a free gift from God. We don't deserve it; we can't earn it. All we do to receive it is accept it by faith. In the same way, our spiritual life after salvation is by grace; we can never deserve or earn it by our own efforts. It, too, is a gift of God received by faith.

Does this mean we no longer need to pray or read the Bible or attend church or give offerings to the Lord? Not to merit righteousness we don't. As good as all these things are, they won't merit righteousness for us any more than they would merit salvation for us. Then why do we do them? We do them because we want to, because we love God and want to communicate with Him, hear from Him, learn more about Him, serve Him, and have a part in His ministry of reconciliation. Any other reason for doing these things is selfish. It's legalistic. It's trying to get God to do something for us because we've done something for Him. That is the wrong motivation. We can never please God by our self-striving efforts.

Some people think they move God by their faith. That's not so. God has already moved by His grace. All we do is accept by our faith what God has already done.

I like to think of it this way. Grace is God reaching out toward us, and faith is us reaching out toward God. God reached out first, and we reach out second. Our faith does not cause God to move; His grace causes our faith to move. We were not saved because God responded to our faith and saved us. Redemption has been completed ever since Jesus Christ rose from the grave. The work is finished. God's part is done. That was grace. Now our part is accepting that which has already been done for us. That's faith. Faith does not move God to action. Faith is our action in response to God's grace. Grace always precedes faith.

We don't attain righteousness by our efforts. It was given to us by God as an act of His grace. Now we accept that righteousness by faith, by responding to what God has already done for us in Jesus Christ.

"I do not frustrate the grace of God: for if righteousness come by the law, then Christ is dead in vain" (v. 21). This word translated *"frustrate"* actually means *"to nullify"* or *"to stop."* What Paul was actually saying here is: "I do not nullify the grace of God by my self-efforts to attain righteousness; because if righteousness could be gained by works of the Law, then Christ died for nothing."

Works of Law or Hearing of Faith?

Galatians 3:1-5

O foolish Galatians, who hath bewitched you, that ye should not obey the truth, before whose eyes Jesus Christ hath been evidently set forth, crucified among you? This only would I learn of you, Received ye the Spirit by the works of the law, or by the hearing of faith? Are ye so foolish? having begun in the Spirit, are ye now made perfect by the flesh? Have ye suffered so many things in vain? if it be yet in vain. He therefore that ministereth to you the Spirit, and worketh miracles among you, doeth he it by the works of the law, or by the hearing of faith?

"O foolish Galatians, who hath bewitched you, that ye should not obey the truth" (v. 1). This word translated *"foolish"* is closer to our word *stupid.* *"Bewitched"* means *hypnotized.* What Paul was saying here is: "O you stupid Galatians, who has hypnotized you? The church in Jerusalem became hypnotized, and so did the one in Antioch. You have been deceived into falling into the same trap they did. Who is responsible for this deception?"

Of course, we know the answer to that question. It

was the legalistic Judaizers who had come in after Paul's departure from Galatia to deceive the ignorant Galatians into giving up their freedom in Christ for bondage to a Law to which they were never subject. Paul obviously had a hard time accepting that anyone would be so foolish as to fall for such a thing. He can only assume these clever Judaizers with their impressive credentials and shrewd arguments have managed to mesmerize these gullible Galatians by dangling the Law in front of them.

"Before whose eyes Jesus Christ hath been evidently set forth, crucified among you" (v. 1). The problem with the Galatians was they had "eye trouble." They had moved their eyes away from the truth to behold a lie. In so doing, they had allowed themselves to become blinded to the truth. They had become so spellbound by the brilliance of the Judaizers and their smooth talk that they had fallen for their line. They had substituted the law of sin and death for the Gospel of grace and life.

The word *"evidently"* here means *"clearly."* Paul was saying to these people: "How could you have been so foolish as to take your eyes off Jesus Christ who was clearly portrayed in front of you, crucified, to turn them to the distortion of the Law?"

"This only would I learn of you" (v. 2). "Just tell me one thing."

"Received ye the Spirit by the works of the law, or by the hearing of faith?" (v. 2). "Did you receive the Spirit of God by keeping the Jewish Law, or by simply receiving Him by faith in Jesus Christ?"

Here Paul was not speaking of the baptism of the Spirit, of being filled with the Spirit, but simply of receiving the Spirit of God through the New Birth. He was asking these people if they were born again of the Spirit by their own efforts, or whether their redemption was a gift from God received by faith alone. The answer, of course, is the latter. As foolish as they were, the Galatians knew it was

83

by grace they were saved, through faith. They knew their redemption was not of themselves but was the gift of God: it was not of works, lest any of them should boast of having achieved it by his own efforts (Ephesians 2:8–9).

"Are ye so foolish? having begun in the Spirit, are ye now made perfect by the flesh?" (v. 3). Paul wanted to know this: "If you were saved by grace, then why are you now trying to be sanctified by works? If you began your New Life by being born of the Spirit, why are you now trying to live that New Life by your own efforts? Are you really so stupid you don't realize that you remain spiritual the same way you became spiritual—by faith in Jesus Christ?"

"Have ye suffered so many things in vain? if it yet be in vain?" (v. 4). What Paul was asking the Galatians here is simply this: "Have you suffered all these trials and tribulations for nothing? Tribulation came to you for your faith. Your faith carried you through, not the Law. After successfully coming through many battles, are you now going to turn to the Law? It wasn't your self-efforts at keeping the Law that brought opposition against you neither was it keeping the Law that brought you through the opposition. It was your faith in Jesus Christ that both made you the target of the Evil One and gave you victory over him. Are you now ready to give up that 'faith which was once delivered unto the saints' (Jude 3), that faith for which you so earnestly contended, to turn back to dead works of the Law?"

Some Christians don't understand the connection between faith and persecution. Either they think having faith exempts a person from all trials and tribulation, or they go to the opposite extreme and think that trials and tribulation are sent by God to test their faith. Neither of these two extreme views is accurate. Christians are not exempt from persecution, but persecution is not from God. Jesus warned that in this world we would have tribulation (John 16:33). But He also told us why tribulation would come upon us: "Persecution ariseth for the word's sake" (Mark 4:17). He further told us the source of that tribulation: "The thief cometh not, but for to steal, and to kill, and to destroy" (John 10:10).

Christians will face trials and tribulation in this world. We will be persecuted for the Word's sake. But this persecution is not sent by God to test our faith, rather it is sent by Satan to destroy our faith. That's why it is so important that we "earnestly contend for the faith which was once delivered unto the saints" (Jude 3). By so doing, we grow in faith power. But it is not persecution that makes us strong; it is the faith we use in that persecution that strengthens us.

As we increase in physical and spiritual prosperity, we will increase our likelihood of becoming the target of Satan's attacks. Some people don't seem to realize that prosperity and persecution go together. Didn't Jesus promise His disciples that along with the "hundredfold return" there would also be a similar increase in persecution (Mark 10:30)? Although Jesus warned them that in this world there would be tribulation, He also exhorted them not to be afraid, because He had overcome the world.

Tribulation always ends in victory for the faithful child of God. That's why Paul reproved these Galatians for being so foolish as to abandon the faith for which they had contended in order to turn back to the Law that has no power to defeat the enemy.

"He therefore that ministereth to you the Spirit, [the New Birth] and worketh miracles among you, doeth he it by the works of the law, or by the hearing of faith?" (v. 5). Paul was speaking of himself in this verse, referring to the first time he came to Galatia to establish these very churches to which he was now writing. He was modestly pointing out that the one who worked miracles in their midst (Paul

85

himself) did so by the presence and power of the Holy Spirit within him, and not by works of the Law. The Law cannot produce miracles any more than it can give the New Birth.

Are miracles worked by the Spirit of God, or by the Law? Do healings take place as a consequence of the teaching of the Law, or as a result of the preaching of the message of faith? The answer to these questions should not be hard to recognize, even for these blinded Galatians.

As we have noted, legalism cannot produce miracles. It is the preaching of the Word, not the teaching of rules and regulations, that God confirms with miracles, signs, and wonders! That's why I am determined as long as I serve as pastor, I am going to preach the Word of God from cover to cover. Other ministers may do as they will, but I am going to hold forth the message of faith, because I know it is by the hearing of faith miracles are wrought. The Word of God never changes. "Jesus Christ is the same yesterday, and to day, and for ever" (Hebrews 13:8).

6
Abraham's Gospel
Galatians 3:6-10

The Righteousness of Abraham

Galatians 3:6

Even as Abraham believed God, and it was accounted to him for righteousness.

Abraham was born, lived, and died before the Law ever came into existence. Yet he was saved. And he was spiritual. If Abraham could do that before the Law existed, surely you and I can do it after the Law was fulfilled. The reason we can do it is because neither salvation nor spirituality is contingent upon keeping the Law but upon believing the Lord:

What shall we say then that Abraham our father, as pertaining to the flesh, hath found? For if Abraham were justified by works, he hath whereof to glory; but not before God. For what saith the scripture? Abraham believed God, and it was counted unto him for righteousness. Now to him that worketh is the reward not reckoned of grace, but of debt. But to him that worketh not, but believeth on him that justifieth the ungodly, his faith is counted for righteousness.
Romans 4:1-5

Paul was pointing out to the Gentile believers that whether in the Old Testament or the New Testament, the means of salvation is the same: faith. Faith is nothing more or less than believing God. That's what Adam and Eve did not do; that's why they fell. Since the fall of man came about because of unbelief, the restoration of man is dependent upon belief. Abraham was not justified because he kept the Jewish Law. That Law didn't even exist in his day. Rather he was justified, declared righteous, because he believed God. Believing God is not limited to the New Testament.

When I am teaching in any group of Christians, one of my favorite questions to ask them is this: "How were the people saved in the Old Testament?" Almost invariably the answer is: "By the keeping of the Law." But that is just not so. If it were, then no one in the Old Testament, including Abraham, could ever get saved, because no one could ever keep the Law. And even if they could, it would not save them because Paul told us plainly that "by the works of the law shall no flesh be justified" (Galatians 2:16). "Well, then, by animal sacrifice." Yet Hebrews 10:4 tells us that "it is not possible that the blood of bulls and of goats should take away sins." So then, how were the Old Testament saints saved? The same way the New Testament saints are saved: by grace through faith. (See Ephesians 2:8–9.)

"Then what was the purpose of the animal sacrifices in the Old Testament? Why did those people have to continually make sacrifices to God?"

In Romans 10:17 Paul told us: "So then faith cometh by hearing, and hearing by the word of God." The Old Testament rituals were only a shadow of the true redeeming atonement that would take place when Jesus Christ, the Lamb of God, would come to shed His own blood for the remission of the sins of the people. By rehearsing that future event symbolically day after day in the tabernacle and temple using sacrificial animals to represent the true Lamb of God, the people actually saw demonstrated continually before their eyes the atoning death of their Savior. With their eyes they "heard" over and over the Word of God, the message of grace, the Gospel of the coming Messiah.

In the New Testament, after the resurrection of the Lord Jesus Christ, people were saved by grace through faith in the finished work of Christ on the cross. In the Old Testament, they were saved by grace through faith in the future work of Christ on the cross. However, in both instances the means of salvation is the same: by grace through faith. That's why Paul referred to Abraham as "the father of faith," "the father of all them that believe....Therefore it [salvation] is of faith, that it might be by grace; to the end the promise might be sure to all the seed; not to that only which is of the law, but to that also which is of the faith of Abraham; who is the father of us all" (Romans 4:11, 16).

Salvation is by grace through faith. That faith comes from hearing. In the Old Testament, hearing came through the ritualistic sacrifices. Every time the people saw their sins placed upon the head of a scapegoat that was then cast out into the wilderness, they saw again the picture of the coming Messiah, "the Lamb of God, which taketh away the sin of the world" (John 1:29). Every time they watched as an animal was slaughtered and its blood sprinkled upon the altar of the temple, they would say to themselves: "That animal speaks of the Messiah who will one day come to take my sin from me. It will be placed upon Him and He will be killed, shedding His blood for the remission of my sin. He will die spiritually that I might be born again spiritually."

Notice, I said the people in the Old Testament were *saved*; I didn't say they were born again. I use the term *saved* to indicate they were *justified* (counted righteous), but they were not born again, because there was no provision for the New Birth until after the resurrection of the Lord Jesus Christ. They were counted righteous, but they did not become righteous until their spirits were re-created and the Holy Spirit came to live within them. That event did not occur until after the Day of Pentecost. Athough they were not born again until after the coming of the Messiah, the Old Testament saints were saved the same way you and I were: by grace through faith. They were saved by believing God, by trusting in His promise of redemption through the shed blood of His own Son. Salvation has always been a gift of God's grace freely received by faith, not a reward attained by works of the Law.

"Even as Abraham believed God, and it was accounted to him for righteousness" (v. 6). So Abraham didn't get saved by keeping the Law. He didn't get saved by works. He wasn't saved by observing a set of do's and don'ts. He wasn't even saved by being circumcised.

"Yes, but Abraham was circumcised."

Yes, he was. But *when* was he circumcised?

> *Blessed is the man to whom the Lord will not impute sin. Cometh this blessedness then upon the circumcision only, or upon the uncircumcision also? for we say that faith was reckoned to Abraham for righteousness. How was it then reckoned? when he was in circumcision, or in uncircumcision? Not in circumcision, but in uncircumcision. And he received the sign of circumcision, a seal of the righteousness of the faith which he had yet being uncircumcised.*
>
> *Romans 4:8–11*

So then Abraham was not saved by being circumcised, but rather circumcision was given as a sign he was saved, separated from the world and joined to God. It wasn't circumcision that saved Abraham; it was only a seal of the covenant between him and God. Circumcision didn't make the covenant; it only attested to it. It was faith that made the covenant a reality in Abraham's life.

Today, New Testament believers are not circumcised

as a sign of our covenant of salvation. Rather we participants in the new covenant are baptized as a sign of our identification with Jesus Christ in His sacrificial death, burial, and resurrection to New Life. We identify with Christ in His death in the same way the Old Testament saints identified with the death of the coming Messiah, through faith.

The Sons of Abraham

Verse 7

Know ye therefore that they which are of faith, the same are the children of Abraham.

Notice, they who are of faith, not of works or the Law, these are the children of Abraham. There are two words in Greek translated either as "children" or "sons" in the King James Version. This is one of them. In this instance the Greek word is *huios*, which would more correctly be translated as "sons" (as it is in most modern translations such as the New American Standard Bible). The other Greek word is *teknon*. We will consider the difference in these two words more closely in chapter 4, but in this particular verse Paul was saying: "Know then that those who are of faith, these are the sons of Abraham."

Now as we remember from Genesis, Abraham had two male children, one by his wife Sarah and the other by her handmaid Hagar. Out of Ishmael, the offspring of Abraham and Hagar, there came the race of people we call the Arabs. From Isaac, the offspring of Abraham and Sarah, there came the Hebrews. So Abraham produced two sets of offspring: the Arabs and the Jews.

Abraham also produced two other sets of offspring: a natural race called the Jews, and a spiritual race called the seed of Christ, the Church universal today.

We can learn a great deal about this spiritual race by looking at the Jewish nation today. The Jew is a natural example of the spiritual hidden Church. Some people today hold the Jews up as an example of how God washes His hands of a people who are unfaithful to Him, but God has never abandoned or forsaken the Jewish nation. Even though they have been in apostasy for two thousand years, God still honors His covenant with them. People may break God's covenant, but He never does. One day that covenant will be fulfilled in every detail, just as God has prophesied through His servants. In the meantime, the covenant is in full effect. That's why there is still a nation called Israel to this day, and why there will continue to be one.

What does that have to do with us under the new covenant? A great deal. Recently I was reading a historical volume entitled Cambridge Ancient History.[1] Although it was not a Christian publication, the author noted it was amazing to trace the rise and fall of nations in relation to how they treated Israel. He went on to give several examples of governments that had fallen as a result of their mistreatment of the Jews. Foremost in that category was the German Third Reich that Hitler boasted would last a thousand years. As we know, it did not last even twenty-five years. The reason is obvious. No government or nation which sets out to oppose and annihilate the people of the covenant can long endure.

Hilton Sutton, Bible prophecy authority, has often spoken about the Shah of Iran, calling attention to the fact that it was only two days after he turned his people against Israel that he was deposed from his throne and his regime began to crumble. God honors His Word.

That should be a source of great comfort and assurance to us today as participants in the new covenant. Even though we may fail, as the Jews have failed through the years, God will not fail. In His Word He has promised never to leave or forsake those who put their trust in Him. God keeps His promises. Once an individual or a group of individuals has entered into a covenant relationship with Him, that person or group becomes special to God. He will see to it that His part of that covenant agreement is kept. One of the provisions of that agreement is protection from those who would harm His covenant people.

It is important how we, as a people and a government, treat the nation of Israel. That also holds true in our relationship with other Christians — even those who are not in fellowship with the Lord at the moment. That doesn't matter: they are still God's covenant people. You do not oppose God's chosen ones without finding yourself in opposition to God — and that is not an enviable position to be in. Jesus warned us not to judge or condemn anyone. In so doing, we only call down cursing upon our own head. Because of the law of sowing and reaping, what we wish upon others, especially those of the covenant, will come back upon us. We would do well to learn to love others, as we would be loved; "for this is the law and the prophets" (Matthew 7:12).

The True Israel

Notice in verse 7, sons come into being through faith. Then how do children come into being? What is the difference between the children of Abraham and the sons of Abraham? The children of Abraham are the physical Jews; the sons of Abraham are those who put their faith in Christ.

In Jesus' day the Jews prided themselves on the fact they were the "seed of Abraham." But Jesus told them God could raise up that kind of physical seed from the stones of the earth (Matthew 3:9). The true seed of Abraham is spiritual. Becoming a seed (a son) of Abraham does not depend upon a person's nationality or race, but upon his faith. Just because a person is a Jew physically does not mean he is one spiritually.

In Romans 9:1-8 Paul made this point very clear:

I say the truth in Christ, I lie not, my conscience also bearing me witness in the Holy Ghost, that I have great heaviness and continual sorrow in my heart. For I could wish that myself were accursed from Christ for my brethren, my kinsmen according to the flesh: who are Israelites; to whom pertaineth the adoption, and the glory, and the covenants, and the giving of the law, and the service of God, and the promises; whose are the fathers, and of whom as concerning the flesh Christ came, who is over all, God blessed for ever. Amen. Not as though the word of God hath taken none effect. For they are not all Israel, which are of Israel: neither, because they are the seed of Abraham, are they all children: but, In Isaac shall thy seed be called. That is, They which are the children of the flesh, these are not the children of God: but the children of the promise are counted for the seed.

Not all those who are Israelites are sons of Abraham. Only those born of the promise; that is, those born again by the Spirit of God through faith in Jesus Christ.

Within the nation of Israel there are *teknon* and there are *huios*. There are the children of Abraham and there are the true sons of Abraham. The children were born Jews, but one day those children exercised faith in the Lord Jesus Christ and were changed from children to sons. In the same way, you and I were born into this earth, but one day exercised faith in the Lord Jesus Christ and became sons of Abraham. We became the true Israel.

Notice again Romans 9: 7: "Neither, because they are the seed of Abraham, are they all children: but, In Isaac shall thy seed be called." What does that mean? How many male offspring did Abraham produce? Two: *Ishmael* and *Isaac*. They were both seed of Abraham, but Paul pointed out that just because they were Abraham's seed it did not make them both sons of Abraham. Only Isaac was called the son of Abraham. Why? Wasn't Ishmael just as much a son of Abraham as Isaac? Why was Ishmael rejected and Isaac accepted?

Some people say Ishmael was rejected because he was born out of wedlock by Hagar, a bondmaid. But that's not so. Natural birth matters nothing to God. It is not the legitimacy of a person's birth that makes him acceptable to God; rather, it is his faith that makes him approved of the Lord. Take the example of Esau and Jacob. Both were legitimate sons of Isaac, twins born of the same mother, Rebecca. Yet even though Jacob was a cheat and a scoundrel, he received the blessing of God, whereas Esau, the firstborn and rightful heir, was rejected of God. This doesn't make sense in the natural. Esau may have been a better person than Jacob. Why was he rejected and his conniving brother accepted? Paul explains:

For this is the word of promise, At this time will I come, and Sarah shall have a son. And not only this; but when Rebecca also had conceived by one, even by our father Isaac; (for the children being not yet born, neither having done any good or evil, that the purpose of God according to election might stand, not of works, but of him that calleth;) it was said unto her, The elder shall serve the younger. As it is written, Jacob have I loved, but Esau have I hated.

Romans 9:9-13

In this passage Paul made it clear that God chose Jacob over Esau while they were still in the womb. Before they were even born, before they had done anything either good or bad, the Lord accepted Jacob and rejected Esau. Why? He looked ahead at their lives and saw the faith of Jacob and the unbelief of Esau. He made His choice based on His foreknowledge of their faith. Because He knew Jacob would believe Him in the future and Esau would not, God made His choice between them. Not according to their actions in the natural realm, but in accordance to their faith. Not of works, good or bad, but by faith in God.

Paul used this point to prove natural birth does not make a person acceptable to God. Jacob went on to become Israel. He produced twelve sons who were born of two different wives and two handmaids. (See Genesis 35:23–26.) Yet all those sons were men of faith, so they became the heads of the twelve tribes of Israel. Natural birth, whether legitimate or illegitimate, is not the determining factor in a person's election by God. It is his faith.

The genealogy of our Lord Jesus Christ is given in both Matthew 1 and Luke 3. Sprinkled throughout His natural family tree we find several Gentiles. Three of the four women mentioned in Matthew's version were Gentiles: Rahab, Ruth, and Bathsheba. So even Jesus was not a "pure" Jew by birth. He was a Son of Abraham not because of His physical descent from Abraham but because He was born of the Holy Spirit of God. It is not natural birth but spiritual birth that makes a person a son of Abraham and therefore a child of God.

In Romans 9:7 when Paul said, "Neither, because they are the seed of Abraham, are they all children: but, in Isaac shall thy seed be called," he was saying Isaac represents faith, and it is the seed of faith that counts with God. This word *seed* is singular. We will be encountering this word throughout chapter 3 of Galatians.

"(For the children being not yet born, neither having done any good or evil, that the purpose of God according to election might stand, not of works, but of him that calleth;) it was said unto her, The elder shall serve the younger" (Romans 9:11–12). Do you remember what Paul said about his call in Galatians 1? He said God chose him by grace from his mother's womb. It has to be grace to choose from the womb because the person has not yet had an opportunity to do anything to merit being chosen by God. Election (redemption, righteousness) cannot be by works. It is entirely God's doing without regard to our actions, either good or bad.

"As it is written, Jacob have I loved, but Esau have I hated" (Romans 9:13). This is a quote by Paul of Malachi 1:2-3. Some people have difficulty with that. They think God is unfair because He judges people before they are even born. However, God is not unfair. His opinion of a person is not determined by that person's actions; it is determined by the amount of faith God sees on the inside of them.

Since He can see the end from the beginning, the Lord doesn't have to wait until an individual has lived out his full life span before He knows what he or she has on the inside. The presence or absence of faith is evident to our heavenly Father from the time of our conception.

God's election or choice before birth is not unfair; it's simply based on foreknowledge. A person's fate is not predetermined or predestined so he or she has no choice in the matter. The apostle Peter addressed his first epistle to the "elect according to the foreknowledge of God the Father" (1 Peter 1:2). God's election is from before the time of birth, but that election is based on His foreknowledge of the person's life, not what that individual will do, but the amount of faith he or she will demonstrate.

Election (salvation) is by grace based upon faith; it is not a product of works. If election is not of works, then neither is righteousness because no one can keep by works of the Law what he never earned by works of the Law. We who are saved by grace through faith "are kept by the power of God through faith unto salvation" (1 Peter 1:5).

Righteousness, like redemption, is all by grace through faith.

The First Jew

Verse 8

And the scripture, foreseeing that God would justify the heathen through faith, preached before the gospel unto Abraham, saying, In thee shall all nations be blessed.

"In thee shall all nations be blessed." This is a quote from Genesis 12:3 in which God promised Abraham that because he believed Him, he would be blessed and that through him all nations would be blessed. "All nations" refers not only to the Gentiles, the non-Jews, but also to the Jews, because as yet the Jewish nation did not exist.

"And the scripture, foreseeing that God would justify the heathen through faith." Who are the heathen? You and I. We non-Jews are referred to as Gentiles or heathen, in the natural. How are we saved? Through faith. If that is so, how are Jews saved? The same way, through faith. At the time God gave this promise to Abraham there were no Jews; everyone was a Gentile, a heathen, even Abraham. As Paul says of Abraham in Romans 4:

> *How was it [salvation] then reckoned [to Abraham]? when he was in circumcision, or in uncircumcision? Not in circumcision, but in uncircumcision....For the promise... was not [given] to Abraham, or to his seed, through the law, but through the righteousness of faith....And being not weak in faith...he staggered not at the promise of God through unbelief; but was strong in faith, giving glory to God; and being fully persuaded that, what he had promised, he was able also to perform. And therefore it was imputed to him for righteousness.*
> *vv. 10, 13, 19–22*

Abraham was not yet a physical Jew when he was

justified. He was saved by faith, just as any other person. Abraham was the first Jew. He was not born a Jew, nor did he become one by circumcision of the flesh. Instead he was circumcised after he believed as a sign of his covenant relationship with God. The first Jew, then, was a heathen who one day exercised faith in God and from that day forth was acceptable to God by his faith. In Abraham, the man of faith, God began a new supernatural race of beings called Jews. If Abraham, the first Jew, was saved by grace through faith and not by works, then his descendants are saved the same way. There is no distinction then between Jews and Gentiles. All are saved the same way, by faith in the finished work of the Lord Jesus Christ.

But how did Abraham know about Christ? The Gospel was preached to him before his conversion:

"And the scripture...preached before the gospel unto Abraham, saying, In thee shall all nations be blessed." Abraham received the Word of the Lord while still a heathen. His belief in that Word changed him from a heathen into a believer. Abraham became the first Jew because of his faith. The mark or sign of Abraham's faith was circumcision. The covenant was established on faith, not works. Circumcision was only the corresponding action of faith in God's promise of salvation by grace. Circumcision did not save Abraham; it was only an outward sign that he had truly been set aside by God and had received salvation.

Who preached the Gospel to Abraham so he could believe and be saved? We find the answer to that in Genesis 12 where the Lord appeared to Abraham while he was still living in Ur of the Chaldees. Jesus Christ preached the Gospel to Abraham. (See verse 17.) The word *Chalde* comes from an ancient Armenian word meaning "moon worship." The Chaldeans were heathens, moon worshippers. Abraham was likely no different from the other pagans of his day and nation. However, seeing his faith, God chose Abraham from that heathen society and appeared to him to preach (declare) to him the Gospel.

What was the Gospel Abraham received of the Lord? What does the word *Gospel* mean? "*Good news.*" What *good news* gets a person saved? The message, "God so loved the world, that he gave his only begotten Son, that whosoever believeth in him should not perish, but have everlasting life" (John 3:16).

People are saved by the good news that the Son of God came to this earth to die for the sin of man, He was dead and buried, and He arose from the grave on the third day to ascend into heaven. He will one day return to receive all those who have put their faith and trust in Him. Isn't that basically what we tell people to confess in order to be saved? Don't we teach them "that if thou shalt confess with thy mouth the Lord Jesus, and shalt believe in thine heart that God hath raised him from the dead, thou shalt be saved" (Romans 10:9)?

In order for a person to be saved, he must hear the Good News. He cannot believe what he hasn't heard. That's what Paul was emphasizing eight verses later when he says "faith cometh by hearing, and hearing by the word of God" (Romans 10:17). If Abraham had to believe God to be saved, he had to first hear from God, because he couldn't very well believe what he had never heard. In order for Abraham to be saved, he had to hear the Gospel. The only person preaching the Gospel in Abraham's day was the Lord Himself. That's the reason He appeared to Abraham in Ur of the Chaldees — to declare to him the Good News. Abraham believed God, he accepted and acted upon the Word of God, and so he was declared righteous. Abraham was saved by the grace of God through faith in His Son.

What proof do we have of this fact? In John 8:56 the Lord Jesus Christ said to the Pharisees: "Your father Abraham rejoiced to see my day: and he saw it, and was glad." Abraham saw the day of Jesus Christ. He was saved by looking forward to the future work of the Savior, just as you and I were saved by looking backward upon that finished work at Calvary.

How was Abraham, the first Jew, saved? By believing the Gospel of the death, burial, and resurrection of the coming Messiah. How did he receive this Gospel? It was proclaimed to him by the Lord Himself. How then were the rest of the Jews saved in Old Testament days? By believing the Gospel. How was it preached to them? By the Lord Himself through the ritualistic sacrifices of the temple worship that portrayed before their eyes continually the sacrificial, atoning work of the future Messiah.

When Jesus told the Pharisees Abraham rejoiced to see the coming of His day, they were incensed:

> *Then said the Jews unto him, Thou art not yet fifty years old, and hast thou seen Abraham? Jesus said unto them, Verily, verily, I say unto you, Before Abraham was, I am. Then took they up stones to cast at him: but Jesus hid himself, and went out of the temple, going through the midst of them, and so passed by.*
>
> *John 8:57 59*

Why did the Jews try to stone Jesus? They were angry because He dared to claim He was God, the All-Knowing One, the All-Sufficient One, the Ever-Existent One, the Great I Am. They didn't see who He really was. They looked at the outward man, but they didn't perceive the Spirit within Him. Abraham recognized the Lord and believed on Him whose day he saw coming. His belief saved him, not his works.

Blessed with Abraham

Verses 9-10

So then they which be of faith are blessed with faithful Abraham. For as many as are of the works of the law are under the curse: for it is written, Cursed is every one that continueth not in all things which are written in the book of the law to do them.

"They which be of faith are blessed" (v. 9). Note, this does not say that "those which be of works are blessed" but "those which be of faith."

"With faithful Abraham" (v. 9). In Greek this word translated *faithful* is closer to our English word *believing*. "They which are of faith are blessed with believing Abraham." Believing is faith in action. It is taking the faith on the inside and putting it into action on the outside.

If you are a Christian, but are not being blessed along with believing Abraham, you may be wondering what's wrong. Why are others around you being blessed continually while you go through life just getting by, never really enjoying life in all its abundance? The answer is probably because you are not taking the faith resident within you and putting it to work for the cause of Christ and of His kingdom.

Abraham wasn't content with just sitting and confessing his faith. He put faith into action. Faith is a little like muscles. We all have muscles, but some of us have much larger and more powerful muscles than others. Why? Those with strong muscles are usually those who continually use the ones they have. In the same way, people are blessed not by having faith but by exercising faith.

It is not hearing the Word alone that matters, though we must hear it. It's doing the Word we hear and believe that actually produces results. It's the doing of faith that brings the blessing of Abraham.

"For as many as are of the works of the law are under the curse: for it is written, Cursed is every one that continueth not in all things which are written in the book of the law to do them" (v. 10). This is a quote from Deuteronomy 27:26: "Cursed be he that confirmeth not all the words of this law to do them."

What Paul was saying here is the curse of the Law existed before the Law was given. What is the threefold curse of the Law pronounced upon anyone who does not keep it in every detail? Poverty, sickness, and death. Didn't each of these things exist before the Law was ever given to man? If these things existed before the Law was given, and if they still exist today after the Law has been given, then the Law does not remove the curse. The curse is still there and will be until the end of the age when it will be totally annihilated and removed forever. Until such time, you and I can live free of the curse only one way, by being in Christ Jesus who took the curse upon Himself for us at Calvary and by walking in the Spirit so we do not fulfill the lusts of the flesh.

As believers, we are not subject to the curse because we are redeemed from it. We were crucified with Christ: nevertheless we live; yet not us, but Christ lives in us; and the life we now live in the flesh we live by the faith of the Son of God, who loved us, and gave Himself for us (Galatian 2:20). Our new life is marked by the blessing of Abraham that comes upon us as we exercise faith to receive it. Because of what God has done for us in Christ Jesus, we, who are of faith, are truly blessed with faithful Abraham.

7

The Abrahamic Covenant

Galatians 3:11–20

The Law Is Not of Faith

Galatians 3:11–12

But that no man is justified by the law in the sight of God, it is evident: for, The just shall live by faith. And the law is not of faith: but, The man that doeth them shall live in them.

In our last chapter we looked at verse 10, which stated that those who are subject to the Law are under a curse, because "cursed is every one that continueth not in all things which are written in the book of the law to do them." We noted no one is able to keep every point of the entire Law; therefore, we all come under the curse of the Law. The Law not only makes us slaves to a system of do's and don'ts, it actually condemns us because we are not able to live up to that system. The Law thus becomes our condemnation rather than our deliverance. That's why we stated the Law was never given by God as a means of salvation but only to cause man to realize his inability to save himself. He can then turn to God to receive the free gift of salvation bought and paid for by the shed blood of His Son Jesus Christ.

Once salvation has been received by grace through faith, believers sometimes make the mistake of trying to please God by works of righteousness. We read our Bible, pray, fast, witness to others about Christ, attend church regularly, pay our tithes, give offerings, do good works, and on and on. All this is well and good. The mistake we make in doing all these things is thinking by doing them we are attaining or retaining righteousness because we are pleasing God. The truth is, the Word of God has made it clear it is faith that pleases God, not works of the Law. If it was not works that saved us, it naturally follows it is not works that make us spiritual. On the contrary, many times our works, our own self-efforts, prevent us from fulfilling righteousness because they get our eyes off the Source of our righteousness and focus them on ourselves.

"But that no man is justified by the law in the sight of God, it is evident: for, The just shall live by faith" (v. 11). Continuing with this same idea, in verse 11 Paul pointed out no one is justified (made righteous) by the Law, but by faith. We are saved by faith to live a life of faith. To begin our Christian life by faith and then attempt to live it by works is to fall back into legalism. A person cannot remain righteous by works any more than he could become righteous by works. The Christian life is one of faith from beginning to end. The Bible tells us "the just [those who are saved by faith] shall live by faith."

Why then do we work? Not to gain the Lord's favor. He was pleased with us before He saved us, that's what grace is, God's favor. It was by His favor we were saved in the first place. Therefore, we cannot now retain His favor by works any more than we received His favor by working for it. No, we work for God because we love Him and are thankful and grateful to Him for His wonderful works on our behalf. We don't work to please God; rather our works are evidence that He is already pleased with us!

Thus the twofold theme of the book of Galatians is

brought out again in verse 11: 1) *Justification by faith* and 2) *Spirituality by faith.*

"No man is justified by the law in the sight of God" (v. 11). Works do not justify a person in the sight of God. They may justify him in the sight of men, but not in God's eyes.

"But didn't James say that Abraham was justified by works?"

Yes, he did, in James 2:21: "Was not Abraham our father justified by works, when he had offered Isaac his son upon the altar?" That action was a work, but Abraham's work did not justify him before God; it justified him before men. You see, men needed to know Abraham believed and God accounted that belief unto him as righteousness. The same is true in our lives. People need to see our good works and glorify our Father in heaven, just as Jesus said in Matthew 5:16. But Jesus did not say we were saved by those good works.

"Then if we are not saved by good works, what is their purpose?"

The purpose of works is not our salvation; it's the salvation of others! What do I mean by that? Simply this: The world cannot see on the inside of us Christians. To them we are simply human beings like them. Judging by our outward appearances, we may seem to be, but God looks at the heart. He sees the faith in our heart, and that faith pleases Him. We don't need to prove our faith to God for Him to save us, but other people need to see some outward manifestation of our faith if they are to be convinced we have something they don't have. The world can't see our faith; it can see only the results of our faith, our good works.

Works, then, like tongues, are not a sign for the believer but for the unbeliever. (See 1 Corinthians 14:22.) Our good works are not the means by which we win points with God; they are the means by which we win souls for God. Do you think God is more interested in our winning points, or in our being like Jesus of Nazareth? Don't you think He's more interested in our being anointed by the

Holy Spirit with power and going about doing good, healing all who are oppressed of the devil, because God is with us? (See Acts 10:38.) Which of these two do you think is more pleasing to God? Which of the two do you think will have the most positive effect on unbelievers?

"For, the just shall live by faith" (v. 11). This is a quote from Habakkuk 2:4: "The just shall live by his faith." Are you just? If so, how did you become just? By faith. How do you live now that you are just? By faith. Faith gets a person into the kingdom of God, and faith keeps him going once he's in. We don't start by faith and then turn to the Law, any more than we start with the Law and stay with the Law. No, we started by faith, and we will stay with faith. We who are just live by our faith.

"And the law is not of faith: but, The man that doeth them shall live in them" (v. 12). This verse is a quote from Leviticus 18:5, part of the Law given by God through Moses to the children of Israel: "Ye shall therefore keep my statutes, and my judgments: which if a man do, he shall live in them." If we shrug off faith and true spirituality to try to attain righteousness by our own self-efforts, then we are obliged to live our whole lives by the Law. Once we have begun to abide by the Law, then we are obligated to abide in the Law. Deuteronomy 28 warns that anyone who does not continue in the Law brings the curse of the Law upon himself. It's not easy to continue in the Law, because to violate one part of it is to violate it all.

When non-Jews refer to the Law, we usually associate it with the Ten Commandments, but that wasn't the whole of the Jewish Law. The Law is the entire first five books of the Bible. There are over 615 separate commandments contained in those five books. To keep 614 of these commandments is not enough—to offend in one is to offend in all. Anyone who thinks he can attain righteousness by keeping the Law has his work cut out for him!

It is impossible to keep every jot and tittle of the Law. That's one reason the Bible teaches no flesh is justified by works of the Law (Galatians 2:16). No flesh is perfect enough to keep the Law a whole lifetime without breaking it in some way. To break the Law is to call down the curse upon the offender. That curse still exists, is still active, still operative. That's why Christians can't live any way we want and still prosper in every facet of our lives.

It's true we are no longer under the old covenant, the Law. We're under the new covenant, but that does not mean we are lawless. Our Lord removed us from the curse of the Law, so the blessing of Abraham could come upon us. However, if we consciously remove ourselves from His circle of protection by committing sin, then the curse can still come back upon us unless that sin is removed.

"Well, if no one could keep the Law, how in the world did the people in the Old Testament become justified? What happened when they kept breaking the Law over and over?"

They kept offering blood sacrifices over and over. Those sacrifices didn't save them; they just pointed to the One who could save them—the coming Messiah. Animal sacrifices were simply a means of teaching the people about the future Christ who would one day come to offer Himself as the Lamb of God to take away the sin of the world permanently. The blood shed on the Old Testament altars was a type of the atoning blood of Jesus Christ, which alone has the power to wash away sin and cleanse unrighteousness.

The Old Testament saints were cleansed of sin the same way you and I are, by the shedding of blood: "without shedding of blood is no remission" (Hebrews 9:22). The difference is the blood of animals could never take away sins; it could only cover them up until the blood of the Lamb would be shed to remove those sins forever. You and I no longer have to continually offer the blood of animals for forgiveness of sin; we simply apply the blood of Christ to our sins. How do we do that? The answer is found in 1 John 1:9: "If we confess our sins, he is faithful and just to forgive us our sins, and to cleanse us from all unrighteousness."

If the blood of Christ cleansed us from our sin so we could be made acceptable to God in the first place, then it is that same blood that continues to cleanse us from all unrighteousness today. If it made us clean, it keeps us clean. The way to fulfill all righteousness and walk in divine protection is not by keeping the Law, but by walking in constant fellowship with the Lord Jesus Christ.

The Great Exchange

Verses 13–14

Christ hath redeemed us from the curse of the law, being made a curse for us: for it is written, Cursed is every one that hangeth on a tree: that the blessing of Abraham might come on the Gentiles through Jesus Christ; that we might receive the promise of the Spirit through faith.

"Christ hath redeemed us from the curse of the law" (v. 13). The Greek tense used in this sentence indicates this is a settled action. Christ has—once and for all—redeemed us from the curse of the Law.

"Being made a curse for us" (v. 13). The way our Lord redeemed us from the curse was to become the curse. What does it mean, *He became the curse*? Since He was absolute righteousness, He had to actually become sin. Since He was God's health, He had to become sickness. Since He had the riches of heaven, He had to lay those riches aside and become poverty. Why did He do all that? For us.

In 2 Corinthians 8:9 Paul told us: "For ye know the

grace of our Lord Jesus Christ, that, though he was rich, yet for your sakes he became poor, that ye through his poverty might be rich." In order for us to become what Christ is, He had to become what we were. He became accursed, that we might become blessed. He became sick, that we might become healthy. He became poor, that we might become rich. These are the three categories of the curse of the Law: poverty, sickness, and spiritual death. In each of these cases, Jesus Christ became the curse for us that we might be set free from the curse.

Let's consider the case of spiritual death. Did Jesus die spiritually for us? Look at 2 Corinthians 5:21: "For he [God] hath made him [Christ] to be sin for us, who knew no sin; that we might be made the righteousness of God in him." The One who knew no sin became sin for us, that we might be made the righteousness of God in Him. We were unrighteous; Jesus Christ was righteous. God made His own Son unrighteous, so you and I could be made righteous. Christ took our unrighteousness, and we took His righteousness. What an exchange!

Our Lord took upon Himself our sinful human nature so we might receive His righteous, divine nature. He took our sin in exchange for His holiness. If that is so, if by receiving Him we received His nature, His holiness, why then would we ever try to achieve a holiness of our own? Could we ever hope to attain by our weak, human efforts what God poured out upon us freely in the person of His own dear Son? Who would be so foolish as to try to attain a righteousness of his own when he has already freely received the divine righteousness of the very Son of God? Can you see why Paul called these Galatians foolish?

That exchange sounds so good some people have a hard time believing it. That's why they have a hard time receiving it — because that is precisely the way it is received, by belief. That belief is called *faith*. The righteousness of God in Christ is received as you would receive any free gift: "For by grace are ye saved through faith; and that not of yourselves: it is the gift of God: not of works, lest any man should boast" (Ephesians 2:8-9). The same Paul who wrote these words also wrote in Romans 5:17 that righteousness is a gift. What did we have to give our Lord in exchange for His righteousness? Nothing. Absolutely nothing. If we'd had to give anything to receive it, then it would not have been a free gift.

There was an exchange. Christ gave us something, and He took something in return, but what Christ took from us was not anything we had to return. He took our sin, sickness, and poverty from us and gave us His righteousness, health, and riches.

"Where does it say that Christ took our sickness?" In Isaiah 53:4-5 we read: "Surely he hath borne our griefs, and carried our sorrows: yet we did esteem him stricken, smitten of God, and afflicted. But he was wounded for our transgressions, he was bruised for our iniquities: the chastisement of our peace was upon him; and with his stripes we are healed."

Matthew wrote: "When the even was come, they brought unto him many that were possessed with devils: and he cast out the spirits with his word, and healed all that were sick: that it might be fulfilled which was spoken by Esaias the prophet, saying, Himself took our infirmities, and bare our sicknesses" (Matthew 8:16-17).

Peter wrote, "Who his own self bare our sins in his own body on the tree, that we, being dead to sins, should live unto righteousness: by whose stripes ye were healed" (1 Peter 2:24).

Jesus became the curse of sickness for us, that we might be made well. Was Jesus ever sick? There is no record that He was. He never knew a day of sickness in His life. He certainly didn't bring any sickness with Him from heaven; there was none there to bring. He proclaimed He came to this earth to do the will of His Father in heaven. While He was here, He went about doing good, and healing all those who were oppressed of the devil. (See

Acts 10:38.) But when Jesus Christ went to the cross of Calvary, there He took upon Himself our sickness, just as He took upon Himself our sins, so we might receive His wholeness as well as His holiness. He also took our poverty, so we might receive His riches. Jesus became our poverty on the cross. He was prosperous when He walked on the earth, just as He was sinless and whole in body and mind.

Where did Jesus become sin? On the cross. When did He become sickness? When did He become poverty? At the cross. Why? Jesus became these things at the cross because it is written, "Cursed is every one that hangeth on a tree" (not "everyone that walketh on the earth"). Therefore, if Christ has become a curse for us, that we might become blessed, if He took upon Himself our sin, sickness, poverty, and spiritual death, that we might receive His righteousness, health, riches, and eternal and abundant life, then why would we ever strive to get these things for ourselves? All we need to do, all we *can* do, is receive them freely as a gift from God the Father who laid our sins on His own Son and nailed them to a tree that you and I might receive His righteousness. That means if Jesus walked a life free from sin on this earth, so can you and I. If He walked free from sickness and disease, so can we. If He lived free from poverty, we can, too.

"But Jesus said He had no place to lay His head."

That's right. That's because He was a minister. It does not mean He was poor, only that He was itinerant. Jesus traveled with a company of twelve disciples, plus many others who accompanied Him wherever He went. Yet we have no record they ever went hungry or naked or without shelter because of a lack of provision. Even when He sent out the seventy and commanded them explicitly not to take anything with them, not even a change of clothes, when they came back He later asked them: "When I sent you without purse, and scrip, and shoes, lacked ye any thing? And they said, Nothing" (Luke 22:35). Jesus was never without means. He had a moneybag carried by Judas Iscariot. It must have been amply filled because we know Judas embezzled from it. Jesus gave to the poor, and poor people don't give to poor people. He wore nice clothes that were gambled over by the soldiers who crucified Him. Jesus was not poor. Not until He went to the cross. There He became poor, that we might be made rich.

Although artists and sculptors always represent Jesus on the cross wearing a loincloth, that is not historically accurate. When the Romans crucified a person, he was always completely naked. That was part of the shame of the cross, which we sing about in many of our old hymns of faith. On Calvary, Jesus Christ, the Son of God, was not only stripped of His vestments, he was stripped of His position, His dignity, His holiness, His righteousness, His riches, His health—even His very fellowship with His Father in heaven: "My God, my God, why hast thou forsaken me?" (Matthew 27:46). He was rejected by men and rejected by God. He became sin, He became sickness, He became poverty for you and me.

Aren't you glad Jesus Christ took the curse, so we might receive the blessing? He did that once and for all. When Christ rose from the grave, He did not arise sinful, sick, or poor. Our Lord is no longer sin, sickness, or poverty because He is no longer dead! He is alive and well and living in glory where all the riches of heaven belong to Him. "As he is, so are we in this world" (1 John 4:17). That means we, too, are alive and well and living in His glory, beneficiaries of all that is His.

The Blessing of Abraham

"That the blessing of Abraham might come on the Gentiles" (v. 14). Notice it was the *curse* of the Law, but it is the *blessing* of Abraham. That's very interesting. If

Christ redeemed us from the curse that we might receive the blessing, why didn't Paul say we have been redeemed from the curse of the Law that the blessing of the Law might come on us? Why did he switch from the curse of the Law to the blessing of Abraham? It is because the two are the same. The same blessing you and I received by receiving the Lord Jesus Christ into our lives is the same blessing we would have received had we been able to keep the Law to absolute perfection. Since Jesus perfectly fulfilled the Law for us, we receive the blessing as though we ourselves had qualified for it. This blessing is the same blessing Abraham received, not because he kept the Law to perfection, there was no Law for him to keep, but because he believed God. Therefore, it is possible to walk in the blessing of the Law and not even know the Law.

The Law was added 430 years after Abraham lived on this earth. Abraham was born, lived out his lifetime, and died before the Law was ever even given. Yet he walked in blessing. Here you and I are today these thousands of years after the Law was given and fulfilled, yet we receive the same blessing as Abraham. If Abraham walked free of the Law, so can you and I. Paul was trying to instruct the people in Galatia: Never let anyone put you under a Law that you, like Abraham, were never subject to in the first place.

"Through Jesus Christ; that we might receive the promise of the Spirit through faith" (v. 14). Notice also it is through Jesus, not through the Law, we are made able to receive the promise of the Spirit. Through what means? Through faith. Again, it is not through the Law we receive the blessing of Abraham; we receive it the same way Abraham received it, through faith.

The Abrahamic Covenant and Us

Verses 15–16

Brethren, I speak after the manner of men; though it be but a man's covenant, yet if it be confirmed, no man disannulleth, or addeth thereto. Now to Abraham and his seed were the promises made. He saith not, And to seeds, as of many; but as of one, And to thy seed, which is Christ.

"Brethren, I speak after the manner of men; though it be but a man's covenant" (v. 15). Here Paul began an analogy between the Abrahamic covenant and a legal agreement. In order to make his point clear, he brought the covenant God made with Abraham down to human terms, likening it to a covenant (contract) drawn up between two individuals on earth.

"Yet if it be confirmed, no man disannulleth, or addeth thereto" (v. 15). Once a contract between two people is drawn up, agreed upon, and confirmed (ratified) by their signatures, from that moment on the agreement is unalterable by either of the two parties to it without the consent and agreement of the other party.

Let's follow Paul's logic and apply this rule to the Abrahamic covenant. This contract between God and Abraham was drawn up and ratified before the Law was ever given. The Law was given to Moses, but the covenant was made between God and Abraham long before Moses was ever born. Therefore, the Mosaic Law could not supersede a previously existing contract, the Abrahamic covenant. If God were to break His agreement with Abraham after his death, He would be worse than a contract-breaker; He would be a cheater, because He would have waited until Abraham was dead to change His contract with him. That would make God lower than the level of men.

"Now to Abraham and his seed were the promises made" (v. 16). As we know, it takes two to make a contract. The two parties to the Abrahamic "contract" were God (Party of the first part who made the promises of blessing) and Abraham and his seed (parties of the second part to whom the promises of blessing were made).

"He saith not, And to seeds, as of many; but as of one, And to thy seed, which is Christ" (v. 16). Who is the seed of Abraham who shared in his promised blessing? Jesus Christ. However, Christ didn't have any need of this contract. The contract releases us from poverty, sickness, and death. Christ had no need of release from these things because He was never subject to them. As the righteousness of God, He was not subject to unrighteousness. As the embodiment of divine health, He was not subject to sickness. As the creator of all riches, He was not subject to poverty. As the author of life, He was not subject to death. As the Son of God, He was not subject to any of these things—until that day when He became sin, until the time He took upon Himself our sickness, poverty, and death, so we might receive His righteousness, health, riches, and life:

> *Who in the days of his flesh, when he had offered up prayers and supplications with strong crying and tears unto him that was able to save him from death, and was heard in that he feared; though he were a Son, yet learned he obedience by the things which he suffered; and being made perfect, he became the author of eternal salvation unto all them that obey him.*
>
> *Hebrews 5:7–9*

As we have said, Christ took our nature as sinners. He took our place on the cross and suffered the chastisement of our sin that we might be made able to take His place as the righteousness of God. He became sin that we might become sons. The promises of God were made to Abraham's seed because God knew it was through the obedience of that Seed that Abraham and all succeeding generations would be made righteous. The only way Abraham could be declared righteous by God because of His faith was because there was coming a Messiah from his own offspring who would fulfill all righteousness for him.

The only way you and I could be declared righteous by God through faith is because we identify with Jesus Christ (the Seed of Abraham) who suffered our penalty and freed us from the law of sin and death. Without the Seed of Abraham in it, the Abrahamic covenant could never redeem anyone. It was through the Seed that the redemption would come.

It is in the Seed of Abraham you and I are included in the Abrahamic covenant. In Ephesians 1:3-12 Paul dealt with this subject of our identity with Christ the Redeemer, the Seed of Abraham:

Blessed be the God and Father of our Lord Jesus Christ, who hath blessed us with all spiritual blessings in heavenly places in Christ: according as he hath chosen us in him before the foundation of the world, that we should be holy and without blame before him in love: having predestinated us unto the adoption of children by Jesus Christ to himself, according to the good pleasure of his will, to the praise of the glory of his grace, wherein he hath made us accepted in the beloved. In whom we have redemption through his blood, the forgiveness of sins, according to the riches of his grace; wherein he hath abounded toward us in all wisdom and prudence; having made known unto us the mystery of his will, according to his good pleasure which he hath purposed in himself: that in the dispensation of the fulness of times he might gather together in one all things in Christ, both which are

in heaven, and which are on earth; even in him: in whom
also we have obtained an inheritance, being predestinated
according to the purpose of him who worketh all things
after the counsel of his own will: that we should be to the
praise of his glory, who first trusted in Christ.

According to verse 3, God "hath blessed us with all
spiritual blessings in heavenly places in Christ." That is
past tense. We have already been blessed.

"According as he hath chosen us in him before the
foundation of the world" (v. 4). This word "chosen" in
Greek means "to call out" or "to speak out." You and I
were called out by God. When? Before the foundation of
the world.

"Having predestinated us unto the adoption of children
by Jesus Christ to himself" (v. 5). According to verse 3 we
were blessed of God before the foundation of the world.
According to verse 4 we were chosen by God in Christ
before the foundation of the world. Now in verse 5 we
find we were predestined to become the children of God
before the foundation of the world.

"Wherein he hath made us accepted in the beloved"
(v. 6). When were we accepted in the beloved (that is, in
Christ)? Before the foundation of the world.

In verse 7 we see that we have redemption. In verse 8
we read God has abounded toward us in all wisdom and
prudence. In verse 9 we are told He has made known unto us
the mystery of His will. In verse 11 we discover that we have
obtained an inheritance. Finally, in verses 11 and 12 we learn
all this was planned and executed by God in accordance to
His own will so that we who first trusted in Christ would
become the praise of His glory.

However, as in the case of Abraham, how could God
do all that for you and me before the foundation of the
world? We weren't even there. How could God have
blessed us along with faithful Abraham when neither
we nor Abraham would even be born for billions upon

billions of years? The only way God could pour out all those spiritual blessings upon us before the foundation of the world was through our Representative who was there. His name is Jesus Christ.

Notice, every one of these statements is qualified. God "hath blessed us." Where? "In Christ" (v. 3). "He hath chosen" us. Where? "In him" (v. 4). God has "predestinated us unto the adoption of children." How? By "Jesus Christ" (v. 5). Who was called out before the foundation of the world? Jesus Christ. But He sat there in the presence of God for you and me.

Christ didn't need to be called out. He didn't need to be chosen. He didn't need any of these things; He already had them. He did all this for you and me. He was our elected Representative. He was not elected by us to represent us, rather He was elected (appointed) by God to stand in for us, to be our Substitute in the heavenly courts, just as one day He would stand in for us as our Substitute on the cross of Calvary. There He paid our penalty for us. Christ's death on the cross was our death. His burial was our burial. His resurrection and ascension into heaven to sit at the right hand of God the Father was our resurrection and ascension and coronation! His victory was our victory!

In Christ Jesus, you and I were called out before the foundation of the world. Before the earth was ever formed, our names were mentioned in the throne room of heaven. That's how personal our relationship to our heavenly Father is. He named us personally. He also named us personally when He made a covenant with Abraham.

"Now to Abraham and his seed were the promises made" (v. 16). You won't find your name or mine mentioned specifically anywhere in the Genesis accounts of the giving of the Abrahamic covenant. Nor will you find them specifically mentioned here in Paul's discussion of the covenant in the sixteenth verse of Galatians 3. But you will find that the covenant was made between God (Party of the first part) and Abraham and his seed (parties of the second part). It is in that phrase "and his seed" you and I are included in the covenant.

As the Seed, Jesus was there representing us. "If ye be Christ's, then are ye Abraham's seed, and heirs according to the promise" (Galatians 3:29). The Abrahamic covenant was actually drawn up between God and us. The Abrahamic covenant actually reads like this: "Now to Abraham and Bob Yandian were the promises made." If you are a Christian, then you can substitute your own name for mine in that paraphrase of Galatians 3:16: "Now to Abraham and _____ were the promises made."

"He saith not, And to seeds, as of many; but as of one, And to thy seed, which is Christ" (v. 16). This is not a physical contract with a physical nation, but a spiritual contract with a spiritual nation, that nation of which you and I are a part, the nation of the Beloved.

"Seeds" are the Jews. "Seed" is the Lord Jesus Christ and all those who believe in Him. The Jews in Jesus' day thought they were the seed of Abraham because of their nationality, but the "seed" of Abraham was to bless "all nations." Abraham produced two offspring: a physical nation called Israel, and a spiritual race called the "seed." The covenant was for the spiritual race.

The promises of that contract were made to us individually through our Representative, the Lord Jesus Christ, the Seed of Abraham. Our part of the covenant agreement was also fulfilled by our Representative, by His life of perfect obedience to the Father in heaven and by His substitutionary death on the cross of Calvary. Now all of us who are in Christ Jesus are entitled to the blessing of Abraham.

The Law and the Covenant

Verses 17–20

And this I say, that the covenant, that was confirmed before of God in Christ, the law, which was four hundred and thirty years after, cannot disannul, that it should make the promise of none effect. For if the inheritance be of the law, it is no more of promise: but God gave it to Abraham by promise. Wherefore then serveth the law? It was added because of transgressions, till the seed should come to whom the promise was made; and it was ordained by angels in the hand of a mediator. Now a mediator is not a mediator of one, but God is one.

"And this I say, that the covenant, that was confirmed before of God in Christ" (v. 17). Once the covenant agreement between Abraham and the Lord was confirmed, it could not be changed by one of those two parties without the consent of the other. This verse actually tells us it was the Lord Jesus who appeared to Abraham and received the covenant from God the Father.

"The law, which was four hundred and thirty years after, cannot disannul, that it should make the promise of none effect" (v. 17). If God had given the Jewish law to replace or supersede the Abrahamic covenant, He would have been guilty of breach of contract. If two parties agree to a contract that is to last forever, and then one of them changes the contract after the death of the other, the agreement has been broken. God could not change the terms of His covenant with Abraham 430 years later, after the death of Abraham, without being guilty of breach of contract.

Did Abraham ever break his part of the contract? Yes, several times. For example, in Genesis we read he took Hagar, his wife's bondslave, and had a child by her. This was a breach of God's commandments upon which the covenant between Abraham and Him was made.

Abraham also lied about his wife's relationship to him, saying she was his sister. Lying also constituted a breach of contract. Yet in spite of these and other offenses by Abraham, the covenant agreement was not disannulled.

God set that agreement into motion, and He intended for it to continue — whether Abraham lived up to his part of the bargain or not. Regardless of man's action, God is determined to keep His part of the agreement. He ratified that covenant, and once a contract is ratified it cannot be altered by only one of the two parties involved.

If this is true, then our actions, our breach of contract, still does not disannul the agreement. It takes both parties to disannul it. Despite the many times we may have fallen down on our part, God still has not agreed with us to void our contract. Therefore, our sin does not alter our covenant relationship with our Father through the Lord Jesus Christ. Our sins and shortcomings do not invalidate our contractual agreement. We are still the righteousness of God in Christ. We're still well, healed, prosperous, and endowed with eternal life.

"Oh, but I'm not well."

That's because you haven't been taking full advantage of the covenant. It's still in force. Your sickness doesn't disannul the contract. Neither does your sin or your poverty or even your death. The covenant still stands. God Himself will not change it. If you're not enjoying all the blessings of your covenant with God, then you don't need a new contract, you just need to avail yourself of the full benefits of the one you already have. You do it the same way you became a party to the agreement in the first place, through faith.

"For if the inheritance be of the law, it is no more of promise: but God gave it to Abraham by promise" (v. 18). The coming of the Law has not disannulled the promises of the covenant. The blessing wasn't given to Abraham by the Law; that came 430 years later. The blessing was given to Abraham by promise.

123

Suppose I promise to give my brother a hundred dollars after church services, and suppose he agrees to accept that gift. Whose obligation is it to fulfill that agreement? His or mine? It's mine, because I was the one who made the promise. I'm not obligated by law, but by our agreement. God made promises to Abraham. The obligation to fulfill those promises was not Abraham's, but God's. This has nothing to do with law, but with agreement.

If God has promised to bless us, and we have agreed to receive that blessing, then whose obligation is it to fulfill the agreement, ours or God's? It's God's. What is our part? To *receive* the blessing. God is obligated to keep His Word of promise to us. We are only obligated to receive the benefit of that promise by simply reaching out and taking it. God promises; we receive and that settles it.

Then why do we feel we have to do something to receive our healing or prosperity or success or any of the other good things promised us in God's Word? Just like God's gift of salvation, all that is required of us it to exercise faith to receive.

We said it was by "the grace of our Lord Jesus Christ, that, though he was rich, yet for [our] sakes he became poor, that [we] through his poverty might be rich" (2 Corinthians 8:9). What are riches? A grace. We also said that God made Christ, who knew no sin, to be made sin for us; that we might be made the righteousness of God in him (2 Corinthians 5:21). What is righteousness then? A grace. We read that God laid on Jesus all our sicknesses and infirmities so that by His death on the cross we might be made whole and healthy (Isaiah 53:4–5).

What is health? What is wholeness? A grace of God.

Grace is unmerited favor. It is favor given, not because it is deserved, but because of the mercy and love of the giver. All the promises of the covenant are graces, gifts of God. Abraham was declared righteous, not by what he did, but simply because he believed God, "being fully

124

persuaded that, what he had promised, he was able also to perform" (Romans 4:21).

The giving of the covenant was accomplished for us by God. The confirming of the covenant was accomplished for us by God. The fulfillment of the covenant was accomplished for us by Christ. The keeping of the promises of the covenant is up to our heavenly Father. What then is our part? Our part in the covenant is to reap the benefits of it! How do we do that? Through faith. We simply believe we have received, as our Lord told us in Mark 11:24. God provides; we appropriate.

"Wherefore then serveth the law?" (v. 19). If all this is true, then what was the purpose of the Law? If Abraham, Isaac, Jacob, and Joseph all survived without it all those centuries, why was it given at all?

"It was added" (v. 19). If the Law was "added," does this mean it was added to the Abrahamic covenant? No, that would be illegal: No "man disannulleth, or addeth thereto" (v. 15). The Mosaic Law could not be an addition to the Abrahamic covenant, not in the sense of a codicil or amendment to that covenant. It was simply a tool used by God in addition to (along with) the covenant. It was not itself a part of that covenant, nor was it ever meant to disannul or alter the original agreement between God and man.

"Then why was it added?"

"Because of transgressions" (v. 19). The Law was "added" because of man's transgressions. This word translated "transgressions" simply means "sins." The purpose of the Law was to point out man's violation of the covenant agreement. Had there been no Law, man would never have been conscious either of what God expected of him or how he had failed to live up to that expectation.

"Till the seed should come" (v. 19). "Seed" is singular. Who is the seed of Abraham? Jesus Christ. The Law was added only until Jesus Christ came. Then He put it away.

He did that, not by destroying (abolishing) it, but by fulfilling it. (See Matthew 5:17.) Since Christ has fulfilled the Law for us, you and I are no longer subject to that Law. It's not for today. It was given to Moses until the coming of the Seed, the Lord Jesus Christ, who would fulfill it in every detail.

In Romans 5, Paul touched on this subject of the Law. Notice how he began verse 20: "Moreover the law entered." This word "entered" is a stage term taken from the Greek theater. It was used to indicate the action of a supporting actor who came on stage to perform until the lead actor made his entrance, at which time the supporting actor retired from the stage.

Paul applied this term to the Mosaic Law, likening it to the role of a minor player whose role it is simply to set the stage for the entrance of the principal player. The Law came on the scene at the time of Moses. It remained on stage only until the arrival of Jesus Christ. Then it gave place to Him, never to reappear again. The Law was introduced by Moses; it exited with the Lord Jesus Christ. It has no bearing on us today because its role in the drama of life is completed.

Now while He was hanging suspended on the cross, our Lord made seven statements. One of them was, "It is finished" (John 19:30). There is a very popular doctrine among many Christians today advanced by a well-known and widely read theologian of the past. This teaching holds that when Christ said, "It is finished," He was referring to the Abrahamic covenant. I do not agree. He was not speaking of the covenant; rather, He was referring to the Mosaic Law. In Colossians 2:14 Paul told us: "Blotting out the handwriting of ordinances that was against us, which was contrary to us...[Christ] took it out of the way, nailing it to his cross." Our Lord took the Law, the "handwriting of ordinances," and crucified it by nailing it to the cross. Jesus said He did not come to destroy the Law, but to fulfill it. He did that by being nailed to the cross Himself, by taking the curse of the Law upon Himself. When He had suffered the full penalty of the curse, He had then fulfilled all righteousness. Therefore the Law is like a check that has been paid and canceled. It is no longer valid. All it serves as now is proof that the debt has been paid in full.

The Abrahamic covenant, with its blessing, is still in effect. It will be fulfilled at the second coming of the Lord Jesus Christ to establish His millennial kingdom on earth.

"To whom the promise was made" (v. 19). This phrase reckons back to the time when the covenant was first made between God and Abraham and his seed. That Seed was Jesus Christ. The promises were given to Abraham and Jesus. Christ fulfilled our part of that covenant when He went to the cross. God has fulfilled His part by giving us (through Christ our Representative) His "great and precious promises" (2 Peter 1:4). We are in covenant relationship with our heavenly Father. In Christ, our Divine Substitute, we are pleasing to God. We also qualify to receive, by faith, the full benefits of sonship.

The Law was not given to provide salvation, but to serve as a sign pointing toward salvation. That salvation is found only in the Seed to whom the promises were given, the Lord Jesus Christ. No one can come to the Father except by Him (John 14:6). For it was only through Him that man's part in the covenant found fulfillment. Anyone who rejects what Christ has done for him personally on the cross of Calvary disqualifies himself from the blessing of the covenant. He is left to try to attain right standing with God on his own merit, and no one can do that. That's why Paul urged the Galatians not to withdraw from grace to follow after the illusion of salvation through works of the Law. The Law was never designed to save, only to point to Christ who is the Savior. Outside of Him, not only is there no salvation, there's not even any hope of salvation.

8

The Law — Our Schoolmaster

Galatians 3:21-29

The Law and the Promises

Galatians 3:21-22

Is the law then against the promises of God? God forbid:
for if there had been a law given which could have given
life, verily righteousness should have been by the law.
But the scripture hath concluded all under sin, that the
promise by faith of Jesus Christ might be given to them
that believe.

"Is the law then against the promises of God?" (v. 21). No,
the Law is not in opposition to the promises; it complements
them. The purpose of the Abrahamic covenant was to bring
righteousness by faith. The Law was added to point people
to the covenant. God would not give us two guides in
opposition to each other. That would be confusing. God is
not the author of confusion, but of order. When people were
so blinded by their sin they couldn't see, they needed the
righteousness by faith provided by the Abrahamic covenant.
The Law was given to turn their eyes to that covenant.

"For if there had been a law given which could
have given life, verily righteousness should have been
by the law" (v. 21). But the Law could only point to

righteousness; it could not provide it of itself. If the Law had provided righteousness, then there would have been no need of a Savior.

"But the scripture hath concluded all under sin" (v. 22). This point is also brought out in Romans 3:23: "For all have sinned, and come short of the glory of God." This is a reference to Deuteronomy 27:26: "Cursed be he that confirmeth not all the words of this law to do them." Since it is obvious no one can ever keep every word of the Law, then everyone is concluded under sin, even under the old covenant. Therefore, no one is justified by keeping the Law, because no one can keep it. If a person were able to keep every jot and tittle of the Law, he wouldn't need the Law to make him perfect, he would already be perfect. So again we see that the Law does not make perfect; it only serves to emphasize human imperfection.

When Galatians 3:22 says all have been concluded under sin, it is not referring to any specific sin, such as adultery, lying, cheating, stealing, or murder. Notice, this word *sin* is in the singular. Whenever the Bible speaks of sin in this way, it is referring to the sin nature, the flesh.

You see, most of the time you and I don't commit sins because we are helpless victims of some evil spirit that gets hold of us. The reason we commit sins is because we have a nature called the flesh. It is this fleshly nature that continually pushes us toward sinfulness. When we became new creatures in Christ, we received a new Spirit within that has power over the flesh. That's why John reminded us He who is in us is greater than he who is in the world (1 John 4:4). Now that we are born again of the Spirit of God, our inward man, our spiritual nature, is stronger than the nature of the outward man of the flesh.

Am I saying we have two natures within us (in our spirit) that are always warring against each other? No, the struggle is the recreated spirit at war with the outward body, the flesh. The only time they war against each other is when we get out of the will of God, when we get carnal. As long as we remain in fellowship with God, the greater power can put down the lesser power. If we are truly spiritual, when our flesh rises up in opposition to our spirits, our spirits take dominion over the flesh, and that ends the rebellion.

I have often heard people describe the battle between the flesh and spirit like this: "As a believer, you are like a person who has two dogs on the inside, a white one and a black one. These two animals are always fighting one another, and the one that will win is the one you feed, because he gets stronger and stronger." That is not really so. We Christians don't have two fighting "dogs" inside us. What we have is a living man and a dead man. It is only when we get out of fellowship with the Lord that the dead man resurrects to cause us trouble. As long as we are walking and living in the Spirit, we are dead to the flesh (Romans 6:11).

In his letter to the Christians in Rome, Paul dealt extensively with this concept of sin versus the spirit. Very little of the book of Romans has to do with personal sins; rather, it deals with the sin nature, or the nature of the flesh. Sins like stealing, lying, and killing are only the symptom of sin. Sin itself is not an act; it's not even an attitude. Sin is a nature that drives a person to think, speak, and do things contrary to the nature of God. That is the whole theme of the seventh chapter of Romans. Paul described how he came to realize there was a force driving him to do what his recreated spirit did not want to do.

In essence Paul said, "I don't understand it. Why is it that I keep doing the things I don't want to do and failing to do the things I want to do? I want to do right, but somehow I always end up doing wrong. Why is that? Why am I so mixed up inside?" One day he discovered the reason: "Oh, it's because my flesh is warring against my mind!" No doubt he recalled the words of Jesus in Matthew 26:41 when He told His disciples to watch and pray because "the spirit indeed is willing, but the flesh is weak." This word "willing" is more than just agreeable, it means "desirous."

What our Lord was saying was: "The spirit desires to do right, but the flesh is not strong enough to fulfill the righteous desires of the spirit." That's exactly what Paul discovered. He realized by looking at his weaknesses, sins, and failures he had been focusing his attention on the symptoms instead of the real cause of his problem, which is not the acts of the flesh, but the flesh itself.

God gives us a new nature when we are born again. How effective that new nature is in controlling our lives depends upon how much attention we give to it, how closely we keep in communication and fellowship with our heavenly Father. Neglect of our spiritual lives produces the same results as neglect of our physical bodies. If we want to remain strong and healthy physically so our bodies throw off the germs and viruses that attack them, we must give our bodies proper rest, nourishment, and exercise. So it is with our spiritual "man."

If we are to maintain dominion over the carnal nature, we must develop our spiritual nature through rest (meditation), nourishment (Bible reading, prayer, hearing the Word), and exercise (living out our faith daily). We don't do these things to please God, we do them to build up our inward man. These activities don't make us righteous; they just make us strong!

Paul spoke from personal experience when he said, "The scripture hath concluded all under sin" (v. 22). The word "sin" here means the sin nature. This verse is speaking specifically about unbelievers, although believers still possess the nature of the flesh after the New Birth. The believer has something to fight back with, the power of the Holy Spirit inside him.

Some people seem to have the mistaken idea that when they were born again, they were relieved of the flesh. That is obviously not so. We Christians were born again spiritually, but as long as we are on this earth, we will be living in the flesh. Didn't Paul himself refer to this truth when he wrote in this same letter, "The life which I now live in the flesh I live by the faith of the Son of God" (Galatians 2:20)?

I believe in sanctification. But sanctification in this life does not come overnight, it is not instantaneous; rather, it is progressive. There is no such thing as a "one-shot" sanctification by which a person becomes born again and never sins again as long as he lives. Some Christians go around "confessing" since they are now the righteousness of God in Christ, they no longer sin. That's self-delusion. It's also hypocritical. We all have the potential to sin. That's why we have 1 John 1:9. We can confess our sins and receive forgiveness. That Scripture was written to believers, not unbelievers

Sanctification is twofold: spiritual and physical. Spiritually we were sanctified the moment we were born again of the Spirit of God. However, physical sanctification, righteous living in the flesh, takes longer. It is a process we begin at the moment of New Birth, but it lasts as long as we live on this earth. In essence, we are sanctified spiritually so we can begin to live a sanctified life in the flesh. That's what Paul meant when he said the life he lived in the flesh, he lived by the faith of the Son of God.

Some people have sanctification backwards. They're trying to live a good life so they can be born again. That's wrong, too. It'll never work. We are born again to live a good life. Unless we are first sanctified by the Spirit of God, we have no power to live a truly sanctified life in the flesh. It is the presence and power of the Greater One within us that gives us dominion and authority over our fleshly, carnal nature.

"That the promise by faith of Jesus Christ might be given to them that believe" (v. 22). This is a mistranslation. It should read: "That the promise by faith in Jesus Christ might be given to them that believe." How do we receive the promises of God? It's by putting our faith in Jesus Christ.

Kept under the Law

Verses 23–25

But before faith came, we were kept under the law, shut up unto the faith which should afterwards be revealed. Wherefore the law was our schoolmaster to bring us unto Christ, that we might be justified by faith. But after that faith is come, we are no longer under a schoolmaster.

"But before faith came, we were kept under the law" (v. 23). This word "kept" means "guarded." Before faith came, we were guarded by a jailer, the Law. We were in prison.

"Shut up unto the faith which should afterwards be revealed" (v. 23). The prison in which we were shut up was our own sin nature. The jailer who kept us in that prison of our fleshly nature was the Law, just as it is the Law that keeps inmates shut away in our state and federal prisons today. The difference is inmates in criminal institutions know they are behind bars; we didn't know we were prisoners of the Law. That's why Paul was having such a hard time convincing the Galatians they were now free; they didn't know they had ever been in bondage. Once they were in bondage to sin and heathenism. Now they were in bondage to the Law. They had gone from one form of bondage to another. They had allowed themselves to come into bondage by subjecting themselves to the Law that Christ had come to fulfill for them.

That's why Paul was so upset with them. They didn't realize the purpose of the Law was only to expose sin, to reveal to people they were in bondage, so they would be set free by faith in Christ Jesus. By turning from faith to the Law, the Galatians were doing just the opposite of what God had intended. He hadn't sent the Law to regulate believers; He had sent it to lead sinners to Christ. Now that they were in Christ, the Galatians had no need of the Law. It had fulfilled its purpose when Christ came and fulfilled it.

Yet so many people don't seem to understand this principle, even today. Many times the hardest people to witness to about Christ are not sinners who know nothing of righteousness, but religious people who think righteousness is something they attain by their own efforts. It is very hard to set free a person who doesn't even know he's in prison. Such people think by keeping religious rules and regulations, they are becoming justified in the eyes of God. The Law keeps them shut up in prison, in spiritual bondage. It is only when they finally come to realize the absolute impossibility of keeping all those codes that they are ever willing to accept God's free gift of justification and redemption through simple faith in His Son Jesus Christ.

"Wherefore the law was our schoolmaster" (v. 24). "Wherefore" means "in conclusion." Here Paul began to draw this part of his argument to a close. The word "schoolmaster" is understood today, but still gives a wrong impression of what Paul was trying to say. When we see that word, we instantly think of a schoolteacher, an instructor in a public or private educational institution. That's not what a schoolmaster was to the people in Paul's day. The Greek word translated "schoolmaster" here in the King James Version is *paidagogos* (*paidos*, a boy + *agogos*, leading = boy-leading). It is from this word that we derive our English word *pedagogue*, meaning "*a teacher."* However, in the culture of the ancient Greeks, a *pedagogue* was a household servant, often a slave. His role was that of tutor-overseer. He was charged with the responsibility of watching over, caring for, training, and instructing the boy child of the family until the son became of age. At that time, the *pedagogue* was relieved of his duties, and the son took full responsibility for his own actions.

"To bring us unto Christ, that we might be justified by faith" (v. 24). What then was the purpose of the Law? The Law was our *pedagogue*. It was a servant of our Father, employed by Him to lead us to Christ Jesus that we might be justified by faith in Him. Notice, the Law itself did not bring faith; it led people to the person of Christ through whom justification was received by faith.

"But after that faith is come, we are no longer under a schoolmaster" (v. 25). Since Christ has come to earth, died, been resurrected, and ascended to heaven where He now sits at the right hand of God the Father, where does that leave the Law, our *pedagogue*? It has accomplished its task, discharged its duties, fulfilled its purpose. Therefore it is dismissed. It no longer has authority or jurisdiction over those of us who are in Christ Jesus. Once you and I came to Jesus, our former *pedagogue* was no longer needed. When we were born again, our *pedagogue* was dismissed, and we became responsible for our own lives. Now that we have reached spiritual manhood, for us to go back and try to submit to a system of do's and don'ts is to try to submit ourselves to a former slave and have him take care of us. Not only is that foolish, it is a denial of our rights as sons.

Then why do people do that? Having once attained their spiritual "majority," why do believers try to return to a system of rules and regulations? One basic reason is laziness. It's easier to follow a set of laws than to think for yourself.

A second reason is fear. Many Christians are so

insecure, they want someone to tell them exactly what to think and say and do. They are afraid of the responsibility that comes with freedom. It's sort of like working all your life for someone else rather than striking out on your own to run your own business.

Most people prefer the security of being an employee to the freedom and responsibility that goes with being their own master. That may be fine in the work market, but it is dangerous in the spiritual realm. There are always those who are happy to appoint themselves as "religious leaders" and to take advantage of the insecurity of immature believers. That's one reason for all the cults so prevalent today inside the church as well as outside. Christians need to learn to take seriously their responsibility as full-grown sons. Part of that responsibility is the duty to think for themselves.

Complete in Christ

Verses 26–29

For ye are all the children of God by faith in Christ Jesus. For as many of you as have been baptized into Christ have put on Christ. There is neither Jew nor Greek, there is neither bond nor free, there is neither male nor female: for ye are all one in Christ Jesus. And if ye be Christ's, then are ye Abraham's seed, and heirs according to the promise.

"For ye are all the children of God by faith in Christ Jesus" (v. 26). This word translated "children" is the Greek word *huios*, which we said was closer to our word sons than to children. *Teknon* usually refers to the physical Jews, whereas *huios* denotes those who have exercised faith in Christ. Paul was telling us we are all sons of God. This word indicates we are mature sons, not little children under the care of a pedagogue.

137

Now in this passage Paul presented spiritual or positional truth rather than temporal, earthly truth. Positionally, the moment you and I accepted Jesus Christ as our Savior, God saw us as mature. In Colossians Paul used the word "complete": "And ye are complete in him [Christ], which is the head of all principality and power" (Colossians 2:10). At the precise moment we were born again, God saw us complete. Where? In Christ. How did we get into that position of completeness? We entered that state through faith. The moment we became "in him," we became complete.

Now you may not feel mature, complete, righteous. You may remember all too well all those unrighteous acts that seem to prove beyond a shadow of a doubt you are not mature or complete or righteous. But you must remember those acts do not make you unrighteous any more than your works of the Law made you righteous. If your righteousness came, not by works, but through faith, then your wrong acts do not destroy your righteousness, not in the eyes of God. Therefore they shouldn't destroy your righteousness, maturity, and completeness in your own eyes.

It is much easier to walk in righteousness once you realize God sees you that way. Once you fix your eyes on your goal, the pathway to that goal becomes clearer and easier to follow. Always keep foremost in your mind the fact that in Jesus Christ you are complete, not because of anything you do or have done, but because you have been granted His completeness. When God looks at you, He sees Jesus Christ. Therefore you are everything He is (1 John 4:17).

If that is so, then if you will fix your eyes and set your affection on things above, you will see that anything you are striving to become in this life, you have already attained. You're already there. It's so much easier to act righteous when you realize you're already righteous.

It's much easier to act sanctified when you realize God already sees you sanctified. It's much easier to act mature when you know God sees you as a mature person.

The key to spiritual maturity is positional truth, you having already become that which you aspire to be.

Paul told us we are the mature sons of God by faith in Christ Jesus. When did that happen? The answer is found in the next verse: "For as many of you as have been baptized into Christ have put on Christ" (v. 27). We became the mature sons of God when we were baptized into Christ Jesus. Now note the expression "put on Christ." This will be discussed more in detail in chapter 4 of Galatians.

"There is neither Jew nor Greek, there is neither bond nor free, there is neither male nor female: for ye are all one in Christ Jesus" (v. 28). In verse 24 we learned about the pedagogue. In verse 26 we learned we are mature sons. In verse 27 we found we have "put on" Christ. Now here in verse 28 we discover that in Christ there is no distinction made between the Jew and the non-Jew, the bond and the free, the male and the female. Again Paul was speaking in spiritual terms. Obviously in the natural, physical realm there will always be distinctions made between the races, social classes, and sexes, but not in the spiritual realm. In Christ we are all one.

"And if ye be Christ's, then are ye Abraham's seed, and heirs according to the promise" (v. 29). Notice, we are "Abraham's seed." This word "seed" is in the singular. Do you recall from verse 16 to whom the promises of God were given in the Abrahamic covenant? "Now to Abraham and his seed were the promises made." In that verse the Seed was the Lord Jesus Christ. Paul told us if we are in Christ, we are the seed. How can that be?

The answer is very simple. When God made promises to Abraham and his seed, Christ was there in spirit (though He would not be born in flesh for hundreds of years). Yet Christ was not actually participating in that

139

covenant agreement on His own behalf, He was there on our behalf. The promises were made by God to Abraham and Christ, but Christ had no need of these promises. He only participated as our Representative. Everything He did was for us, for you and me. In reality, the promises made by God to Abraham and his seed were actually made to Abraham and us. That's where we came into the Abrahamic covenant. How did we get into it? By faith. Because we are Abraham's seed, through faith in Jesus Christ, we are heirs according to the promise.

9

Paul's First Trip to Galatia

Galatians 4:1-16

Our Redemption from the Law

Galatians 4:1-5

Now I say, That the heir, as long as he is a child, differeth nothing from a servant, though he be lord of all; but is under tutors and governors until the time appointed of the father. Even so we, when we were children, were in bondage under the elements of the world: but when the fulness of the time was come, God sent forth his Son, made of a woman, made under the law, to redeem them that were under the law, that we might receive the adoption of sons.

"Now I say, That the heir, as long as he is a child, differeth nothing from a servant, though he be lord of all; but is under tutors and governors until the time appointed of the father. Even so we, when we were children, were in bondage under the elements of the world" (vv. 1-3). In this opening passage Paul likened us to an heir, born of the head of the house, who must serve a time under tutors and governors. These are types representing the Law that kept us as our pedagogue until the time appointed by God for us to be given the full rights of manhood.

"But when the fulness of the time was come, God sent forth his Son, made of a woman, made under the law" (v. 4). The expression "made of a woman" refers to the virgin birth of our Lord. "Made under the law" indicates the Messiah was born under the Law. In fact, Jesus Christ was born, lived His life, was crucified, died, was buried, was resurrected, and ascended into heaven, all under the dispensation of the Law. The New Dispensation, which is the church age, did not begin until the Day of Pentecost with the outpouring of the Holy Spirit.

That's why you and I today don't have to live by the Law. We have the Holy Spirit living in us as our Guide. Since we are in Christ, positionally speaking, we cannot become any more complete. Can Christ become any more fully mature? However, in our Christian walk, in this fleshly body, you and I do continue to grow and mature. We start out as babes in Christ, and by feeding on the sincere milk of the Word, we grow and develop until we are ready for meat. We grow in God's Word and learn to be led by the Spirit of God Himself. That's when we become full-grown sons of God: "For as many as are led by the Spirit of God, they are the sons of God" (Romans 8:14). Holy Spirit leadership is a sign of spiritual maturity.

Some people tell me, "Oh, I wish I knew how to be led by the Spirit." I ask them how they make decisions. "Oh, when I'm faced with some problem or circumstance in my life, I just go by the Scriptures. Usually some verse or passage will come to my mind and I'll apply it to my situation."

"Then you are being led of the Spirit. The Spirit of God always leads in line with the Word of God. The Spirit has been sent to lead and guide us into all Truth (the Word)."

"Oh, but that's so simple. I thought God would speak through some great prophet or dream or vision or unusual event."

"He can speak that way," I tell them, "and sometimes He does. But most of the time, God speaks to His children just as He spoke to His prophet Elijah: not in the strong wind or the earthquake or the fire, but in a still small voice. (See 1 Kings 19:11-12.) That's why, in the midst of all the busy activity of our daily lives, and even in our exuberant worship, we still need a time to be still and know He is God. Too often we're seeking some great manifestation, some overwhelming pronouncement or personal prophecy, some miraculous or spectacular occurrence, when we should be simply listening for the gentle, sweet voice of the Spirit. The truly mature son of God hears more in silence than the frenzied crowd hears in a trumpet blast."

"To redeem them that were under the law, that we might receive the adoption of sons" (v. 5). Jesus Christ came to redeem those who were under the Law first. Who was that? The Jews. Then Paul went on to say, "that we might receive the adoption of sons." When he used the pronoun "we," he was talking about himself and the Galatians to whom he was writing. Christ came to redeem not just the Jews, but the Gentiles as well, everyone. Jesus came to the Jew first, then the Gentile.

Isaiah spoke for the whole of mankind when he said, "All we like sheep have gone astray; we have turned every one to his own way; and the LORD hath laid on him [Christ] the iniquity of us all" (Isaiah 53:6). Whether they had the Law or not, whether they tried to keep the Law or not, all mankind was lost, condemned, without hope, until Christ came to give His life a ransom for many.

What was the threefold curse of the Law? Sickness, poverty, and spiritual death. Everyone, Jew and Gentile alike, was subject to that curse.Everyone, both Jew and Gentile, needed redemption through Jesus Christ. Jesus came to redeem all those who were under the curse of the Law, which was all mankind: "For all have sinned, and come short of the glory of God" (Romans 3:23,). He came to redeem the whole world. Jews were under the Law and couldn't keep it. Gentiles were under the curse even though they did not have the Law. ALL needed redemption. Redemption came in the form of the Messiah who was sent by God "that we might receive the adoption as sons" (Galatians 4:5).

Our Adoption as Sons

This phrase about our being adopted as the sons of God is one of the most misunderstood in the whole Bible. Most Christians don't have the foggiest idea of what it really means. Even pastors and teachers of the Word sometimes miss the whole point of Paul's analogy here. I once read a book in which the author used this text as evidence for his theory that when a person is saved by faith, he is just a sinner who has been adopted by God; he is not really God's blood relative. That is totally false. Nothing could be further from the truth.

Jesus told Nicodemus that in order to enter the kingdom of heaven a person must be "born again" (John 3:3). Paul told us, "If any man be in Christ, he is a new creature: old things are passed away; behold, all things are become new" (2 Corinthians 5:17). If we became Christians by being born again, and become totally new creatures, then it is ridiculous to say we are just sinners who have been adopted by God. I'm not "just an old sinner saved by grace." Neither are you, not if you are in Christ Jesus. We used to be sinners, but now, according to 2 Corinthians 5:21, we have become the righteousness of God in Christ. We are now the sons of God, and I can assure you God doesn't have any sinners in His family. We're not sinners; we're saints and became saints when we were washed in the blood of Jesus.

Paul didn't say believers are "adopted sinners." He told us we are the very sons of God: "For as many as are led by the Spirit of God, they are the sons of God. For ye have not received the spirit of bondage again to fear; but ye have received the Spirit of adoption, whereby we cry,

Abba, Father. The Spirit itself beareth witness with our spirit, that we are the children of God: and if children, then heirs; heirs of God, and joint-heirs with Christ" (Romans 8:14–17).

"If we are the sons of God, then why did Paul speak of our 'adoption' as sons?"

When Paul used the term *adoption* in his day, it had a totally different meaning to the New Testament Greeks than it does to us Americans today. We think of adoption as taking a child from outside the family and making him a son by legal means. Such a child is not a true blood offspring. Throughout the New Testament the word adoption referred to the action of parents who "adopted" their own children into the family. Let me explain.

The Greek word translated *adoption* in the King James Version is *huiothesia*. It is a compound word made up of two elements that literally mean "son placing" (in the sense of "adult son placing.") It was used to refer to the ceremony in which a minor son was formally initiated into full family status by being vested with the rights and privileges of an adult.

To the Greek, the word adoption didn't convey the image of taking a child from outside the family and bringing him into it by a legal process. Rather, it symbolized maturity, the imparting of the full rights of sonship upon a minor child who was already a member of the family.

In the time of Paul, a boy child born into a Greek family was considered a ward of his appointed pedagogue who exercised authority over him. The pedagogue was charged with the responsibility of teaching and training the boy until the time he was ready to accept full responsibility for himself, which was usually at about age 14. Until that time, the child, though he was heir to his father's name and estate, was totally subject to his pedagogue. Though a son, for all practical purposes, he had no more rights or privileges than a slave in the household.

145

Until the boy reached the age of consent, he was required to wear a cloak of childhood to indicate to others he was not yet responsible for his own actions and decisions. When he had attained sufficient maturity to take care of himself, the boy was presented to the head of the family by his *pedagogue* as a candidate for adoption. If he successfully demonstrated his maturity, he then went through a ceremony called the *toga virilis*, which simply means *"the ceremony of the cloak of manhood."* His cloak of childhood was formally removed from his shoulders, and he was invested with the cloak of manhood.

With that ceremony, the boy became a man. Henceforth, he was no longer just a child, a servant under a *pedagogue.* He was a son, an heir of the father, with all the rights and privileges that went with that title.

This is what Paul was referring to in this passage: our "adoption" as sons by God the Father: "wherefore thou art no more a servant, but a son; and if a son, then an heir of God through Christ."

What happened to the *pedagogue* after the boy had been declared a man? He was no longer needed. His task had been completed. He was assigned a new charge. Never again would he be placed in a position of authority and dominion over the son.

That's what happened in our case. When we accepted Christ into our lives, when we "put on" Christ (our cloak of manhood), our *pedagogue,* the Law, was dismissed. It no longer has authority or dominion over us because we are full-fledged sons of the Father. It still remains, but now it pertains only to those who are still under its jurisdiction, those who have not yet come to the Father through faith in Jesus Christ. The Law is for the unrighteous. (See 1 Timothy 1:9–10.)

No More Servants, but Sons

Verses 6-7

And because ye are sons, God hath sent forth the Spirit of his Son into your hearts, crying, Abba, Father. Wherefore thou art no more a servant, but a son; and if a son, then an heir of God through Christ.

"And because ye are sons" (v. 6). Now if you are a woman, you may be thinking, "How can I be a 'son' of God?" You are just as much a "son" of God as any man, because this word simply indicates a mature offspring. Paul already told us that in Christ there is neither Jew nor Greek, bond nor free, male nor female (Galatians 3:28). We are all one in the body of Christ. If that is so, then we don't need to join movements to "fight for our rights" either as males or females. All we need to do is to recognize the freedom and equality that is already ours through our Lord Jesus Christ. There is no one as free as the person who walks in line with the Word of God and in harmony with His Spirit, for the one whom the Son has set free is free indeed (John 8:36).

"God hath sent forth the Spirit of his Son into your hearts, crying, Abba, Father" (Galatians 5:6). This word "Abba" is Chaldean for father, just as the Greek word *pater* here was translated father. Some people seem to think "Abba" has some deep, mystical significance. They go around chanting it as though it is a sort of magic word that somehow moves them closer to God. All Paul did here was repeat the same word in two different languages. The Chaldean word "Abba" was simply left untranslated. We cry, "Father, Father."

"Wherefore thou art no more a servant, but a son" (v. 7). There is an implied intimacy with God here, the kind that allows us to call Him "Daddy" as well as "Father." The people under the old covenant could not

147

do that. Until the coming of the Holy Spirit to live in the individual believer, no Jew ever looked upon himself as a son of God. This new relationship between God and man was what Jesus was preparing the Jews for when He began to teach His disciples to address God as their heavenly Father. Prior to this time, no one had dared to approach God in that way. He was not their Father; He was Elohim, the Almighty, the Eternal. He was their Creator, their Lord, their Sovereign. Yet Jesus began to give them a glimpse of the new relationship that would be theirs once they had become participants in the new covenant God was establishing with them through Him.

The truth Paul was sharing with the Galatians is the fact that when they received the Spirit of Christ into their hearts, they, too, had become the children of God. No longer were they servants, but sons. If they were sons of God, as Jesus is the Son of God, they were heirs of God just as Jesus is. The way they became sons and heirs was by being born again of the Spirit of God.

It was previously stated that the Old Testament saints were saved, but were not born again until after Pentecost. The reason is because no one could be born of the Spirit of God until the Spirit had been given to all mankind. At Pentecost the Spirit didn't come exclusively upon those in the upper room; He came upon all who had put their trust in God through Jesus Christ His Son. The same Spirit is still with us today, He has never left. He is still bearing children of divinity, still giving birth to new sons of God. He is still filling believers with His presence and power.

In the Old Testament, no one was a *son* of God because the only way to come into the family of God is by birth, the *new birth*. Moses, as great as he was, was not a son of God; he was a servant in the household of God. (See Hebrews 3:5.) Elijah, the great prophet, was not a *son* of God, but only a servant of the Most High. When Jesus Christ arose from the dead, He became the firstborn of many brethren (Romans 8:29).

He ascended into heaven from where He poured out the Holy Spirit upon those who had believed on Him. The Holy Spirit began in Jerusalem and encircled the globe, bringing believers into the family of God.

John said of Jesus Christ: "As many as received him, to them gave he power to become the sons of God, even to them that believe on his name" (John 1:12). John does not say Jesus made sons of God out of those who believed in Him; He only gave them "power to become the sons of God." That event took place after Jesus had returned to His Father in heaven. It was not Jesus who made His followers into sons of God; it was the Holy Spirit who gave them New Birth. They had the power to become sons of God by their faith in Christ. In essence, they had their "ticket" to sonship by faith, but they had to hold onto that "ticket" until the Day of Pentecost when they presented it for admission into the family of God. Rebirth came through the "washing of regeneration, and renewing of the Holy Ghost" (Titus 3:5).

"And if a son, then an heir of God through Christ" (Galatians 5:7). That New Birth brought with it a new relationship to God. No longer were they servants of the Most High; now they were sons of God. He was no longer just their Creator and Lord, now He was their heavenly Father.

I imagine one of the things the followers of Jesus were saying on the Day of Pentecost as they burst forth into praises to God in their new tongues was, "Abba, Father!" That's why I always try to get new converts to say to God, "Lord, thank You for saving me; now I can call You Father." That gives the new believer a whole new perspective of God and of himself. He begins to see God as His loving heavenly Father rather than as a faraway, all powerful being. He also sees himself differently from then on. No longer is he a mere subject, or servant of the Lord God Jehovah; he has become a son of God, an heir of God and a joint heir with Christ.

If Jesus is the heir of God, and if we believers are joint

149

heirs with Him, what is it we are heirs of? "All things" (Hebrews 1:2).

When you and I were born again, born into the family of God, we went through a spiritual ceremony of *toga virilis.* Our cloak of childhood was removed and the cloak of manhood, the cloak of mature sonship, was placed upon us. From that moment on, we were declared by God to be full-grown sons, heirs to all that is His. We can see this inheritance illustrated in the story we usually refer to as the parable of the Prodigal Son. Do you remember what the loving father told the older brother who was angry because his younger brother had received such a welcome home after "wasting his inheritance"? "Son, thou art ever with me, and all that I have is thine" (Luke 15:31). That's the way it is with us as the sons of God: All He has is ours. (See 1 Corinthians 3:21–23.)

Wouldn't it be foolish if we, after having been granted the freedom and fullness of sonship, would suddenly decide to go back, take upon ourselves the cloak of childhood, and deliberately place ourselves under the authority and dominion of our old pedagogue, the Law? Yet that is precisely what the Galatians were doing. How stupid. They had just been brought out of bondage to sin, just been set free from the law of sin and death, just been received into the family of God as heirs of all that is His — only to turn right around and place themselves back under bondage. This kind of ignorance and foolishness Paul just could not understand.

Why Turn Back to Bondage?

Verses 8–9

Howbeit then, when ye knew not God, ye did service unto them which by nature are no gods. But now, after that ye have known God, or rather are known of God, how turn

*ye again to the weak and beggarly elements, whereunto
ye desire again to be in bondage?*
"Howbeit then, when ye knew not God, ye did
service unto them which by nature are no gods" (v. 8).
This expression "by nature" simply means "in essence."
Paul was asking these people: "How is it that when you
were sinners, in essence you served those things that are
not gods at all?" Before their conversion to Christ, the
Galatians were heathens; they were idol worshippers.
They bowed down and worshipped images carved from
wood and stone. Of course, we know that man-made
"gods" are not gods at all. Yet notice Paul didn't say they
worshipped these "non-gods"; he said they "did service
unto them." That is, the Galatians served idols. To serve
something is to be a servant or slave of that thing.

Paul was telling these people that before they came to
know Christ, they were slaves; they were in bondage. As
Gentiles, they were never in bondage to the Jewish Law;
rather, they were slaves to the law of sin and death. They
were under condemnation because they had not believed
on Him who has the power to set men free, the power to
cause them to become the sons of God.

"But now, after that ye have known God, or rather
are known of God, how turn ye again to the weak and
beggarly elements, whereunto ye desire again to be in
bondage?" (v. 9). "Now that you have come to know God
through His Son Jesus Christ, now that He has set you
free from the law of sin and death, why do you turn back
to another form of death, the Law? Once you were in
bondage, trapped by your ignorance of God and His love.
Now that Christ has delivered you from that trap, why do
you want to turn back to another form of enslavement?"

To Paul what the Galatians were doing made no sense
at all. He couldn't understand why anyone who was
once set free from the bondage of heathenism would ever
want to fall into the bondage of Judaism. To him, one was
as bad as the other. Both were mere forms of bondage.

151

Both were forms of religion, man's puny efforts to gain spiritual favor and right standing by giving service to a dead system of physical rules and regulations. Paul was much too intelligent and enlightened to be fooled into thinking external rules could ever produce a new internal spirit. He knew the only way man could ever truly please God was by becoming one with Him through the New Birth. Once that had happened, once the person had become a true son of God by spiritual rebirth, then he was no longer a slave to a system of external rules. From then on he was led from the inside by the indwelling Spirit of God.

Led of the Spirit, Not by the Law

Verse 10

Ye observe days, and months, and times, and years.

"Ye observe days" (v. 10). Here Paul began to rebuke the Galatians for allowing the legalistic Judaizers to influence them into observing the Jewish calendar instead of holding fast to the freedom that was won for them through the suffering of the Lord Jesus. The "days" the Galatians had taken to observing were Jewish Sabbath days. These Gentiles in Galatia had become Sabbath-keepers. Remember, this is Saturday, not Sunday, the Christian day of rest and worship.

Now we remember how legalistic the Jews had become about keeping the Sabbath. Through the centuries they had worked out an elaborate and complicated system of laws regulating every possible aspect of Sabbath-keeping. For example, they had determined the exact number of steps allowed to be taken on the Sabbath without constituting work. They had become so minutely involved in keeping the Law, they had missed the whole point of it. They actually broke the Sabbath by trying to keep it because they worked so hard at trying to avoid work. They also worked very hard at trying to force their own self-righteous standards on everyone else. They had succeeded in making the Law a stumbling block instead of a stepping-stone.

That kind of attitude and behavior did not die out with the ancient Jews. I remember well when I was growing up how strictly many Christians kept the "Lord's Day." There were laws about what could and couldn't be done on Sunday just like the Pharisees had about Saturday. Christians were not supposed to do any kind of work for any reason on Sunday. They couldn't even play baseball. Of course, you wouldn't dare think of going hunting or fishing or even swimming on Sunday (especially not in "mixed company")!

Moviegoing on Sunday was definitely out (I still cannot figure out why some perfectly legal activities six days a week suddenly became such enormous sin on Sunday. The same roller skating rink that was a wholesome place of entertainment on Saturday night somehow got devilishly transformed into a den of iniquity on Sunday afternoon!) But one thing was sure: If it was in any way restful, it wasn't supposed to be done on the Day of Rest!

Then there were the "Blue Laws." Some well-meaning souls somewhere obviously became so concerned about all the sinning going on every Lord's Day, they decided it was their Christian duty to jump in and help God keep it holy. They managed to get legislatures and city councils to pass strict laws about what could and could not be sold on Sunday.

I remember going into a store in Kansas City on Sunday and seeing certain departments roped off because the religious zealots had come in to decide what was sinful to be sold. It was such a relief to see you could buy a baby bottle, but not detergent. I know the Lord was so grateful to those good church people for seeing to it that housewives in Kansas City could feed their babies on Sunday just as long as they weren't able to wash their dirty diapers!

"Blue Laws" are a prime example of how the church of Jesus Christ has totally misunderstood its purpose and role on this earth. As Christians, we are called and commissioned to go into the entire world and spread the Good News of Jesus Christ. We are not sent to tell businesses what they can and cannot sell, on Sunday or any other day. We are ambassadors for Christ, not shelf inspectors!

Nor are we "sin fighters." Our calling is not to fight sin; it's to save sinners. We don't have to spend our time and energy trying to close down bars and clubs. Once we get all the clientele of those establishments saved and filled to overflowing with the Holy Spirit, they will close themselves down because they won't have any customers to keep them going. The answer to alcoholism or drug addiction or prostitution is not prohibition; it's regeneration! If the church of Jesus Christ had ever worked as hard to fulfill the Great Commission as it has to stamp out sin, by now the whole world would be saved, and sin wouldn't be a problem anymore. I wonder how many souls have ever been saved from hell because some church group somewhere succeeded in forcing the neighborhood Sears store to close on Sunday?

In the church I pastor, we don't believe it is our duty to set out to close down the local shopping mall. Even if we managed to close it down, there would be no guarantee that either the merchants or their customers would be in church on Sunday. Who would want to go to a church that has just closed down his store? Besides that, we don't believe we have a right to try to force anyone to close his business to conform to our religious convictions. If we in the church of Jesus Christ want and expect our freedom to be respected, we must be very careful we are not guilty of depriving others of theirs, whether we agree with their beliefs or practices or not. Our church is persuaded that as Christians we have only one obligation, one responsibility to our fellowman, and that is to preach to him the glorious Gospel of Jesus Christ. How can we effectivly preach if we are out picketing his store and driving away his customers?

It's high time we in the church come to our senses and quit trying to force our beliefs and practices onto others. It's high time we quit judging and condemning the world for not abiding by our standards of conscience or behavior. Why should they? They're lost. It wouldn't do them any good to abide by our codes anyway; it wouldn't save them. That's the whole point of this letter to the Galatians, the fact that no one is saved by keeping religious laws. Like Jesus, we're not sent to judge, but to save. The only way we'll ever save the world is not by condemning people for being sinners, but by loving them into becoming saints.

Finally, it's high time we Christians quit judging and condemning each other, regardless of our differences of doctrine and practice and belief. John had these strong words to say to the people of his day: "If a man say, I love God, and hateth his brother, he is a liar: for he that loveth not his brother whom he hath seen, how can he love God whom he hath not seen?" (1 John 4:20). Let's paraphrase that quote a bit: "If a Christian says, 'I love God,' and judges and condemns his fellow Christians, he is a liar: for how can he possibly love God whom he cannot see if he doesn't love his brothers and sisters in Christ whom he can see?" There will never be brotherhood among men until there is first brotherhood among brothers.

"And months" (Gaatians 4:10). "Months" refers to the fast initiated by the Jews during their Babylonian captivity. Here the Galatians had gone way back into Hebrew history to resurrect a commemoration that had nothing

155

whatsoever to do with them personally. "And times" (v. 10). "Times" refers to the seven regularly established Jewish feast days. The Galatians were now observing Passover, the feast of Unleavened Bread, the dedication of the Firstfruits, Pentecost, Trumpets, Atonements, and Tabernacles. Can you see why Paul was so disgusted with these Gentiles? Why would they ever think they had to keep these Jewish commemorative feast days—none of which applied to them in its original context?

We, too, can see how foolish it was for Gentiles to allow legalistic Jews to intimidate them into trying to keep special observances that had no relation to them personally. We like to think we would not be so gullible as to let anyone else put his or her religious straitjacket on to us.

Yet the same thing happens today. People come into a Christian church or fellowship where they are born again and filled with the Spirit of God. Once set free from their bondage to the law of sin and death, many times they turn right around and fall into the trap of legalism. They will be taught now that they are free, they must give up the ways of the world and learn to abide by the way of the Word, usually as interpreted for them by some self-appointed religious leader or group.

The end result is things haven't changed at all. They are no more "free" in the church than they were outside it. Their lives are still bound by traditions, taboos, and "thou shalt not's." They are told if they do not worship God in the prescribed manner, they are not "spiritual." They soon realize they are expected to conform to accepted standards, to adapt to someone else's ideas of the proper mode of dress and code of conduct. They are told what to wear, what to read, what to listen to, what to think. Although they are supposed to be free, they still don't have the right to determine the truth for themselves by listening to the Spirit of God or by studying the Word for themselves.

Despite their glowing testimonies and phony smiles, so many times church people are not out to win people to Christ or to set people free from bondage nearly as much as they are out to get them onto their roll and into their mold. In religious terms that is called *proselytizing*, and it is every bit as legalistic as attempting to impose the observance of Jewish Law on Gentile believers.

Most of the seven feast days in the Jewish calendar have already been fulfilled by the Lord Jesus Christ; those which are left will be fulfilled by Him when He returns to this earth in glory. The first feast was Passover, the ancient Jewish celebration of the passing of the death angel over the homes of the children of Israel while the firstborn of the Egyptians died. Each Hebrew family took a lamb and slaughtered it, smearing the blood on the doorpost as a sign that they were under God's protection.

Jesus Christ was our Passover Lamb who shed His blood that we might be saved. That's why His crucifixion took place at the time of the Passover Feast. The same religious Jews who were responsible for Christ's crucifixion hurried home from Calvary to partake of the Passover Feast, never realizing they were eyewitnesses to the very event they had been proclaiming all those centuries by their commemoration.

Next came the weeklong Feast of Unleavened Bread during which time the women were required to thoroughly clean their houses to remove all dust from them because leaven, represented by dust, was a type of sin. Removing all the dust was a sign of the removal of our sins by Christ during His three days and nights in the bowels of the earth.

The first Sunday during the Feast of Unleavened Bread was called Firstfruits. In the Jewish tradition this commemorated the bringing of the first and best of the fruits of the harvest to be dedicated to God. It was on the day of Firstfruits that our Lord was resurrected, representing the First and Best of a long line of souls who will be raised to new and eternal life because of Him. You and I are part of that huge harvest that is yet to be completed.

Then fifty days after Passover came the feast of Pentecost, which was fulfilled when the Holy Spirit was poured out on all believers.

Between Pentecost and the next feast there was an interval of five months. Pentecost was in April; the next feast day, Trumpets, came in October. The interval of five months between the two represents the church age in which you and I are now living. The next feast day to be fulfilled will be that of Trumpets, referring to the fanfare that will mark the triumphant return of our Lord to this earth to begin His millennial reign.

After that comes the Feast of Atonements, looking forward to the day when Jesus Christ will cleanse the earth of all sin, remove all sinners from it, and lift the last curse from it. Paul wrote in Romans 8:19–23 that this is the moment for which all creation has been groaning and travailing so long, the moment when final atonement will have been fulfilled on the earth.

The final feast day to be fulfilled is that of Tabernacles, which was instituted to remind the Jews of the time in which God dwelt in a tabernacle with them. Its fulfillment will come when Jesus Christ sets up His kingdom here on earth, inaugurating a thousand-year reign of peace.

There is no need for Gentiles to observe these "times" of the Jewish calendar because those that have not already been fulfilled soon will be. We should know about them and their significance to us as the body of Christ on this earth, but we are not obliged to keep them in their original context because they all point to Christ in whom we are already complete.

"And years" (v. 10). This is a reference to the seven seven-year periods of the ancient Jewish calendar, culminating in the fiftieth year, the year of Jubilee. In that year all slaves were set free and all property that had changed hands returned to its original owner. Now we Christians don't need to observe the year of Jubilee; we're living in it. In Luke 4, we read where our Lord went into the synagogue and was handed the scroll to read. Notice the passage He read, and His reason for doing so:

> *The Spirit of the Lord is upon me, because he hath anointed me to preach the gospel to the poor; he hath sent me to heal the brokenhearted, to preach deliverance to the captives, and recovering of sight to the blind, to set at liberty them that are bruised, to preach the acceptable year of the Lord. And he closed the book, and he gave it again to the minister, and sat down. And the eyes of all them that were in the synagogue were fastened on him. And he began to say unto them, This day is this scripture fulfilled in your ears.*
>
> *Luke 4:18-21*

This Scripture has been fulfilled. The "acceptable year of the Lord" has already come. It is here. Jubilee has arrived. The slaves are set free. The property of the just is being returned to its rightful owners. Throughout the land, there is rejoicing and praise to God the Father because He has redeemed us from our oppressors, has opened our blind eyes, has healed our brokenness, and has restored to us our inheritance just as He promised.

This was just as true in Paul's day. The "acceptable year of the Lord" had already come before Paul ever set foot in Galatia with the Gospel. In fact, that was the Good News he had brought to these Gentiles. Hearing it had set them free from their bondage. Now here they are turning from that liberty to submit themselves to Jewish Law and observance that was only a shadow of what had already taken place by the coming of the Lord Jesus Christ. That's why Paul spoke in such harsh terms to these people. He wanted them to realize how foolish it was to turn their backs on the Good News of liberation and to surrender to the very Law that Christ had come to fulfill in every last detail.

Be as I Am

Verses 11–12

I am afraid of you, lest I have bestowed upon you labour in vain. Brethren, I beseech you, be as I am; for I am as ye are: ye have not injured me at all.

"I am afraid of you" (v. 11). This is a mistranslation. It should read, "I am afraid for you." Why? What was Paul's fear concerning the Galatian believers?

"Lest I have bestowed upon you labour in vain" (v. 11). Paul was afraid that by their actions they were undoing all the work that he put in on them. He was concerned that they were in danger of destroying the foundation of faith and freedom that he had built in them during his first visit.

"Brethren, I beseech you, be as I am" (v. 12). This word "be" would better be translated become. Paul was telling these people, "Become as I am." What does he mean by that? He means that he began his Christian walk in faith, and he remained in faith. Paul fully understood the message of grace that he had preached to the Galatians. He lived by it himself. Now he urged them to remain in God's grace, just as he had done in his own life.

"For I am as ye are" (v. 12). Whenever Paul's message of faith is preached today, people tend to say, "Sure, it was easy for Paul to live by faith; he was an apostle, a great man of faith. But it's hard for me to live that way; I'm nobody special."

Realizing these Gentile converts in Galatia might have that attitude, Paul assured them what he was prescribing to them is not impossible. He was saying he lived by faith, and he had confidence they could, too, because humanly speaking he was no different from them. Paul wanted the Galatians to understand that of himself he was in no way superior to them. What he could do, they, too, could do. That's part of the message of grace: it's not our great faith that makes us special; it's God's great grace. That grace is freely available to anyone who will simply receive it. In that sense, Paul had no unique gift. He had the same gift that is freely offered to everyone: the free gift of God's favor.

"Ye have not injured me at all" (v. 12). Here Paul was simply saying, "By your actions, you haven't harmed me. I'm just the same as I was." He was implying, "You're not harming me by your actions; it's yourselves who are being injured."

Paul's Infirmity

Verses 13-16

Ye know how through infirmity of the flesh I preached the gospel unto you at the first. And my temptation which was in my flesh ye despised not, nor rejected; but received me as an angel of God, even as Christ Jesus. Where is then the blessedness ye spake of? for I bear you record, that, if it had been possible, ye would have plucked out your own eyes, and have given them to me. Am I therefore become your enemy, because I tell you the truth?

Too many times people have taken these verses out of context and quoted them as evidence that Paul was a sickly man. In their efforts to discredit the message of healing in the atonement, they link this passage with others from various sources in an attempt to prove Paul's "thorn in the flesh" (2 Corinthians 12:7) was a physical sickness or disease. Sometimes they even go so far as to take this expression about the Galatians being willing to have plucked out their own eyes and given them to Paul as an indication that Paul's infirmity was an eye disease. All such teaching is mere speculation. We have no conclusive proof of exactly what it was that Paul was referring to when he spoke of his "thorn in the flesh."

Surely Paul was buffeted in his flesh wherever he went, as we will see. But to interpret Paul's physical hardships and persecutions as an indication that God does not will for His children to be healthy and well is as much a mistake as interpreting our own children's "hard knocks" in life as evidence we don't will for them to be healthy or prosperous or successful. Where did we ever get the idea that we humans are better parents than God?

"Ye know how through infirmity of the flesh I preached the gospel unto you at the first" (v. 13). Paul spoke here of preaching to the Galatians "through infirmity of the flesh," but I think a bit of investigation of the Scriptures can give us some clue as to what that infirmity might well have been.

Note the last phrase of this verse: "at the first." This tells us *when* Paul came to preach the Gospel to these people to preach the Gospel to them "through infirmity." It was during his very first missionary trip to Galatia (which we remember is not a city, but a province in which Paul established churches in four cities: *Antioch, Iconium, Derbe,* and *Lystra*). Let's read about this first journey to the province of Galatia, picking up Paul and Barnabas as they leave Antioch:

> *And it came to pass in Iconium, that they went both together into the synagogue of the Jews, and so spake, that a great multitude both of the Jews and also of the Greeks believed. But the unbelieving Jews stirred up the Gentiles, and made their minds evil affected against the brethren. Long time therefore abode they speaking boldly*

in the Lord, which gave testimony unto the word of his grace, and granted signs and wonders to be done by their hands. But the multitude of the city was divided: and part held with the Jews, and part with the apostles. And when there was an assault made both of the Gentiles, and also of the Jews with their rulers, to use them despitefully, and to stone them, they were ware of it, and fled unto Lystra and Derbe, cities of Lycaonia, and unto the region that lieth round about: and there they preached the gospel. And there sat a certain man at Lystra, impotent in his feet, being a cripple from his mother's womb, who never had walked: the same heard Paul speak: who stedfastly beholding him, and perceiving that he had faith to be healed, said with a loud voice, Stand upright on thy feet. And he leaped and walked.

Acts 14:1–10

Paul and Barnabas were quite successful on their first trip to Galatia, but their success was not achieved without opposition. They had to flee from Iconium to Lystra to avoid being stoned by the angry crowds the Jews stirred up against them. It was in Lystra that the Holy Spirit, who had granted signs and wonders be done by the hands of Paul and Barnabas, worked another mighty miracle. The lame man, who had been crippled from birth, was healed.

In the healing classic, *Christ the Healer*,1 we find quite a lengthy discussion of the views of various theologians on the subject of Paul's supposed "weakness of the flesh." One theory advanced was that Paul suffered from a serious eye disease called ophthalmia, which was marked by constant pain and a continual drainage of water and pus. The person advancing this theory suggested because of this infectious condition, Paul was a hideous man to look at. He also pointed out the pain caused by this condition would be like that of a stake piercing the eye (hence Paul's reference to a "thorn" in his flesh).

When Paul gazes steadfastly into the eyes of the lame man in Lystra, is there any indication that Paul had difficulty focusing his eyes on the man upon whom he so steadfastly fixed his attention? No. Any mention of Paul's having pain or discomfort in his eyes? No. Does it seem reasonable that this cripple would be moved to great faith for his own physical healing if the man who was preaching the message of healing to him was himself hard to look upon because of his own hideous eye disease? Not likely.

Notice what happened after this healing took place. What might have actually been the cause of the infirmity from which Paul suffered during his first stay in Galatia?

And when the people saw what Paul had done, they lifted up their voices, saying in the speech of Lycaonia, The gods are come down to us in the likeness of men. And they called Barnabas, Jupiter; and Paul, Mercurius, because he was the chief speaker. Then the priest of Jupiter, which was before their city, brought oxen and garlands unto the gates, and would have done sacrifice with the people. Which when the apostles, Barnabas and Paul, heard of, they rent their clothes, and ran in among the people, crying out, and saying, Sirs, why do ye these things? We also are men of like passions with you, and preach unto you that ye should turn from these vanities unto the living God, which made heaven, and earth, and the sea, and all things that are therein: who in times past suffered all nations to walk in their own ways. Nevertheless he left not himself without witness, in that he did good, and gave us rain from heaven, and fruitful seasons, filling our hearts with food and gladness. And with these sayings scarce restrained they the people, that they had not done sacrifice unto them.

Acts 14:11–18

As a result of the healing of the lame man, the people of Lystra were convinced Paul and Barnabas were Greek gods in the form of men. Notice what Paul told them in verse 15: "Sirs, why do ye these things? We also are men of like passions with you." That reminds us of his words in Galatians 4:12, "I beseech you, be as I am; for I am as ye are." Why did these people want to worship Paul and Barnabas? It was because the Holy Spirit had performed miracles through them, so the people looked upon them as gods.

Note again in Galatians 4:14 what Paul said about the way he had been received when he first brought the Gospel to Galatia: "And my temptation which was in my flesh ye despised not, nor rejected; but received me as an angel of God, even as Christ Jesus." Paul reminded the Galatians that when he first brought them the Gospel of grace, they had received him as if he were Jesus Christ Himself

Paul and Barnabas had to talk fast and hard to persuade the people of Lystra they were not Greek gods in human flesh, but were representatives of the One True God, Creator of heaven and earth. All this commotion in Lystra attracted the attention of the Jews. The following passage describes what happened next:

> *And there came thither certain Jews from Antioch and Iconium, who persuaded the people, and, having stoned Paul, drew him out of the city, supposing he had been dead. Howbeit, as the disciples stood round about him, he rose up, and came into the city: and the next day he departed with Barnabas to Derbe. And when they had preached the gospel to that city, and had taught many, they returned again to Lystra, and to Iconium, and Antioch, confirming the souls of the disciples, and exhorting them to continue in the faith, and that we must through much tribulation enter into the kingdom of God. And when they had ordained them elders in every church, and had*

*prayed with fasting, they commended them to the Lord,
on whom they believed.*

Acts 14:19-23

Paul was stoned by the Jews in Lystra. Most biblical scholars agree Paul was actually dead, but was restored to life by God. Some even go so far as to speculate that this might have been the time during which he was taken up into the third heaven where he saw unspeakable things. (See 2 Corinthians 12.) Whether this is so or not, Paul was assumed dead by the crowds who dragged him out of the city where they discarded what they thought to be his dead body. As the disciples stood around his prostrate form, Paul was revived, got to his feet and immediately went right back into the city. From there, he and Barnabas continued their missionary journey, retracing their steps throughout the whole province of Galatia, visiting the cities of Derbe, Iconium, and Antioch, besides returning to visit Lystra.

What do you think might have been Paul's appearance and physical condition after having just been stoned and dragged out of the city of Lystra? Is it likely he showed any signs in his body of the beating he had just experienced? I'm sure he did. He was probably black and blue all over. His reference to the Galatians having been willing to have plucked out their own eyes for his sake could be an indication his own eyes were temporarily damaged, perhaps black or even swollen shut, as he and Barnabas made their way through the cities of Galatia.

In any case, I believe there is much stronger evidence that the infirmity through which Paul preached while in Galatia was a temporary, man-induced condition he eventually overcame, rather than being some chronic debilitating physical disease that he just had to live with all his life.

"And my temptation which was in my flesh ye despised

not, nor rejected; but received me as an angel of God, even as Christ Jesus" (Gaatians 4:14). The expression "my temptation" actually means "my test." Paul was simply saying here, "When I came to you the first time, I was suffering from the test of faith that I had just endured, but you did not let my repulsive physical condition deter you from receiving me as you would have received the Lord Himself."

"Where is then the blessedness ye spake of? for I bear you record, that, if it had been possible, ye would have plucked out your own eyes, and have given them to me" (v. 15). "Since you were so gracious to receive me as a messenger of God, why have you now rejected the message I brought you to turn to a different messenger with a different message? My message is the same. You loved me at first and hate me now. I have not changed, but you have. Then, you were in such sympathy with my physical pain and suffering, if you could have, you would have given your own eyes (your right arm) to be a help to me."

"Am I therefore become your enemy, because I tell you the truth?" (v. 16). "What has happened to change that spirit of loving brotherhood we shared? What have I done to betray you so that now you no longer trust me? All I have ever done is what I did when I first came to you, tell the truth. For that have I now become your enemy?"

10
Sarah and Hagar
Galatians 4:17–31

Paul's Concern for the Galatians

Galatians 4:17–20

They zealously affect you, but not well; yea, they would exclude you, that ye might affect them. But it is good to be zealously affected always in a good thing, and not only when I am present with you. My little children, of whom I travail in birth again until Christ be formed in you, I desire to be present with you now, and to change my voice; for I stand in doubt of you.

"They zealously affect you, but not well" (v. 17). "They" refers to the legalistic Judaizers. The Greek word translated "affect" is *zeloo*, from which we derive our English word zealous. According to Strong, this word means "to have warmth of feeling for or against" someone or something.1 So this verse could be paraphrased: "These legalistic Judaizers are eager to court you, but their intentions are not honorable."

"Yea, they would exclude you, that ye might affect them" (v. 17). "They are trying to woo you away from us in order to win your affection for themselves." Paul likened the Judaizers to adulterers who try to seduce people from their mates into becoming involved in an extramarital affair. He was trying to warn the Galatians not to be misled by the feigned ardor and enticing words of these clever Jews because their ultimate motive was selfish: they just wanted to destroy the relationship the Galatian believers had with the Lord.

"But it is good to be zealously affected always in a good thing, and not only when I am present with you" (v. 18). Paul was telling the Galatians it is fine to be courted by someone when that person's intentions are good. Paul wanted someone to court them who preached his same message. But, now that he was far away from them, he warned them about being led astray from their covenant relationship by unfaithful seducers.

"My little children, of whom I travail in birth again until Christ be formed in you" (v. 19). Here it would seem that Paul was addressing these Galatians as though they were unbelievers, saying that he was "travailing" (praying strongly) to bring them to new birth. That was not what he meant. These were believers; they had already been born again, but they had turned away from the Word of God and slipped into legalistic works. Paul's travail here refers to his intercessory prayer for them. The first time Paul went through travail for the Galatians, it was to bring them to the new birth. Now that they were in the kingdom of God, he wanted them to know his labor for them had not ended. He continued to pray for them, that their nature would be conformed to the image of the Christ who lived within them in the person of the Holy Spirit.

That should be a lesson for us today. Just because people have been born again does not mean we no longer need to pray for them. Once they are reborn, they are still just "babes in Christ," like these Galatians. They still need to be formed, shaped, developed. They need us to pray for them now through our intercession.

Even mature believers and established churches need

our prayer support. Paul said he prayed for the Ephesians "after I heard of your faith in the Lord Jesus, and love unto all the saints" (Ephesains 1:15). He did the same for the Colossians. (See Colossians 1:3-4.) None of us is so fully developed, so mature in the Lord, that we don't still need the support of other believers to overcome the trials, temptations, and obstacles that our enemy throws up in front of us to discourage and destroy us. In the church we should be praying together with our brothers and sisters in Christ, pulling together, strengthening and encouraging one another, bearing each other's burdens, forgiving each other, lifting up the weak and the fallen, drawing hope and encouragement from each other, and edifying each other, "till we all come in the unity of the faith, and of the knowledge of the Son of God, unto a perfect man, unto the measure of the stature of the fulness of Christ" (Ephesians 4:13).

"I desire to be present with you now, and to change my voice; for I stand in doubt of you" (Galatians 4:20). In this letter Paul had not been dealing gently with these people. He had to be harsh with them. He had to rebuke them for their foolishness and error. He had to verbally correct them, even going so far as to call them "Galatian idiots" (Phillips Translation). Now he made it clear he didn't like to speak to them in that tone of voice. The only reason he did so was because he had real doubts about their commitment.

The New International Version captures Paul's mood here when it translates Galatians 4:17-20 in these words:

Those people are zealous to win you over, but for no good. What they want is to alienate you from us, so that you may be zealous for them. It is fine to be zealous, provided the purpose is good, and to be so always and not just when I am with you. My dear children, for whom I am again in the pains of childbirth until Christ is formed in

171

you, how I wish I could be with you now and change my tone, because I am perplexed about you!

Abraham's Two Sons

Verses 21–23

Tell me, ye that desire to be under the law, do ye not hear the law? For it is written, that Abraham had two sons, the one by a bondmaid, the other by a freewoman. But he who was of the bondwoman was born after the flesh; but he of the freewoman was by promise.

"Tell me, ye that desire to be under the law, do ye not hear the law?" (v. 21). The Greek word translated "hear" actually means "understand." In verse 21 Paul began to introduce chapter 5 in which he emphasized two themes: freedom in Christ and life by the Spirit. He began his introduction to these themes by asking the Galatians a puzzling question: "You who want to be under the Law, don't you understand the Law?"

That seems a strange question for Paul to ask people whom he has been reproving for three and a half chapters for observing the Law. Doesn't he realize these people had to know about the Law in order to keep it? Yes, he does. He also knows there is a difference between knowing the Law or knowing *about* the Law and fully understanding the Law. It's possible to have knowledge of something and still never understand the meaning of it.

For example, how many orthodox Jews today fully understand the Law they are so careful to observe? How many of them realize everything in it, every ritual and ceremony and requirement of it, points to Jesus Christ? They know the letter of the Law, but they really don't know what the letter symbolizes. They see the Law well, but they are not able to look beyond the jot and tittle of it to the One to whom it points.

That's nothing new. It was true of the Jews in Jesus' day. Do you remember what He told the Pharisees who questioned His authority? "You search the Scriptures because you think that in them you have eternal life: but the Scriptures point to Me!" (See John 5:39.) The scribes and Pharisees knew the Law perfectly. They kept it in minute detail. Yet they missed the whole point of it.

The Law could not save them; it only pointed to the Savior. That Savior now stood before them in flesh and blood, and they refused to recognize and acknowledge Him. They held to the letter of the Law and rejected the Living Fulfillment of the Law. That was not only foolish, it was also tragic. By their misguided zeal, the Pharisees missed the very salvation they were so desperately seeking. That's the message Paul tried to get across to these foolish Galatians who had turned their backs on the Door to go back to the signpost.

"For it is written, that Abraham had two sons, the one by a bondmaid, the other by a freewoman. But he who was of the bondwoman was born after the flesh; but he of the freewoman was by promise" (vv. 22–23). Here Paul began to unfold to these spiritually blind Galatians what the Law was all about. To explain the Law and its purpose, he went all the way back to the time of Abraham who lived 430 years before the Law ever came into existence. He used the two sons of Abraham as examples of Law and grace, and the works of the flesh and the fruit of the Spirit. We will look at these in more detail as we follow Paul's logic through a comparison of the offspring of the bondmaid and the offspring of the free woman.

Sarah and Hagar

Verses 24–27

Which things are an allegory: for these are the two covenants; the one from the mount Sinai, which gendereth to bondage, which is Agar. For this Agar is mount Sinai in Arabia, and answereth to Jerusalem which now is, and is in bondage with her children. But Jerusalem which is above is free, which is the mother of us all. For it is written, Rejoice, thou barren that bearest not; break forth and cry, thou that travailest not: for the desolate hath many more children than she which hath an husband.

"Which things are an allegory" (v. 24). When Paul said the two offspring of Abraham are an "allegory," he meant they are an analogy. They represent something beyond themselves.

We know this is true, because Abraham himself represented something far more universal and everlasting than he ever imagined in his own lifetime. In this context, Abraham is a type of the individual believer. The two women living in his tent with him are a type of the two messages to which the believer is exposed and is free to devote himself. The free woman, Sarah, symbolizes grace or the promise of God. The bondmaid, Hagar, symbolizes the Law. In the story of the relationship between these three Old Testament figures and their offspring, we see portrayed symbolically the whole conflict between the Law and grace.

By faith in Christ, the Seed of Abraham, you and I became participants in the Abrahamic covenant with the patriarch of old. Therefore, the things that affected him still affect us today because he represents us. Although the Law did not technically come into existence until 430 years later, Abraham had a type of the Law right there in his tent. Her name was Hagar. He also had a type of grace

174

living in his tent. She was called Sarah. From which of these two are you and I descended? To answer that question, let's consider each of these two women separately.

First, what was Hagar's position in the family? She was a bondmaid, a slave. What was her country of origin; where did she come from? She was an Egyptian. Think about that for a moment. What was Egypt a type of in the Old Testament? Egypt always represented exile and bondage, our life as unbelievers.

Before you and I were converted, we were living in a spiritual Egypt. We were exiled from our loving heavenly Father, held in bondage, slaves to sin. But then there came a day when we crossed the Red Sea, a type of the blood of the Lord Jesus Christ, and we walked out of bondage into liberty. Our enemies were cut off from us, washed away by the blood of Jesus. We walked away free men.

As we traveled, we had to do some growing up. We developed and matured spiritually. Following the Lord, we crossed the Jordan and entered into our Promised Land of the life of faith.

Even though we were set free, when we left Egypt we brought a part of it with us. Like Abraham, we had with us in our tent (body) not only our Sarah of grace, but we also had our Hagar of the Law. Our Hagar, our Egyptian, was the flesh. Although we were redeemed by grace, born again of the Spirit, we still have not rid ourselves of the flesh. That is something with which we must contend as long as our regenerated spirit is in this body of flesh. One day, we will be released from this earthly, natural body and caught up to heaven where we will live forever in perfect freedom and holiness. Until that day, you and I must dominate the flesh by the spirit.

The New Testament writers like Paul understood this principle. That's why they wrote things like this: "For I know that in me (that is, in my flesh,) dwelleth no good thing" (Romans 7:18, emphasis added). That is not to

175

say that we are to hate our flesh, to abhor or neglect or "punish" it through asceticism. It just means we are to take authority and dominion over our fleshly lusts and not allow them to dictate to us. I like the answer Smith Wigglesworth gave one day when someone asked him if he ever felt bad: "I never ask myself how I feel," he replied quickly, "I tell myself how I feel!" As free men, that's the way we are to live in relation to our Egyptian bond slave. We are to exercise dominion over it, making it conform to our desires and wishes rather than the other way around.

We will always have the flesh to contend with in this life, but the flesh is not our wife. Our wife is Sarah, the type of the inward man, the regenerated spirit, the new creation. We are to live with her in harmony and peace. We are to become one in union with her.

In the case of Abraham, although he was promised offspring through Sarah (representing the spirit), he became impatient and took unto himself Hagar (representing the flesh). As a result of that union, Hagar gave birth to a son named Ishmael. Later on, Abraham did father a child through Sarah whom they called Isaac. Consequently, there were produced two sets of offspring by Abraham: those of the flesh (through Ishmael, a type of the works of the flesh) and those of the spirit (through Isaac, a type of the fruit of the spirit).

Like our father Abraham, we, too, have a choice of which of these two "women" we will unite ourselves with. We have two voices calling out to us for our attention, seeking our commitment. One voice is that of the flesh; the other is that of the spirit. We must decide which we will give ear to, which one we will "mind." Paul told us: "To be carnally minded is death; but to be spiritually minded is life and peace" (Romans 8:6). Notice, both of these two states of mind produce something: one produces death, the other produces life and peace. Thus, our choice of "mates" will determine the offspring or fruit produced in our lives.

The fruit of our union does not end with the first generation. It has the ability to go on reproducing itself indefinitely. The fruit Abraham produced through Hagar and Sarah kept on multiplying itself. Ishmael produced only a natural race, the Arabs. Isaac produced a natural race, the Jews, which was also a spiritual race, the redeemed. One is temporal; the other is eternal. One lasts for a space of a few hundred earth years; the other endures forever and ever. One is illegitimate (because there is no true marriage to the Law); the other is legitimate (a product of the marriage of the human spirit with God's Spirit). One produces death; the other produces life and peace.

The Two Sons

"For these are the two covenants; the one from the mount Sinai, which gendereth to bondage, which is Agar" (v. 24). Hagar represents the old covenant that was handed down to Moses on Mount Sinai, which is in Arabia. The Law was not given in the promised land of Israel; it originated in Arabia, in the land of cursing. That is an important point.

"For this Agar is mount Sinai in Arabia, and answereth to Jerusalem which now is, and is in bondage with her children" (v. 25). "Answereth" means "corresponds." The first covenant, the old covenant symbolized by Hagar, corresponds to the Jewish nation centered in ancient Jerusalem, which was in bondage both literally and figuratively at the time Paul wrote these words. Literally, the city of Jerusalem was under the yoke of Rome. Spiritually, it was under the yoke of the Law. "With her children" is a reference to the two sets of offspring fathered by Abraham: 1) a natural race, the Jews, who were and are in bondage to the Law; and 2) a spiritual race, the church of Jesus Christ, which is free. This second race is the true Israel, as we read in the ninth chapter of Romans:

> *Not as though the word of God hath taken none effect. For they are not all Israel, which are of Israel: neither, because they are the seed of Abraham, are they all children: but, In Isaac shall thy seed be called. That is, They which are the children of the flesh, these are not the children of God: but the children of the promise are counted for the seed. For this is the word of promise, At this time will I come, and Sarah shall have a son. And not only this; but when Rebecca also had conceived by one, even by our father Isaac; (For the children being not yet born, neither having done any good or evil, that the purpose of God according to election might stand, not of works, but of him that calleth;) It was said unto her, The elder shall serve the younger. As it is written, Jacob have I loved, but Esau have I hated.*
>
> *vv. 6–13*

Now God did not hate Esau and love Jacob for no reason, as we saw previously. Even before they were born, He could look ahead and see their lives. Through foreknowledge, He was aware of the faith resident in Jacob and the unbelief that would motivate Esau. God did not hate Esau personally; He hated the unbelief he stood for. Likewise, God didn't love Jacob as much personally (certainly not his human nature and actions) as He loved the faith he represented.

When Paul spoke of the two offspring of Isaac, he was doing more than examining their individual, personal lives. He was using the two to symbolize the two types of people in the world: 1) those, like Esau, who doubt and disbelieve, and 2) those like Jacob, who though far from perfect, humanly speaking are yet counted righteous by God because of their faith in Him.

This same analogy applies in the case of Ishmael and Isaac. They represent two totally different heritages. One was a product of the flesh, the result of human planning, the fruit of man, a child of the Law. The other was a product of the spirit, the result of divine planning, the fruit of the Holy Spirit, a child of the promise. In other words, Ishmael was Abraham's idea; Isaac was God's idea. That's why Ishmael, the natural child, had no part in the inheritance of Isaac, the spiritual child. This was what Paul was referring to when he said that not all of Israel (the natural seed of Abraham) are part of the true Israel (the spiritual seed of Abraham).

The Two Mountains

"But Jerusalem, which is above is free, which is the mother of us all" (Galatians 4:26). In verses 24 and 25 Mount Sinai represents the giving of the Law. Because it came to be identified with those who held to the Law and rejected the risen Christ, the promised Messiah, it came to be a type of the rejection of the promises of God. As such, Mount Sinai symbolizes legalism, which is bondage.

According to Paul, the Old Jerusalem, the Jerusalem of the natural Jews, is an example of the bondage in which those people live who look to the Law for their justification. Since justification comes not by works of the Law, but by faith in the promises (the integrity) of God, the true Israel is made up of all those who look to Him for their redemption. Their holy city then is not an earthly habitation built by the hands of men; it is the New Jerusalem, "which is above." (See Hebrews 11:10.)

Paul said this New Jerusalem is "the mother of us all." "The mother" is a reference to the new birth. "Us all" refers to all who have been born again, not of the flesh but of the Spirit. The center of Jerusalem is Mount Zion. It is to this mount Israel looks for its deliverance. But the true Mount Zion, like the true Jerusalem, is not a natural, physical place; it's a spiritual one. Just as Mount Sinai corresponds to the Old Jerusalem, the earthly Jerusalem, Mount Zion corresponds to the New Jerusalem, the heavenly Jerusalem.

The writer of Hebrews told us:

For ye are not come unto the mount that might be touched, and that burned with fire, nor unto blackness, and darkness, and tempest, and the sound of a trumpet, and the voice of words; which voice they that heard entreated that the word should not be spoken to them any more: (for they could not endure that which was commanded, And if so much as a beast touch the mountain, it shall be stoned, or thrust through with a dart: and so terrible was the sight, that Moses said, I exceedingly fear and quake:) but ye are come unto mount Sion, and unto the city of the living God, the heavenly Jerusalem, and to an innumerable company of angels, to the general assembly and church of the firstborn, which are written in heaven, and to God the Judge of all, and to the spirits of just men made perfect, and to Jesus the mediator of the new covenant, and to the blood of sprinkling, that speaketh better things than that of Abel.

Hebrews 12:18–24

What mountain did Moses stand before in the midst of thunder and lightning and darkness? Mount Sinai, where the Law was given. But you and I have not come to that mountain. As this passage points out, we have come to Mount Zion, "and unto the city of the living God, the heavenly Jerusalem" (v. 22). We came to that mountain when we "married Sarah," when we joined ourselves in union with God through faith in His promises. Faith always connects a person to the promises.

At Mount Zion, we became a part of "the general assembly and church of the firstborn," those whose names are "written in heaven." We became one with "God the Judge of all." We found our home in the "company of angels" and with the "just men made perfect." Who are these "just men made perfect"? All those who have come to God through faith, "being justified freely by his grace through the redemption that is in Christ Jesus" (Romans 3:24).

The Two Nations

"For it is written" (Galatians 4:27). This expression refers to Isaiah 54:1: "Sing, O barren, thou that didst not bear; break forth into singing, and cry aloud, thou that didst not travail with child: for more are the children of the desolate than the children of the married wife, saith the LORD."

"Rejoice, thou barren that bearest not; break forth and cry, thou that travailest not" (v. 27). The barren one here refers to Sarah. She was told of the Lord to break forth into singing and rejoicing. When? Before she had even yet become pregnant. Why was she to be so joyful when she was still barren?

"For the desolate hath many more children than she which hath an husband" (v. 27). Sarah was told to rejoice because of the promise of the Lord. Her joy was not to be based on what she saw with her eyes, but on what she heard from God.

Does that remind you of a Scripture? "So then faith cometh by hearing, and hearing by the word of God" (Romans 10:17). Faith does not wait for the physical manifestation before it finds expression; it rejoices upon hearing from God. Why? Faith knows what God promises He provides. Nothing in all the world is as sure as a promise from God, provided we, like Abraham, are "fully persuaded that, what he [has] promised, he [is] able also to perform" (Romans 4:21). For that kind of assurance we receive not only the manifestation of what was promised, but we also receive something far greater, the righteousness of God: "And therefore it was imputed to him for righteousness" (v. 22).

The beauty of the faith life is it is a double blessing. When we believe God, we freely receive what we have been promised; then, in addition, God rewards our faith by calling us righteousness. In other words, God does all the work, all the giving; all we do is believe Him. Yet we get both the promised blessing and a reward — as though we had done the giving! This is what justification means to the individual believer: "All I did was believe God, and I received a blessing and a reward, 'just-if-I'd' been the one doing the work."

Notice again when this belief, this rejoicing, is to take place: *before* the physical manifestation. Do you recall what Jesus told His disciples about how to get their prayers answered? "Therefore I say unto you, What things soever ye desire, when ye pray, believe that ye receive them, and ye shall have them" (Mark 11:24). "When ye pray, believe." The key to answered prayer is to believe at the time of the prayer. In essence, that's what Abraham did. He believed when he heard the Word of God, not when he saw the manifestation of what was promised him. For that, he received the double blessing of manifestation and righteousness.

"The desolate" in Galatians 4:27 refers to righteous Sarah who, though she was barren, rejoiced at the promise of God that she would one day produce more offspring than the one in her household who had already given birth to a son. The offspring of Hagar, the bondmaid, would go on to produce a long line of earthly descendants who would multiply and cover the earth. We call the people of that physical nation Arabs. Sarah produced two nations through her offspring, a spiritual race of believers and the natural nation of Israel. The difference is the offspring of Sarah would last not only for the short span we call time, but being spiritual, would endure throughout all eternity.

There is a lesson here. What we do in the natural, physical realm is important because by our actions we plant seeds that will produce a harvest either of good or of evil long after we are gone.How much more important is it that we give attention to our spiritual sowing because it has eternal significance. The fruit produced by that seed will never die.

The Children of Promise

Verses 28–31

Now we, brethren, as Isaac was, are the children of promise. But as then he that was born after the flesh persecuted him that was born after the Spirit, even so it is now. Nevertheless what saith the scripture? Cast out the bondwoman and her son: for the son of the bondwoman shall not be heir with the son of the freewoman. So then, brethren, we are not children of the bondwoman, but of the free.

"Now we, brethren, as Isaac was, are the children of promise" (v. 28). You and I are the children of promise.

"But we're not Jews."

That doesn't matter. The children of promise include all nations around the world. (See Genesis 12:3.) Anyone who has received the Lord Jesus Christ as his personal Savior has entered into the Abrahamic covenant and has become the seed of Abraham. Abraham's seed is not determined by flesh, but is counted by spirit, according to the promise. We become heirs of the promise with Isaac.

"But as then he that was born after the flesh persecuted him that was born after the Spirit, even so it is now" (v. 29). Paul

183

was here referring to the fact that Isaac, the son of promise, the son born after the Spirit of God, was persecuted by Ishmael, the natural son, the son born after the flesh. He was saying those who were born of God have always been the object of scorn, ridicule, and abuse by those who were born only of the flesh. This was especially true in the day in which Paul wrote these words, since the Christian church was hounded and persecuted not only by the paganistic Romans, but especially by the legalistic Jews.

"Nevertheless what saith the scripture? Cast out the bondwoman and her son: for the son of the bondwoman shall not be heir with the son of the freewoman" (v. 30). This is a quote from Genesis 21:

And Sarah saw the son of Hagar the Egyptian, which she had born unto Abraham, mocking. Wherefore she said unto Abraham, Cast out this bondwoman and her son: for the son of this bondwoman shall not be heir with my son, even with Isaac. And the thing was very grievous in Abraham's sight because of his son. And God said unto Abraham, Let it not be grievous in thy sight because of the lad, and because of thy bondwoman; in all that Sarah hath said unto thee, hearken unto her voice; for in Isaac shall thy seed be called. And also of the son of the bondwoman will I make a nation, because he is thy seed. And Abraham rose up early in the morning, and took bread, and a bottle of water, and gave it unto Hagar, putting it on her shoulder, and the child, and sent her away: and she departed, and wandered in the wilderness of Beersheba.

vv. 9–14

Sarah realized that she had made a mistake in offering her handmaid to Abraham to bear him the child she was not able to give him herself at the time. (See Genesis 16:1–16.) Finally she warned Abraham to get rid of Hagar and her son because Ishmael could not be allowed to have any part in the inheritance that rightfully belonged to Isaac, the child of promise. Being a just and honest man, Abraham was reluctant to cast out Hagar and Ishmael, because the boy was his son just as Isaac was. However, the Lord commanded Abraham to do as Sarah had said, noting that it would be through Isaac alone that the covenant would be fulfilled. In obedience to God, Abraham sent Hagar and Ishmael away.

Abraham's feelings reflect our own. Many times we are hesitant to put away the seed of our carnal nature to give total place to the seed of our spiritual nature. We want to hang on to our fleshly nature because it, too, seems to be a vital part of us. Yet God knows that nothing must come between us and Him; nothing must be allowed to keep us from devoting our full attention and devotion to the things of the spirit.

Abraham was ordered not only to get rid of Ishmael, but also Hagar. So many times we want to try to rid ourselves of the product of our flesh, but still pet and excuse the flesh itself. In Galatians 5:24 we will see where Paul said that those who "are Christ's have crucified the flesh with the affections and lusts" of it. It is not only the flesh we must subdue, but also its affections and desires. Not only did Hagar have to depart, her seed also had to depart with her.

In Colossians 3:9–10 we read these words: "Lie not one to another, seeing that ye have put off the old man with his deeds; and have put on the new man, which is renewed in knowledge after the image of him that created him." In this case, the "old man" is Hagar, and the "deeds" are Ishmael. Notice, we are not to rid ourselves of Hagar and keep Ishmael, nor are we to rid ourselves of Ishmael and keep Hagar. We are to put off both the old man and his nature and put on the new man. The "old man" is a reference to our flesh. We are to put it back on the level of a slave, exercising authority and dominion over it, not

185

allowing it to dictate to us or lord it over us.

When Paul spoke of crucifying the flesh, he did not mean we have to kill our old nature every day. Our old man was put to death at the cross. He is dead, and the life we now live in the flesh, we live by the faith of the Son of God who loved us and gave Himself for us (Galatians 2:20). Even though our old man, our flesh, is dead, in God's sight, we need to count it dead in our own lives. We need to see it as God sees it. We have to dominate it by operating in the power of the Spirit. "So then, brethren, we are not children of the bondwoman, but of the free" (v. 31). You and I are the product of the faith of Abraham. We who are of faith are blessed with believing Abraham. We are the seed of Abraham. We are heirs according to the promise. We are the children of the promise. We have been set free from the curse of the Law to live in the blessing of Abraham.

11
Circumcision
Galatians 5:1-18

Stand Fast in Liberty

Galatians 5:1

*Stand fast therefore in the liberty wherewith Christ hath
made us free, and be not entangled again with the yoke
of bondage.*

In our last chapter we saw that both Ishmael and Isaac
were offspring of Abraham, yet each represents a totally
different approach to God. Ishmael, the child of the flesh,
represents works of the flesh, while Isaac, the child of the
promise, represents the grace of God. The two lived for a
time in the same household, growing up together in their
father's home. But there came a time when the child of
flesh was cast out in order to give way to the child of
promise. This, we saw, was an illustration of the Law and
the Abrahamic covenant.

Just as Isaac was promised to Abraham and Sarah
before the birth of Ishmael by the flesh, so the covenant
God made with Abraham was given before the Law came
on the scene. After the birth of Ishmael (representing the
giving of the Law), the promise of the son was fulfilled;
Isaac was born. This is a symbolic representation of the

fulfillment of the Abrahamic covenant. For a time the two existed together, but the child of the flesh, the child of the bondwoman, never had a part in the inheritance of the child of promise, the child of the freewoman. That's why eventually the illegitimate son (the Law) had to go to give place to the true son and heir of Abraham (the product of faith), the one who came not by natural means but by the promise and power of God.

By this allegory, Paul tried to show the Galatians that they were not the offspring of the illegitimate son, the Law, but were the offspring of the legitimate son, the one given by the grace of God and received by faith. As such, they had no part in the Law, and the Law had no part in them. In Christ Jesus they had been set free from the Law of sin and death that they might freely live unto righteousness and peace.

"Stand fast therefore in the liberty wherewith Christ hath made us free" (v. 1). This expression "stand fast" was a military term meaning "to hold one's ground." Paul was telling these people that once they had gained ground in their spiritual life, they were to hold fast to it and not allow the enemy to wrest it from them.

Liberty is freedom, but freedom is not free. It doesn't come easy. Nor does a person remain free without effort. Just as it takes courage and commitment to hold on to political freedom, so it requires dedicated effort to preserve spiritual liberty. As citizens of the kingdom of God, we must be every bit as vigilant to preserve and protect our spiritual freedom as we must be as citizens of the United States in preserving and protecting our political freedom. In both cases we have an enemy who will destroy and enslave us if we are not continually on our guard.

Paul was warning these people that now that they were free, they had to be careful to stand firm in that freedom lest it be taken away from them by their enemy. But notice he told them to stand fast "in the liberty wherewith Christ hath made us free." Paul knew we must be aware of both the enemy without and the enemy within. He also knew often those we must guard ourselves against most are not those who come against us openly, but those in our own midst who would like to see us yield to their authority and viewpoint. In other words, Paul warned against religion, the manmade system of rules and regulations that gives an appearance of godliness and devotion by its imposed restraints but which has no real power to bless and heal and set free.

"And be not entangled again with the yoke of bondage" (v. 1). Paul urged the Galatian believers not to allow anyone to put them back into slavery to a set of man-imposed laws, which he called *bondage*. He wanted the believers in Galatia to be free, totally free. That includes freedom from religion as much as freedom from sin.

Wherever I preach this message of liberty in Christ, someone always accuses me of "giving people a license to sin." It seems so hard for some people to accept true liberty, either for themselves or for others. They seem to view freedom from the stranglehold of religion as some sort of spiritual anarchy in which people are just turned loose to commit all the pent-up sins that have been held in check all these years by rules and regulations. That is a false concept of Christian righteousness and responsibility.

If God's own children cannot be set free to think, speak, and act as they choose, if they must be kept chained by a system of do's and don'ts, then the New Birth is no better than the life of sin. In that case, God simply took us out of one bondage into another. Grace is not a license to sin; it is a license to serve. God gives us freedom to serve Him and binds us only with love.

Churches that preach rules and regulations eventually dry up from within, because God is not a dictator; He's a Liberator. Jesus said He came to do the will of His Father in heaven, which is to loose bonds, to free captives, to set at liberty them that are bruised. It is Satan who binds, not God. Our Father wants us to be free. That means free to worship and love and serve Him as we will, not as we are forced to do. That's why the message of freedom always attracts crowds. People want to be free, not to sin, but to live. They don't come to church to hear the message of grace and love so they can go out and "sin all they want to." They come to hear it so they can go out and enjoy the abundant life their Savior bled and died to purchase for them.

The only people who are afraid to set the church free are those who don't trust it. The reason they don't trust others with freedom is because they don't trust themselves. They are the very ones who need to be set free the most from their own self-imposed legalism. Once they are free, then they can allow the church to be liberated so it can go and liberate others. That's God's plan as revealed in the book of Galatians.

Circumcision or Christ?

Verses 2–6

Behold, I Paul say unto you, that if ye be circumcised, Christ shall profit you nothing. For I testify again to every man that is circumcised, that he is a debtor to do the whole law. Christ is become of no effect unto you, whosoever of you are justified by the law; ye are fallen from grace. For we through the Spirit wait for the hope of righteousness by faith. For in Jesus Christ neither circumcision availeth any thing, nor uncircumcision; but faith which worketh by love.

The big issue in Galatia at this time was circumcision, which was part of the Mosaic Law, part of the old covenant. Even in the day in which it was instituted, it was never meant to provide salvation, because the Law

190

itself was not given as a means of salvation but only to reveal to man his need of a Savior. Circumcision was an outward physical sign of the covenant between God and Abraham. Circumcision didn't save Abraham; it was simply intended to symbolize outwardly what had happened to him inwardly.

Like the Law of which it was a part, circumcision was only a sign to the Jews to teach them about faith. In a way, it was the Old Testament equivalent of the New Testament practice of water baptism. Baptism is an outward sign of an inward occurrence. It presents in symbolic language the spiritual truth of a person's being dead, buried, and raised to new life in Christ. Down through the years this practice has lost some of its significance because some segments of the church have misinterpreted it. They have taken the outward sign of salvation and made it the means of salvation, which is a mistake. Water baptism does not save; it only tells the world that salvation has taken place in a person's life. To substitute the physical symbol for the spiritual reality is to miss the reality.

This is what happened down through the years since the practice of circumcision had been given by God to Abraham as a sign of his covenant relationship with the Lord. Now it was necessary for Paul to write to Gentiles to explain to them that by depending on a physical symbol of an old covenant relationship, they were actually depriving themselves of the spiritual reality the symbol represented.

"Behold, I Paul say unto you, that if ye be circumcised, Christ shall profit you nothing" (v. 2). Circumcision has natural or medical benefits, but no real spiritual benefits. If a person allowed himself to be circumcised thinking by doing so he was achieving salvation, then Christ could be of no value to him. How could he be saved by grace through faith in the finished work of Jesus on the cross if he was trusting a physical sign of the Law in his own body? His faith in his own shed blood would be keeping him from true faith in the shed blood of Jesus Christ.

"For I testify again to every man that is circumcised, that he is a debtor to do the whole law" (v. 3). Again Paul was speaking here of circumcision for spiritual reasons. In verse 2 he refers to circumcision as an attempt to obtain salvation and in verse 3 of circumcision as an attempt to attain spirituality. Paul explained if a person thinks he should be circumcised to keep the Law, to be "holy," then logically he should not stop at circumcision; he should keep the whole of the Jewish Law. If keeping the Law makes a person "holy," then he is obligated to keep *all* the Law if he intends to be completely holy. He can't just pick and choose some parts and neglect others; he is obliged to keep every tiny detail of it. Once he begins in the Law, even the most minor aspects, he is obligated, a debtor, to keep the whole Law.

In our day, there are those who are so legalistic in their thinking they believe they should go back and keep the Jewish Sabbath. Consequently, Saturday becomes their day of rest and worship, which is fine. However, Paul pointed out if they really believe they should keep the Law, they ought to keep the whole Law, not just one minor requirement of it. To be consistent, such people ought to build a temple in accordance with the instructions given by God in the Old Testament; anoint priests and Levites, dressing them in the robes and turbans of ancient Israel; bring in grain and meal and drink offerings to the Lord; offer up burnt animal sacrifices; and do everything else required by Jewish Law because the Law stipulated that to violate one part of it was to violate it all.

James 2:10 says, "For whosoever shall keep the whole law, and yet offend in one point, he is guilty of all." Paul explained to the Galatians: "If you keep one part of the Law, the part about circumcision, then you're obliged to keep the entire Law." That would put the Gentile Galatians in the position of keeping every jot and tittle of a system of laws and regulations they knew virtually nothing about because they had never been subject to it. Paul wanted them to see how blessed and free they are in Christ Jesus who fulfilled all those minute details for them once and for all.

"Christ is become of no effect unto you, whosoever of you are justified by the law; ye are fallen from grace" (v. 4). When Paul spoke here of being "justified," he was referring to the new birth experience. He explained that anyone trying to be born again by keeping the Law is destined to failure because the New Birth does not come by the Law but by grace through faith.

Another way to look at it is this: If anyone thinks he can be saved by the righteousness he achieves in keeping the Law, he is doomed, because no one has ever kept the Law perfectly. Even if he could keep it to perfection, he would still be doomed, because no flesh will be justified by works of the Law. Therefore, to trust in the Law for salvation is to deny the only real means of salvation offered to man, redemption through the grace of God by faith in His Son Jesus Christ.

Jesus had already told the people of His day that no one could come to the Father except by Him (John 14:6). To try to get to God through the Law is to try to reach Him other than by Jesus, and there is no other way. That's what Paul meant when he said such people have fallen from grace. He meant as long as they are trying to win salvation, they will never have it, because it can be received only as a free gift of God's grace. If a person insists on winning it by his own efforts, he will never have it. Those self-efforts include water baptism, church membership, good works, acts of penance, anything other than simple faith in the finished work of Jesus Christ on the cross of Calvary.

"For we through the Spirit wait for the hope of righteousness by faith" (v. 5). One of the fruits of the Spirit is patience. Patience always looks forward to the

193

hope of righteousness that lies ahead. Many times it may look as though it would be easier to have our needs met by some works of the Law rather than by simply trusting God, but this is usually evidence of a lack of patience. We get tired of waiting on the Lord so we jump up and take some action on our own, which is usually a mistake that ends up costing us more than if we had simply exercised faith a little while longer. Paul was telling the Galatians to be patient; their righteousness would be revealed, not by their attempts at self-righteousness, but through faith in the Lord who imputes righteousness.

"For in Jesus Christ neither circumcision availeth any thing, nor uncircumcision; but faith which worketh by love" (v. 6). Circumcision is done on the outward man, but faith is an action of the inner man. Man looks on the outward appearance, but God looks on the inside. Faith pleases God, not an outward work like circumcision. Whether a person is circumcised or not circumcised is of no significance to God; it avails nothing. What matters to God is faith that manifests itself in love, love for God and love for our fellowman.

The Race of Faith

Verse 7

Ye did run well; who did hinder you that ye should not obey the truth?

"Ye did run well" (v. 7). Here Paul likened the faith life to a race in which many runners compete. He commended the Galatians for running their race well. When was that? The first time Paul came to Galatia. We have seen in Acts 14 how the Galatians received Paul graciously, how they listened to him intently, how they were quickly born again, filled with the Spirit, set free from idolatry, liberated from their bondage to the Law of sin and death to become new creatures in Christ Jesus. They began their Christian race well, but now it seems something has happened.

"Who did hinder you, that ye should not obey the truth?" (v. 7). The Greek word translated "hinder" is drawn from the ancient Greek footraces. It refers to the action of one runner who cuts across the path of another, knocking him off his stride and slowing him down, perhaps even causing him to fall. In his analogy, Paul was saying to these people: "You began your race so well. Who has cut in front of you to trip you up?" Of course, we know the answer to that question. It was the legalistic Judaizers who had come in behind Paul, teaching their doctrine of strict observance of the Law. Paul recognized these teachings as a hindrance to the Galatians.

In Hebrews 12:1 we find a similar image:

Wherefore seeing we also are compassed about with so great a cloud of witnesses, let us lay aside every weight, and the sin which doth so easily beset us, and let us run with patience the race that is set before us.

Again we see a picture of a runner who is weighed down with unnecessary encumbrances causing him to falter and stumble. That weight is the weight of the Law and does not set free, but like the sin it exposes, actually entangles itself about the feet to cause defeat and failure. That's why Paul warned the Galatians in verse 1 not to become entangled again with the yoke of bondage.

Leaven of the Law

Verses 8–9

This persuasion cometh not of him that calleth you. A little leaven leaveneth the whole lump.

"This persuasion cometh not of him that calleth you"

(v. 8). In other words, "It is not God who is cutting you off or persuading you to follow the Law."

"A little leaven leaveneth the whole lump" (v. 9). Here Paul likened the Law to leaven (yeast). Now in the Bible, leaven is never used to symbolize anything good. For example, in Mark 8:15 Jesus cautioned His disciples: "Take heed, beware of the leaven of the Pharisees, and of the leaven of Herod." The disciples didn't understand what He meant. They thought He was referring to actual bread, when what He was really speaking about was the teaching of the Pharisees.

This is precisely what Paul was referring to in verse 9. He was explaining that if the Galatians heeded the leaven of the legalistic Judaizers, they would be led off into error. A little bit of the Law would obligate them to keep all of it, just as a little sin in a person's life will spread throughout his being and cause his downfall.

What is the answer to this problem? The solution is to purge the leaven out of the lump. It must be cast out, just as Ishmael and Hagar were cast out of Abraham's household. By allowing the leaven of Egypt into his household, Abraham brought disruption into his home. That leaven had to be purged before it affected the child of promise.

So it is in our lives today. The Spirit of God cannot cohabit with sin. That's why we must take heed, to beware the leaven of sin. We must also be on our guard against the leaven of the Law that brought sin. To live a life truly pleasing to our Lord, we must avoid works of the Law as carefully as we avoid works of iniquity. One gets us out of God's will; the other gets us out of His grace. Neither gets us any closer to righteousness.

The Offence of the Cross

Verses 10-11

I have confidence in you through the Lord, that ye will be none otherwise minded: but he that troubleth you shall bear his judgment, whosoever he be. And I, brethren, if I yet preach circumcision, why do I yet suffer persecution? then is the offence of the cross ceased.

"I have confidence in you, through the Lord, that ye will be none otherwise minded: but he that troubleth you shall bear his judgment, whosoever he be" (v. 10). Paul expressed confidence in the Galatians that they would see and understand what he was explaining to them, and would fall back upon the foundation he had left in them before his departure. He was trusting they would yet realize the truth of his message of grace and would remove the person (or persons) from their midst who was causing confusion and doubt in their minds.

"And I, brethren, if I yet preach circumcision, why do I yet suffer persecution?"(v. 11). Obviously part of the confusion caused by the legalistic Judaizers was telling the gullible Galatians that Paul himself, being a Jew, believed in and practiced circumcision. This one point was enough to thoroughly disrupt the churches in Galatia and to throw them into a state of turmoil. If the great apostle Paul believed in and practiced circumcision, then who were they to refuse to adhere to the practice? Paul was setting the record straight once and for all by pointing out to the Galatians that if he ascribed to the practice of circumcision as the Judaizers said he did, he would not still be persecuted by them and the proponents of Judaism.

"Then is the offence of the cross ceased" (v. 11). Paul emphasized if he were trusting in circumcision and the keeping of the Jewish Law for his salvation, the cross of Jesus Christ would have no significance. If it was the Jewish Law that saved men, then what would it matter whether another Jew had died on the cross at the hands of the Roman conquerors? The cross would be meaningless.

The "offence of the cross" to which Paul referred here is its simplicity: simplicity of salvation, simplicity of spirituality. Once people grasp the truth that the cross of Calvary paid fully for all their sins so God can now forgive those sins, clothe them in robes of righteousness, and grant them eternal and abundant life because of it, no more room remains for great involved intellectual or religious discussion or debate. That's what Paul meant when he wrote to the Corinthians: "But we preach Christ crucified, unto the Jews a stumblingblock, and unto the Greeks foolishness" (1 Corinthians 1:23).

The cross was a stumbling block to the Jews because it was too simple spiritually. To them salvation required the keeping of every jot and tittle of a huge and complicated system of rules and regulations. The cross was foolishness to the Greeks because it was too simple intellectually. As members of a highly cultured civilization and culture, what possible significance could there be to them in the crucifixion of some unknown Jewish carpenter from Nazareth?

That's why Paul made such efforts to keep his teaching simple, even though the truths he shared were tremendously profound. That's why he prayed the eyes of the understanding of those who heard the Gospel would be opened. He knew people would never really be able to appreciate the simplicity and beauty of the Gospel until they had once truly grasped the full significance of the message of salvation through the grace of God by faith in His Son who was crucified so every person on earth could be set free from the law of sin and death.

Religion and Heathenism

Verse 12

I would they were even cut off which trouble you.

In the King James Version this verse sounds reasonable, even nice. However, in Greek it is much stronger. In this verse Paul addressed the question of circumcision once and for all, expressing his viewpoint about it (and those who preach and require it) in very explicit terms. The New American Standard Bible translates Paul's statement this way: "Would that those who are troubling you would even mutilate themselves." The New International Version makes Paul's meaning even clearer: "As for those agitators, I wish they would go the whole way and emasculate themselves!" But the truth is, what Paul really meant to express was this idea: "If those Jewish troublemakers think cutting off a little foreskin pleases God, then in order to fully please Him they ought to go all the way and cut off the whole male organ!"

Although this statement may seem rather crude and extremist to us in our modern and refined thinking, the Galatians understood Paul's meaning perfectly. So did the religious Jews at whom this statement was aimed. In one area of Galatia in the city of Pessinus there flourished a heathen cult, the worship of Cybele. To the followers of this religion, the highest form of worship was self-mutilation. And the highest form of self-mutilation for a man was self-castration. Paul was saying to the Galatian Christians, "If these teachers of the Law really believe that cutting some part of the physical body pleases God, then why don't they carry that belief out to its logical conclusion and cut that part off entirely?"

Paul warned against the heathenistic practice of self-mutilation because it is an abomination before the Lord. He reasoned that the practice of circumcision for salvation or spirituality, carried to its logical extreme, does not bring a man closer to God; in fact, it is sin: "He that is wounded in the stones, or hath his privy member cut off, shall not enter into the congregation of the LORD" (Deuteronomy 23:1). That's why Paul spoke out so strongly against circumcision in Philippians 3:2: "Beware of dogs, beware of evil workers, beware of the concision [those who preach circumcision]." This warning is his message to believers throughout the New Testament.

This theme of attempting to reach God or to please Him through asceticism (self-denial or self-inflicted punishment) is one Paul dealt with strongly in the book of Galatians. He wanted these believers to understand that to practice asceticism is to become "religious." Religion is defined as man's efforts to please God. In that sense, the religious person is no different from a heathen. Both attempt to reach God or to please Him by their own self-efforts.

Paul saw very clearly the foolishness of trying to substitute self-righteousness for the righteousness of God in Christ Jesus. True righteousness can never be earned or merited; it can be received only as a gift by the grace of God who bestows it freely upon those who simply ask for it in faith. Thus, the religious Jews who worked so diligently to be righteous missed it, while the "unreligious" Gentiles who did nothing but believe God, received His righteousness without doing anything for it. That is part of the mystery of the Gospel.

After Paul laid the axe to the root of the tree of circumcision, he left the subject to move on to a more positive aspect of his message.

Called unto Liberty

Verse 13

*For, brethren, ye have been called unto liberty; only use
not liberty for an occasion to the flesh, but by love serve
one another.*

"For, brethren, ye have been called unto liberty"
(v. 13). There are always those who will be afraid to teach the
message of liberty because they fear it will lead people to live
self-indulgent, sinful lives. That may happen to some degree.
Out of every 100 Christians who are set free from bondage to
the Law, there may be two or three who will take advantage of
that freedom to serve their own selfish interests. Some few will
give in to the desires of the flesh. But I would rather preach the
message of love and liberty and see 98 percent of those set free
go on to live fuller, happier, more devoted Christian lives, than
I would deny them fullness and joy and service just because
some people can't handle it. God forbid we ever let our own
fear and doubt keep in bondage the very people for whom
Christ gave His life that they might be set free.

I once heard a foreign missionary say he didn't preach
the message of prosperity to his new converts. He was
afraid once they began to prosper they wouldn't know how
to handle the increase and would turn away from God.
However, people are basically the same everywhere. If a
believer is likely to turn away from his God the moment he
gets a little ahead financially, then he never was much of
a disciple to begin with. What loving parent would want
to keep his child hungry and naked just to insure the child
stayed dependent on the parent? Such an attitude is not
real love, because true, mature love is not possessive; on
the contrary, it sets the object of its love free.

An old saying states: "What you love, set free. If it
returns to you of its own accord, you will have it forever.

If it does not return, you never had it to begin with." I believe God treats His children this way. He wants our love only if it is voluntarily given. If the only way He can have it is by keeping us in bondage, He never had our love in the first place.

"Only use not liberty for an occasion to the flesh" (v. 13). Paul brought out this same idea in Romans 6:1–2 in which he wrote, "What shall we say then? Shall we continue in sin, that grace may abound? God forbid. How shall we, that are dead to sin, live any longer therein?" Even though we are not under the Law but under grace, that still does not mean we are free to indulge ourselves in sin. We may have the freedom of choice to engage in sin, but we are not free from the consequences of that sin.

"But by love serve one another" (v. 13). The flesh always calls attention to itself, but love draws attention to others. Use your liberty to choose love, not the desires of the flesh. Selfishness demands its own desires be fulfilled; love seeks to fulfill first the desires of another. In fact, that is the definition of true love. Love is that force within a person causing him to desire someone else's welfare more than his own. Unless we can honestly say we desire the other person's happiness more than we desire our own, we shouldn't flippantly tell that person, "I love you," especially if that person is God. To love God is to desire His will be done more than we desire our own will be fulfilled.

To love others is to desire to see them blessed more than to see self blessed. Obviously, the flesh cannot love like that. Nothing short of the Spirit of God Himself can empower us to truly love others, to desire their welfare more than our own: "Greater love hath no man than this, that a man lay down his life for his friends" (John 15:13).

We may not be called upon to give our lives for someone else, but we may well have opportunities to give part of our material possessions someone else may be benefited. That's when we must be led of the Spirit, because our flesh will rebel. The flesh is not capable of such love because by its very nature it is self-centered.

Scientists tell us the drive for self-preservation is one of the strongest of the inborn human traits. It goes against the grain of our human nature, our flesh, to put others first, especially when it means we will suffer loss. That's why our natural human nature is never able to please God; it's too centered on self. The only way anyone can be freed from the selfish human nature is by receiving within him a new nature, a new Spirit that is not self-centered but "other-centered." That Spirit, if heeded, will lead the person in paths of righteousness and truth and blessing.

Learn to heed the Spirit within you. His counsel may not always seem logical, but that's because it's not based on human logic but on God's logic. When He says give away what you desperately need for yourself, don't be afraid to comply. It may not seem "natural," but if it were the "natural thing to do," it probably wouldn't be the "God thing to do." "Give, and it shall be given unto you; good measure, pressed down, and shaken together, and running over" (Luke 6:38). God rewards obedience to His Spirit, *not* obedience to the Law, but to the Spirit.

The Spirit of God is the nature of God. And what is God's nature? John, the beloved apostle, told us "God is love" (1 John 4:16). Therefore to be led of the Spirit of God is to be led by love, the force that puts the other person's welfare ahead of our own. Christians are under law. We are not under the Mosaic Law, but the *law of love*. There is a difference between being under the Mosaic Law, and being under the law of love. Law is imposed from the outside, love impresses from the inside. Law compels; love impels. Law is what we do because we have no choice; love is what we must do because we do have a choice. Law is what our bodies are forced to obey; love is what our hearts won't allow us not to obey. Law binds us to service; love frees us for service.

203

This law of love becomes the central issue and the culmination of Paul's message from here on to the end of the book.

Fulfilling the Law

Verse 14

For all the law is fulfilled in one word, even in this; Thou shalt love thy neighbour as thyself.

It is only natural that Paul would end his remarks by concentrating on love because love is the fulfillment of the Law. In Romans 5:5 Paul told us that "the love of God is shed abroad in our hearts." In Romans 8:16 he said that the Holy Spirit bears "witness with our spirit, that we are the children of God." If we are led of the Spirit of God, who is love, we will always be led in ways of love. If we walk in love, we will fulfill the Law.

God gave the Mosaic Law because the people under the old covenant didn't have the Holy Spirit to lead them from within as we do today. They had to have an outward, physical law to constrain them and guide their actions. Now that the Spirit of God Himself has come to take up residence within our bodies, why would we ever want or need to return to being led by an outside rule? That's why we are free of the Law, not to do as we please, but to do as the Spirit pleases.

To follow the Spirit is to fulfill the Law because the Spirit of love will always lead us in conformity to the Law. God's Spirit will never lead us to commit murder, adultery, bear false witness, steal, or do any of those things forbidden under the old covenant. The Holy Spirit will never guide us into actions that are in disobedience to God or harmful to our neighbor, but only into those that please God and benefit our neighbor. Putting God's will ahead of our own, and desiring our neighbor's welfare more than our own welfare is love. That's why following the Spirit, walking in love, is the fulfillment of the whole of the Law.

Walk in the Spirit

Verses 15–18

But if ye bite and devour one another, take heed that ye be not consumed one of another. This I say then, Walk in the Spirit, and ye shall not fulfil the lust of the flesh. For the flesh lusteth against the Spirit, and the Spirit against the flesh: and these are contrary the one to the other: so that ye cannot do the things that ye would. But if ye be led of the Spirit, ye are not under the law.

"But if ye bite and devour one another, take heed that ye be not consumed one of another" (v. 15). What does a person bite with? The mouth. Paul was speaking here of sins of the tongue, gossiping and maligning. It's not necessary to be around other people to bite and devour them. All it takes is malicious talk. That talk can go on in their presence or out of it, at home or in church, around town or a thousand miles away. The result is the same. Biting and devouring always results in someone's being consumed. Bite an apple enough times and it will be gone.

I once heard a person say he had noticed no great man or woman of faith ever talked negatively about others. I believe there is a great deal of truth in that observation. Godly people don't speak evil of anyone, even if it's true. They know nothing kills faith faster than an uncontrolled tongue. Godly people speak faith and love. The reason they do so is because the two go together.

Galatians 5:6 says faith works by love. If Christians bite and devour one another, we will never be great men and women of faith. Paul noted in 1 Corinthians 13, even if we have the faith to move mountains, without love it profits us nothing. Our faith works not so much by how much Word we have in our talk, but in accordance to the amount of love we have in our walk.

If you have been guilty of biting and devouring other people, especially your brothers and sisters in Christ, it's not enough to change or confess your wrong to the Lord. In addition, there is something else you need to do. If you have openly gossiped about and maligned someone, you need to go to that person and make things right. Until you do that, your prayers will be hindered. Answers to prayer depend upon faith, and faith depends upon love. If you know someone "has ought against you," you will never have a truly successful prayer life or ministry until that hindrance has been forgiven and removed.

Verse 15 speaks of biting and devouring "one another," just as verses 13 and 14 speak of loving and serving "one another." Love serves one another, but biting and devouring consumes one another. Here is the principle: Love edifies, but hate demolishes. Love encourages, helps, and builds up; but sins of the tongue discourage, hinder, and destroy. In the past, we've had enough division and demolition in the church. Let's join hands and hearts with our brothers and sisters in Christ (despite their doctrines or creeds) and work together to build rather than destroy.

If we really want to win the world for Christ, let's learn to walk in love, especially with those "who are of the household of faith" (Gal. 6:10).

"This I say then, Walk in the Spirit, and ye shall not fulfil the lust of the flesh" (v. 16). "Walk in the Spirit." What does that mean? It means to be led of the Spirit of God who witnesses to our reborn human spirits. The Holy Spirit in our spirits will always lead us in line with God's will, which is His Word. If we are always led in line with God's will, we will always walk in love.

Some people seem to have trouble with this concept of following the leadership of the Holy Spirit within. They say they can never tell if it is God's Spirit or their own spirit they are listening to. That's no problem. It really doesn't make any difference whether the leading is coming directly from the Spirit of God or through the enlightened, reborn human spirit. The test is the same for both. Does the leading line up with the Word of God? If so, then follow it. If there is not a specific Scripture to test the leading, then does it bring peace and assurance? If not, then don't yield to that leading no matter how reasonable or attractive it may appear.

Never be afraid of following your own heart, in line with the Word of God. Since God now lives within you, you can trust your own spirit. It has been reborn, renewed in the likeness of God's Spirit. Your spirit will never lead you counter to the will and Word of God. It's only when you begin to listen to your flesh that you get into trouble.

"For the flesh lusteth against the Spirit, and the Spirit against the flesh: and these are contrary the one to the other: so that ye cannot do the things that ye would" (v. 17). Abraham had no trouble in his home until he became involved with Hagar, the symbol of the flesh. As long as Hagar was kept on the level of a slave, everything was fine. But the moment she rose in position equal with Sarah, things began to go wrong. So it is with you. Your flesh is fine as long as you keep it on the level of a slave. But the moment you begin to comply with its desires, instead of forcing it to conform to yours, you are in trouble. To be led by the Spirit means keeping the flesh in its place.

"But if ye be led of the Spirit, ye are not under the law" (v. 18). Remember, the Law is synonymous with the flesh. If you allow yourself to become subject to the Law, your flesh, you begin to reap the harvest of the flesh. But if you subject yourself to the Spirit, you walk in the blessing of Abraham.

The flesh leads contrary to the will and Word of God because it leads by what you hear, see, taste, and feel from the outside world. The Spirit leads through an inner witness, by the intangible and eternal. That's why God doesn't lead His children by signs or fleeces or outward manifestations. These may be used by God to confirm His inward leading, but not as direct guidance. Those who are sons of God are those who are led of His Spirit. Although the Spirit may lead contrary to outward signs and circumstances, never be afraid to follow Him. For the paths of God are the paths of peace and truth and light. If you are led of the Spirit, you are not under Law.

12

The Fruit of the Spirit
Galatians 5:19–26

Walking in Love

In our last chapter we learned that walking in the Spirit fulfilled the Law. We discovered walking in the Law was bondage to an outside force, while the inner voice of the Spirit leads in love, which does not bind but sets at liberty.

In this chapter we will examine more closely this Spirit-walk. In Galatians 5:16–18, the first letter of the word *Spirit* is capitalized, making it appear that Paul was referring to the Holy Spirit, which he is in a sense. Actually the capitalization was added by the translators, since the Greek does not indicate whether this word is capitalized or not. *Spirit* then could be referring to the Holy Spirit of God, or it could be referring to our human spirits, as in the statement: "For the flesh lusteth against the (s)Spirit, and the (s)Spirit against the flesh: and these are contrary the one to the other: so that ye cannot do the things that ye would" (v. 17).

Whichever way we interpret this verse, Paul's point is the same: *we can allow ourselves to be led by our flesh* (which is our old man, sold to sin) *or by our spirits* (which are reborn in the image of God's Holy Spirit). The one we choose to follow will determine the direction our lives will take.

To walk in the Spirit (or by our spirits), is to walk in love. If we will listen to the dictates of our own reborn human spirits, we will walk in the Spirit of love and, therefore, will not fulfill the lust of the flesh. We will not need an outward law but will fulfill all righteousness because our spirits (quickened by the Holy Spirit) will never lead us into disobedience to God or in opposition to His desires and will.

It is not hard to walk in the spirit. You can do that while you drive the car, do housework, teach a class, or run a business. Walking in the spirit is not a mystical exercise in which a person falls into some sort of trance. Nor is it a feeling. Walking in the spirit is simply walking in constant fellowship and communion with the Spirit of God resident within us. It is walking in line with the Word of God, moment by moment.

The Works of the Flesh

Galatians 5:19–21

Now the works of the flesh are manifest, which are these; adultery, fornication, uncleanness, lasciviousness, idolatry, witchcraft, hatred, variance, emulations, wrath, strife, seditions, heresies, envyings, murders, drunkenness, revellings, and such like: of the which I tell you before, as I have also told you in time past, that they which do such things shall not inherit the kingdom of God.

"Now the works of the flesh are manifest, which are these" (v. 19). It is important we understand the list of the works of the flesh Paul gave us is not comprehensive. It does not include every possible work of the flesh. There is no such list available because no one could ever enumerate every way the fleshly nature can manifest itself. That's why Paul ended this list with the expression "and such like" (v. 21). However, this partial list is sufficient to instruct us in the types of things the flesh produces.

Note also these are "works" of the flesh. This word is plural, indicating there are many manifestations of the fleshly, carnal nature of man.

In addition to the "works" of the flesh, let's consider for a moment the "wages" those "works" earn. When you and I work in the physical sense, we earn a salary or wages. So it is in the spiritual sense. Works produce *wages*. We know from Romans 6:23 what those wages are: "For the wages of sin is death; but the gift of God is eternal life through Jesus Christ our Lord."

Walking by the flesh does result in a product. That product may seem pleasurable and appealing. In fact, it almost always does for a while. Even the Bible admits there is pleasure in sin for a season (Hebrews 11:25), but that pleasure is short-lived. On the other hand the psalmist says of God, "In thy presence is fulness of joy; at thy right hand there are pleasures for evermore" (Psalm 16:11). The product of the sin-filled life is temporal pleasure while the product of the Spirit-filled life is peace and joy.

The fruit of the Spirit keeps on producing long after the original seed is sown. What is sown to the flesh yields temporary results because being corruptible it eventually goes back to corruption. That which is sown to the Spirit, being incorruptible seed, goes on producing forever. The two may appear indistinguishable for a while, just as Ishmael and Isaac may have both seemed to look alike in the natural realm. However, there was a difference between them, an internal difference. Ishmael was born of the fleshly desire, while Isaac was born of the promise of the Spirit. The natural race of Ishmael exists today, but will pass away at the end of the age. The spiritual race of Isaac will never end but will go on forever after the flesh is gone.

"Adultery" (v. 19). Whenever this word is used in the Bible, it usually refers to illicit sexual activity by an individual who is married to someone other than his sexual partner.

"Fornication" (v. 19). This word is usually used to refer to illicit sexual activity by an unmarried person. So if an unmarried man had sex with a married woman, he would be guilty of fornication while she would be committing adultery. When two people who are married but not to each other engage in a sexual union, their relationship is adulterous. Two unmarried people who engage in sex together would be guilty of fornication.

"Uncleanness" (v. 19). This word deals more with the thought leading to the physical sex act rather than to the act itself. No sin, especially sexual sin, ever begins from the outside; rather it begins in the mind of the person who commits it. Uncleanness deals with evil sexual thoughts and desires. In this respect it could be translated as "lust."

"Lasciviousness" (v. 19). When unclean thoughts control the person, it is called "lasciviousness." This causes the person to seek after sexual activity such as dirty magazines and movies. He mentally undresses women and has a cheap attitude toward sex. The lascivious person has given himself over to his sexual craving.

"Idolatry" (v. 20). In the day in which these verses were written, idolatry referred to the worship of graven images. Today it includes giving preeminence to anything other than God. It could be money, power, position, fame, glory, even a business, club or amusement (such as a hobby, sport, or pastime). None of these things is evil in itself, but it becomes evil when a person elevates that thing to a higher position than God. In that sense, we must constantly be on our guard against spiritual idolatry.

"Witchcraft" (v. 20). This word is interesting. In the Greek it is *pharmakeia*, from which we derive our English word *pharmacy*. Witchcraft has always revolved around the use of drugs, as evidenced by the origin of this word.

To us in our modern-day world, the word conjures up images of an old woman in a long black gown and tall hat flying through the air on a broomstick.

True witchcraft is no joking matter. It is not to be confused with innocent child's play. It is a multi-million-dollar business involving not only spiritists and the occult, but also the thriving drug culture threatening to destroy our way of life.

"Hatred" (v. 20). Hatred is defined as personal hostility toward someone else. Like lust, it is a mental sin. A person can be smiling and cheerful on the outside and still be seething with internal hatred. Sooner or later that emotion will find expression through words or deeds or by destroying the mind and body of the one who harbors it inside. Like all mental sins, hatred is a cancer. It harms the one it inhabits far more than the one to whom it is directed. That's why Christians are warned to put away all anger, wrath, and malice (Colossians 3:8). It's for our own good.

"Variance" (v. 20). Variance simply means "disagreement." It has to do with being at odds with people. The result is dislike between two people or two groups simply because of a difference in viewpoint. As Christians we are not required to agree on every issue of life, but we are warned against allowing our differences of opinion to lead to animosity, another of the mental sins with its attendant power to destroy the one who harbors it.

When we find ourselves in variance with someone, we are not to respond in kind. Whatever their attitude or action toward us, we are to respond in love. We cannot allow ourselves to become a party to anger, wrath, or malice, because if we do, we will reap the bitter fruit of our own wrong attitude.

"Emulations" (v. 20). This is akin to jealousy but usually revolves around spiritual matters. In a sense, it is trying to play spiritual "king of the mountain." It is an attitude that will not cooperate with others unless it gets its own way. We would call it *ambition* or *rivalry*.

"Wrath" (v. 20). Wrath is the outward manifestation of inward hatred. It refers to emotional outbursts, explosions of anger.

"Strife" (v. 20). Strife simply means *discord* or *disharmony*. These are musical terms relating to musicians playing together so their instruments or voices blend together as one. It is impossible for one person alone to be in discord or disharmony (unless it is with himself). To have discord or disharmony there must be more than one person involved. Strife is a group-related activity. It manifests itself in temper tantrums, complaining, troublemaking, but its root source is lack of love. Just as darkness is the result of the absence of light, strife is the result of the absence of love.

As light always overcomes darkness, so love always overcomes strife. It is important to walk in love because it is the greatest power on earth. Nothing can stand against it. It will always be triumphant over evil and cover a multitude of sins.

"Seditions" (v. 20). Seditions are factions or divisions over points other than personalities. What causes religious groups to split apart one from the other? Isn't it usually over some minor viewpoint rather than an individual? One person or group decides a specific doctrine or tradition must be kept at all costs. Unless it is done, they threaten to draw apart and dissolve their union with the rest of the group. That is sedition. It is spiritual treason.

"Heresies" (v. 20). A heresy is an opinion contrary to the Word of God. Most heresies begin as seditions, group disruptions over a point of order or law. Eventually these disputes result in a separation. One group, holding to its opinion, splits away to follow its own interpretation. Many times this interpretation is in opposition to the Word of God. If so, it is heresy.

"Envyings" (v. 21). Envy is jealousy without a particular target. It, too, is an inward or mental sin. It is the attitude that "everyone gets a better break than me." Whereas jealousy is directed toward one particular person, envy is toward all.

"Murders" (v. 21). Notice, Paul did not say "killing" is wrong, but *murders*. Murder is always condemned in the Word of God. The Bible is explicit in its condemnation of murder, which it defines in Proverbs 6:17 as the shedding of innocent blood. Therefore the Bible does condone capital punishment, or the shedding of guilty blood, which was instituted of God thousands of years before it became a political issue.

In Genesis 9:6 the Lord said to Noah and his family: "Whoso sheddeth man's blood, by man shall his blood be shed: for in the image of God made he man." This is the basis for capital punishment for murder. It also applies to the shedding of blood during times of warfare. Those who make war against others will have their own blood shed by their fellow man. No Christian should ever feel guilty for serving in the armed forces to defend his nation, even if it means shedding the blood of her enemies. God ordained for man to shed the blood of those who would take the lives of the innocent. That's why we have policemen who carry deadly weapons not to "murder," but to protect them against the evil that is loose in this world.

"But doesn't the Bible say, 'Thou shalt not kill?'" No, it says, "Thou shalt not murder." There is a difference. Confusion has arisen because of a mistranslation of the Hebrew word that means to take the life of an innocent person. The only time the word is correctly translated is when Jesus quoted this commandment to the rich young ruler, "Thou shalt do no murder" (Matthew 19:18). We read in Ecclesiastes 3:3 that there is "a time to kill, and a time to heal." The Bible does not contradict itself. When it says there is a time to kill, it is referring to the taking of life by legal means. When it says not to murder, it is referring to the taking of life by illegal means. One is justifiable; the other is not.

"Drunkenness" (v. 21). The Word of God has always condemned drunkenness, which is the excessive use of alcohol.

"Revellings" (v. 21). This simply refers to wild parties, carousing, and brawling that usually accompany drunkenness.

"And such like" (v. 21). As we have noted, this is Paul's way of indicating the sins he has listed are not inclusive. Instead, it is a partial listing of the many manifestations of the flesh.

Why Should Saints Act like Sinners?

"Of the which I tell you before, as I have also told you in time past, that they which do such things shall not inherit the kingdom of God" (v. 21). Now we must be very careful in our interpretation of this verse or else we will destroy Paul's message up to now. It would seem Paul was saying any believer who has envy or strife in his heart will not go to heaven. If so, we are all condemned, for who has not been guilty of at least one of these kinds of behavior or "such like"? Does this mean we will not inherit the kingdom of God?

No, God does not categorize sins. The concept of degree of sins is man's invention, not God's. He doesn't rank sins in order of their importance. In Romans 14:23 Paul told us "whatsoever is not of faith is sin." Envy is sin and murder is sin. Jealousy is a sin and adultery is a sin. God views the sin of inward thought just as evil and sinful as those of outward action. Jesus said that to think evil is to commit murder. He said that to look upon a woman to lust after her is to commit adultery with her. We have our list of greater and lesser evils; God calls all evil "sin."

All outward sins begin as inward thoughts. If we can

stop the inward thought, the outward deed will never take place. We need to see the evil of sin and God's hatred of it, whether it is a sin of thought or of deed.

The problem with this verse is that it seems Paul was saying that if we are guilty of any of these sins, we will not inherit the kingdom of God. If God does not categorize sin, then we are all bound for hell. Which one of us has not had a thought of envy or jealousy? A closer look at this verse, however, will reveal its simplicity and true meaning.

The Greek word for *do* in this verse means "to practice." Paul was saying those who practice sin will not inherit the kingdom of God. Unbelievers are being referred to in this verse, not believers.

The unbeliever has a different nature from that of the believer. Sin is his way of life. He may have a godly thought now and then, but it is not his usual attitude. He practices sin because sin is his nature.

The believer cannot practice sin. He may sin at times, but righteousness is his way of life. Despite his occasional failures, he practices godliness.

He that committeth sin is of the devil; for the devil sinneth from the beginning. For this purpose the Son of God was manifested, that he might destroy the works of the devil. Whosoever is born of God doth not commit sin, for his seed remaineth in him: and he cannot sin, because he is born of God.

1 John 3:8–9

Paul was saying, "Why are you Galatians looking and acting like those who will not inherit the kingdom of God? You are born of God but are acting like those who are of the devil. I have told you (believers) in the past that they (unbelievers) who do such things will not inherit the kingdom of God."

217

Carnal or Spiritual?

For four chapters Paul spoke to the Galatians about legalism versus true spirituality. Then beginning with chapter 5 he began to tell them to learn to listen to their reborn spirits rather than their flesh. He wanted them to understand they were slaves to their unregenerated flesh *before they were born again,* which could not please God. But now that they are born again of His Spirit abiding within them, they should put away the flesh and its desires and habits; they should begin to live by the Spirit of life that does not practice sin but that, like Jesus, always does those things that please the Father (John 8:29).

In 1 Corinthians 3:1-3 Paul wrote these words:

And I, brethren, could not speak unto you as unto spiritual, but as unto carnal, even as unto babes in Christ. I have fed you with milk, and not with meat: for hitherto ye were not able to bear it, neither yet now are ye able. For ye are yet carnal: for whereas there is among you envying, and strife, and divisions, are ye not carnal, and walk as men?

This passage sounds as though it had been written to the Galatians, especially since Paul called them "carnal" and refered to their "envying, and strife, and divisions." In the last verse he said they were walking as men. The Amplified Bible says "mere...men." Paul pointed out that although these people were believers, they were behaving like unbelievers. Carnal believers look and act like unbelievers.

In Ephesians 5:1-7 Paul wrote to the church in Ephesus:

Be ye therefore followers of God, as dear children; and walk in love, as Christ also hath loved us, and hath given himself for us an offering and a sacrifice to God

218

for a sweetsmelling savour. But fornication, and all uncleanness, or covetousness, let it not be once named among you, as becometh saints; neither filthiness, nor foolish talking, nor jesting, which are not convenient: but rather giving of thanks. For this ye know, that no whoremonger, nor unclean person, nor covetous man, who is an idolater, hath any inheritance in the kingdom of Christ and of God. Let no man deceive you with vain words: for because of these things cometh the wrath of God upon the children of disobedience. Be not ye therefore partakers with them.

Again this sounds like Paul's message to the Galatians as he spoke of walking in love as opposed to fulfilling the desires of the flesh through "fornication, and all uncleanness, or covetousness,...filthiness,...foolish talking,...jesting," emphasizing again that those who practice such things have no inheritance in the kingdom of God. Who are these whoremongers and unclean persons, these covetous men, these idolaters? Paul told us in verse 6: "the children of disobe-dience." In other words, these people are the children of their father, the devil, who "sinneth from the beginning" (1 John 3:8). Paul told the Corinthians the same thing he told the Galatians: they should have no part in such activity because they are not the children of the devil, but the children of God. As such, they should be "followers" (imitators) of their heavenly Father, not followers or imitators of the father of the children of disobedience.

Those who engage in sin, those who are the children of Satan, will spend eternity with their father in the place reserved for him and his angels. But those with the new nature, the children of God, have a different inheritance and destiny. They will spend eternity in heaven with their Father and Lord.

Between now and the time we get to heaven, Christians

still have the freedom of choice as to how we will behave: as the children of God or as the children of disobedience. In other words, as spiritual people or as carnal people. Paul said those who become involved in the natural activities of the carnal are like babies. They need to grow up. Although they are believers, children of God, because of their immaturity they act like the children of disobedience.

In verse 14 of Ephesians 5, Paul wrote to those who are in this situation: "Wherefore he saith, Awake thou that sleepest, and arise from the dead, and Christ shall give thee light." The image presented here is one in which those who are out of fellowship with God appear to be dead, just like those who are dead in their sins. They aren't dead; they're only asleep, but to the world they seem to be dead. There appears to be no distinction between them and the children of disobedience.

Paul said God is calling such people to awake and to arise from their sleep. The Greek expression rendered "arise from the dead" means "to arise from among the dead." That's the problem with the church today, too many of the children of God are asleep among the dead. If they will only awaken and arise, the Lord Jesus Christ will give them light. They will have renewed fellowship with Him and with their brothers and sisters in Christ, and His blood will cleanse them from all unrighteousness.

This is what the Galatians needed to do. Any sinner can live by the Law, but he will not be any nearer to heaven. The Galatians didn't need to live like sinners. They needed to use the Spirit of God inside them and live like God in this world.

The Fruit of the Spirit

Verses 22–23

But the fruit of the Spirit is love, joy, peace, longsuffering, gentleness, goodness, faith, meekness, temperance: against such there is no law.

In verses 19 through 21 Paul talked about the works of the flesh. Here in verses 22 and 23 we have contrasted the fruit of the Spirit. There are several differences between works and fruit. Flesh produces works. The Spirit produces fruit. Works are recompensed by a reward that comes at a definite stated moment, like a paycheck at the end of the week. On the other hand, fruit does not have a predetermined moment to appear.

The rewards for work come as soon as the work is completed. Fruit, since it is the product of a seed that must grow and develop through a long process, takes longer to materialize. Even when it makes its appearance, it must still remain attached to its support for a while before it is ready to be used to meet needs. Therefore, although sowing to the flesh and sowing to the Spirit both eventually produce results, the rewards of spiritual seed will many times manifest themselves later than those of the carnal seed. However, being spiritual, their fruit is much longer-lived than that of a carnal nature and has the ability to reproduce itself indefinitely.

Throughout human history, carnal man has been sowing seeds that have produced a harvest of sin and death. That process of sowing and reaping will go on until the end of the age. But throughout human history, the Spirit of God has been sowing spiritual seed that has also produced fruit. Sowing and reaping will also go on until the end of the age, but it won't end there. The end of time is just the beginning of the era of righteousness and peace on this earth called the Millennium. This will be the thousand-year earthly reign of the Lord Jesus Christ, the Seed of Abraham. That Seed was sown thousands of years before it made its appearance in the days of Caesar Augustus. That Seed, has produced and will continue to produce literally millions of other seeds that will continue producing in ever-increasing numbers as the end draws near. One day that Righteous Seed will return in glory to redeem unto Himself His bride, the Church of Jesus Christ.

The Fruit of that Seed was poured out upon all believers on the day of Pentecost. It had taken a long time in coming, but once it arrived it blossomed forth abundantly, spreading everywhere within a short while until it covered the whole earth. Although it seems the Fruit was hidden for a time, today it is once again bursting forth into an abundant harvest around the world. We are living in the last days of that mighty harvest. The results of the harvest won't end here; they will live on throughout eternity. That's the difference between works and fruit. Fleshly works prosper for a season, but the fruit of the Spirit flourishes forever and ever.

This is not the fruit of the Holy Spirit but of the human spirit. Jesus is the Vine; we are the branches. Fruit does not grow on the vine; it grows on the branches. Jesus wants us to bear fruit. The Holy Spirit does not need love; He *is* love. We need love.

"But the fruit of the Spirit is love" (v. 22). There is one final difference between works and fruit. Notice "works" (Galatians 5:19) is plural while "fruit" is singular. There is but one fruit of the Spirit. That fruit is "love."

"But I thought there were nine fruits of the Spirit," you may say.

No, there's only one. All the other eight are manifestations of love. What was the one great commandment Jesus gave the Pharisee? "Thou shalt love the Lord thy God with all thy heart, and with all thy soul, and with all thy mind" (Matthew 22:36–37). Then He went on to say, "And the second [commandment] is like unto it [the first], Thou shalt love thy neighbour as thyself" (v. 39). The reason He gave for summarizing all the Law into two commandments was that love fulfills the whole Law. We saw in verse 14 it is the Holy Spirit who sheds love abroad in our hearts. There is only one spiritual substance shed in the heart by the Spirit. The other eight qualities mentioned here are simply manifestations of the one great fruit of love.

As confirmation of this truth, let's look at what Paul had to say about this "more excellent way" (1 Corinthians 12:31) in the great love chapter, 1 Corinthians 13:

> *Charity suffereth long, and is kind; charity envieth not; charity vaunteth not itself, is not puffed up, doth not behave itself unseemly, seeketh not her own, is not easily provoked, thinketh no evil; rejoiceth not in iniquity, but rejoiceth in the truth; beareth all things, believeth all things, hopeth all things, endureth all things. Charity never faileth.*
>
> *1 Corinthians 13:4–8*

It is interesting to note that every one of the other eight manifestations of the fruit of the Spirit can be found in this descriptive passage about love. If we are filled with the Spirit of God, we have within us the power to display all these attributes of our heavenly Father, who is love. That power comes from the Holy Spirit, but the fruit is manifested in our reborn human spirits because we are the ones who need these qualities, not God. Let's look at these divine traits one by one.

"Love" (v. 22). This word in Greek is *agape*, meaning "divine love," the kind of selfless love God displayed toward us in His Son Jesus Christ. It is the product of a mature human spirit in tune with God's Holy Spirit. This God-type love is directed toward our heavenly Father and toward our fellowman. Filled with this kind of divine love, we fulfill all the Law because we love the Lord our God with all our hearts, souls, and minds, and we love our neighbor as ourselves. This is the primary fruit of the Spirit, the one from which all the others are derived.

"Joy" (v. 22). This is not happiness, which is an outward

223

expression of pleasure, a superficial emotion dependent upon our current situation or circumstances. Joy is a deep-seated sense of well-being no outside circumstance can alter. The joy of the Lord is our strength (Nehemiah 8:10).

Possessed with this divine strength, we can face the worst life can hand us and, though our outward faces may reflect the heartbreak or turmoil we are experiencing at the moment, deep within we are secure, knowing God has not left us, nor has He forsaken us. It is this joy that sees us through those times, such as the passing of loved ones. Although we miss them, we are comforted within because we know they are not dead, but are at that very moment being received into glory where one day we will meet them again.

Some people misunderstand joy. They know it's something we Christians are supposed to have, so they try to work it up through some kind of activity, such as worship or praise or confession. The joy of the Lord is not produced by physical manifestations or verbal affirmations (as good and sincere as these may be). This joy is deep, abiding assurance that, come what may, God is still on His throne and therefore we will emerge victorious from every fiery trial. It is closer to confidence than to exuberance. It's not something we "work up"; it's something we rest in.

"Peace" (v. 22). Peace is inward stability when everything about us is falling apart. Like joy, it is a deep-seated assurance, a calm in the midst of the storms of life. The joy of the Lord allows us to sing at midnight while chained in prison with our feet in stocks. The peace of the Lord allows us to lie down and get a good night's sleep in the den of lions.

"Longsuffering" (v. 22). This simply means patience, the kind of patient endurance that works hand in hand with faith so that we inherit the promises of God (Hebrews 6:12).

"Gentleness" (v. 22). This is kindness toward others.

"Goodness" (v. 22). Goodness refers to treating others in grace as Christ treats us.

"Faith" (v. 22). This is a mistranslation. It should be faithfulness. It is possible to operate in faith and not in love, as Paul noted when he wrote, "And though I have all faith, so that I could remove mountains, and have not charity [love], I am nothing" (1 Corinthians 13:2). Faithfulness simply means dependability. Of all the traits listed here, this one is probably the most sought by God, and the one He rewards the most:

> *His lord said unto him, Well done, good and faithful servant; thou hast been faithful over a few things, I will make thee ruler over many things: enter thou into the joy of thy lord.*
>
> *Matthew 25:23*

Notice also the joy of the Lord does not come from hand clapping and praise shouting, but as the result of faithfulness in carrying out His assigned tasks. Through praise and worship we can again find the joy and peace of the Lord. Praise and worship do not bring the fruit. God gives it to us at the New Birth.

That's why we are exhorted not to grumble and complain but to be faithful in whatever the Lord has put before us to do. A faithful person is a humble person, one who accepts his assigned task and fulfills his calling with devotion and integrity. He knows that in due time the Lord will exalt him as he humbles himself under His mighty hand. When that promotion comes, it is a source of real joy, one that does not have to be manufactured, one that cannot be contained.

"Meekness" (v. 23). Some people tend to confuse this with *weakness*. Meekness does not mean being a doormat for others to walk on. It simply means being teachable. A meek person is a teachable person. The Bible tells us to "receive with meekness the engrafted word" (James 1:21). That Word may sometimes come from a totally unsuspected source. After all, God is not limited to teaching us only through those with whom we agree on all points. The truth is the truth whatever its source. If we are meek, we will receive that truth as from the Lord. We will be teachable, even by those with whom we differ.

Jesus said the meek will inherit the earth (Matthew 5:5). We are told by the psalmist: "The meek will he guide in judgment: and the meek will he teach his way....The meek shall eat and be satisfied....The meek shall inherit the earth; and shall delight themselves in the abundance of peace" (Psalm 25:9; 22:26; 37:11).

What is the *Lord's way* He will teach us so we may eat and be satisfied and delight ourselves in abundance? The way of peace. That's what a meek person is, a person of peace. He has no need to fight for what's rightfully his; he learns to receive it directly from the Lord's hand, just as his Master did.

"Temperance" (v. 23). Temperance is self-control in all aspects of life. It is summarized by the rule: Moderation in all things. This obviously does not refer to moderation in sin; it is the legitimate needs or pleasures of life that need to be controlled. Food and drink are fine, but overindulgence becomes a sin. Television, magazines, radio, and movies are fine, but they can become idols if given too much of our attention. We need to control our every need and desire in order to give God as much of our time as possible. "So teach us to number our days, that we may apply our hearts unto wisdom" (Ps. 90:12).

In Titus 2:11–12 Paul wrote, "For the grace of God that bringeth salvation hath appeared to all men, teaching us that, denying ungodliness and worldly lusts, we should live soberly, righteously, and godly, in this present world." This word "soberly" refers to temperance in every aspect of life.

"Against such there is no law" (v. 23). When we walk in the Spirit and produce its fruit, the Law has no power over us. We fulfill it, not by keeping it, but by following the Spirit of God.

Life in the Spirit

Verses 24–26

And they that are Christ's have crucified the flesh with the affections and lusts. If we live in the Spirit, let us also walk in the Spirit. Let us not be desirous of vain glory, provoking one another, envying one another.

"And they that are Christ's have crucified the flesh with the affections and lusts" (v. 24). We have already seen in Galatians 2:20 that we were crucified with Christ so the life we now live in the flesh we live by the faith of the Son of God who loved us and gave Himself for us. Therefore, while we are free, we also have a responsibility to live our lives in accordance with the will and desire of the One who loved us so much He gave His only begotten Son that we might have life in Him.

"If we live in the Spirit, let us also walk in the Spirit" (v. 25). When did we start living in the Spirit? At the time of the New Birth. Since that time we should be daily walking in the Spirit. Paul was telling these Galatians, who did not seem to realize this truth, that *now* was the time for them to awaken to who they were in Christ Jesus and begin to allow the Spirit to bring their outer walk into conformity with their reborn inner natures. That's living life in the Spirit, the essence of Christianity.

"Let us not be desirous of vain glory, provoking one another, envying one another" (v. 26). If we are now new creatures in Christ, the Son of the Living God who freely gives us all things to enjoy, there is no longer any need of our seeking after power or position to make us somebody in the eyes of others. Again, we do not need to act like unbelievers. Sinners seek power. We need to seek the kingdom.

We can now freely receive everything we need for righteous living directly from our loving heavenly Father. All we have to do is ask, remembering the words of our Lord Jesus that when we pray, we are to believe we receive and it will be ours. If this is true, none of us ever needs to be jealous of anyone else or to be envious of anything he has, whether material possessions, power, position, health, or any other good thing. As heirs of God and joint heirs of Christ, all things are ours. Therefore, living life in the Spirit not only frees us from bondage to the Law, it also frees us from bondage to our own selfish nature that causes us so much grief and pain.

13
Ministry of Restoration
Galatians 6:1–18

Restoring in a Spirit of Meekness

Galatians 6:1

Brethren, if a man be overtaken in a fault, ye which are spiritual, restore such an one in the spirit of meekness; considering thyself, lest thou also be tempted.

"Brethren" (v. 1). Notice, Paul began this last chapter by addressing the Galatians as *brethren*. This is a title used in the New Testament only between fellow believers. In falling for the deception of the legalistic mentality, these people have fallen "short of the glory of God" (Romans 3:23 NIV). But by using the form of address, *brethren*, Paul indicated the Galatians were still members of the family of God. They may have failed, but it did not change their relationship with God, their heavenly Father.

"If a man be overtaken in a fault" (v. 1). The Greek word for "fault" here is *paraptoma*, which is sometimes translated as "sin," but which Strong defines as "a side-slip (lapse or deviation), i.e. (unintentional) error or (willful) transgression." 1 This word differs from the usual word used to express "sin." That word is *harmartia*, which Strong defines as an "*offence*."2 In the Greek it implies *missing the mark,* while *paraptoma* implies *an unintentional blunder.*

By the use of this word *paraptoma* to describe what the Galatians have done, Paul was saying they had unintentionally stumbled and fallen into error. Their action was a sin, in the sense that it was an offence against God because by it they missed the mark of His intention for them. Yet it was not as though they had deliberately and purposefully chosen to disobey Him or rebel against Him. They had simply blundered.

Most of these people were completely unaware that by walking into the trap of legalism they had missed the mark. They had not realized what they had done. As we saw in Galatians 3, the reason they had been so foolish as to fall for this deception was because they had been "hypnotized" by the shrewd Judaizers who had taken advantage of their ignorance and gullibility.

"Ye which are spiritual, restore such an one" (v. 1). The question arises in such cases: If a person has fallen into error like this, how can he be rescued from his error and restored to fellowship with God and his fellow believers? Many Christians have found themselves mired in something they know is wrong, but they don't know how to extricate themselves from it. What they need is someone who is spiritual enough to perceive their need and concerned enough to show them, not so much where they missed the mark, but how to get back on track again.

That's where you and I come in. As the sons of God, our calling and ministry is not so much to rescue those caught in sin as it is to warn others before they become trapped by it. Many times our fellow believers are suffering just as much from the wages of sin as the unbelievers. That's why Paul wanted these people in Galatia to understand it is not their job to condemn those who have stumbled and fallen into error, but to be the instruments by which the Lord can reach out and restore them to fellowship with the Lord. The church of Jesus Christ needs to learn it is here to redeem from debt, not to foreclose on it!

The Greek word for "restore" in this verse means "to reset a dislocated bone." Notice, the bone is not broken, but dislocated. This can be painful in our physical bodies and also in the body of Christ. We who are spiritual are to restore that person to the place of full usage in the body of Christ. Legalism puts him out of place. Love restores him.

Some Christians seem to think their failure and lack of fellowship with the Lord will not affect anyone but themselves. That's not so. As the bride of Christ, we are to our Lord what Eve was to Adam, bone of his bone and flesh of his flesh (Genesis 2:23). The psalmist said of the righteous man that the Lord "keepeth all his bones: not one of them is broken" (Psalm 34:20). Since Jesus is the personification of the righteous man, none of His bones were ever broken, in fulfillment of Scripture. (See John 19:36.) Yet earlier David spoke prophetically of Jesus' suffering on the cross, saying, "all my bones are out of joint" (Psalm 22:14).

As "bones" of the body of Christ, we cannot be broken, but we can be "out of joint." A bone out of joint is painful. Paul told us in 1 Corinthians 12:26, when one member of the body suffers, the whole body suffers with it. None of us should ever think that his suffering is his alone, or that his failure or blunder does not have an effect upon other members of the body. That's why people of prominence in the body of Christ must be very careful of their words and actions because their mistakes can be costly not only to themselves but especially to the hundreds and thousands of people who look to them for spiritual leadership.

Sin, whether *paraptoma* (a blunder) or *harmartia* (an offence), affects our fellowship with our Father in heaven and our brothers and sisters here on earth. If it's not dealt with, it clogs the channel of communication and blessing between God and us, and consequently between us and those to whom we are to minister. It is vitally important we keep ourselves as free from sin as possible, so that

231

channel will remain free and clear of obstruction. As the saints of God, as those "which are spiritual," part of our ministry is the restoration of those of our number who have been "overtaken in a fault." In many ways, it is every bit as important to restore those who are saints as it is to make new ones.

"In the spirit of meekness; considering thyself, lest thou also be tempted" (Galatians 6:1). Do you recognize this "spirit of meekness" as one of the manifestations of love, the fruit of the Spirit? We who are spiritual (full of the Spirit of God) are to demonstrate meekness in restoring those who have fallen. Why? We remember the words of Solomon who warned that a haughty spirit goes before a fall (Proverbs 16:18). We are meek (gentle) with others who have fallen because we know if we are haughty, we ourselves are liable to fall into temptation just as they have done. We also know none of the other fruit gifts will operate in our lives as long as we are out of fellowship with God because of a haughty spirit.

When we come across someone who has fallen, it is the easiest thing in the world to become prideful. The devil will tempt us into thinking how glad we are such a thing could never happen to us because of our great spirituality. But such a thought is itself an evidence of pride. Iin a sense, when we think that way we have already fallen, we reject that thought and refuse to allow it to take root in our hearts.

To look down upon the fallen is to sit in judgment upon them. When we judge someone because he has sinned, we have just joined him in his fall by our sin of passing judgment. Actually, in that case, we are in worse shape than he is because while he's repenting and coming back to God we're looking down upon him in pride and thus separating ourselves from God. Among the sevens sins listed in Proverbs 6:16–19 as those God hates most, number one is a proud look. God does not like pride.

232

Sharing Burdens

Verses 2–5

Bear ye one another's burdens, and so fulfil the law of Christ. For if a man think himself to be something, when he is nothing, he deceiveth himself. But let every man prove his own work, and then shall he have rejoicing in himself alone, and not in another. For every man shall bear his own burden.

"Bear ye one another's burdens" (v. 2). Now at first glance, verse 2 and verse 5 of this passage might seem to contradict each other. One says we are to bear each other's burdens and the other says each person is to bear his own burden. We will look at this more in detail when we consider verse 5. Right now let's see why we are to share in carrying each other's burdens.

"And so fulfil the law of Christ" (v. 2). What law was Paul referring to when he spoke of burden-sharing as fulfilling "the law of Christ"? This is the law where we are to love our God with all our hearts, and love our neighbor as ourselves. If we truly love our neighbor as our own selves, we will not only refrain from doing him wrong, but we will also actively seek to do him good. Are we satisfied with just not hurting ourselves? Doesn't our self-love push us to much greater lengths, to see we are made happy? That's why we are told to bear each other's burdens. By helping our neighbor bear his load (because we love him as ourselves), we are bearing our own burden because when he became us, his burden became ours. No longer is there your burden and my burden; now there is only *our* burden.

"For if a man think himself to be something, when he is nothing, he deceiveth himself" (v. 3). When we go to lift up someone who has fallen into sin, we must be careful not to think more highly of ourselves than we ought. We must remember we, too, are always liable to fall just as he has. This attitude will keep us from thinking we're something when we're really nothing.

Paul did not say that we are nothing. That would be a denial of his whole teaching throughout the New Testament. Every person is important to God. Each of us is somebody in God's eyes. We were important enough to Him, He sacrificed His own Son so we could live.

Paul did not mean we are to assume an attitude of self-depreciation. He simply meant we are to avoid an attitude of self-exaltation. We are to keep ourselves from becoming self-righteous. Otherwise we will be in danger of pride, of thinking that we are the ones who lift up the poor from the dust and the needy out of the dunghill. (See Psalm 113:7.)

Nowhere is humility needed more than in the process of restoring the fallen to fellowship with God because then there is a real danger of thinking we're doing it by our own power or because of our own righteousness. A person who thinks this way deceives himself. It's bad enough to be deceived by Satan or by others, but it is more tragic to deceive yourself.

"But let every man prove his own work, and then shall he have rejoicing in himself alone, and not in another" (v. 4). In the Old Testament, David said, "Examine me, O LORD, and prove me; try my reins and my heart" (Psalm 26:2). But in the New Testament, Paul said, "Let a man examine himself" (1 Corinthians 11:28), and "Examine yourselves, whether ye be in the faith" (2 Corinthians 13:5). The difference is the presence of the indwelling Holy Spirit to enlighten our reborn human spirit. Under the old covenant, God examined people from the outside. Under the new covenant, He has written His laws on our hearts God now trusts us to examine ourselves on the inside in the light of the law of love.

This is what Paul was telling the Galatians: "Don't judge others by what they are able to do. Instead, examine your own work. Then you can be happy about what you have done, not jealous or angry because of what someone has or has not accomplished." In other words, while we are to examine our own selves, we are not to run around examining (judging) others. That's not our business; that's strictly between them and God. "For every man shall bear his own burden" (Galatians 6:5). This verse seems to contradict verse 2, which says we should bear one another's burdens. The reason they seem contradictory is because two different Greek words are translated *burden* in the King James Version. In verse 2 the Greek word is *baros*, which means a *heavy* "burden (-some), weight." 3 In verse 5 the Greek word is *phortion*. According to Strong, a *phortion* was *"an invoice"* or a *bill of lading*. In this sense, it figuratively represented "a task or service," as well as an individual "burden."4

When Paul spoke in verse 2 of our carrying each other's *baros*, he was speaking of a large and burdensome weight, whereas in verse 5 when he said each one of us must carry his own *phortion*, he meant we must carry out our own individually assigned task or service. The two are not synonymous. In one instance, we are called upon to help shoulder a weight that has become too heavy for one individual to bear by himself. This is the load of legalism brought on by the fault of sin. In the second, we are reminded not to shirk our own individual responsibility or duty. We help others come to the place of strength to carry their own *phortion* again. One case involves a joint effort, the other an individual effort. Both are part of our overall task as laborers together with Christ.

235

Sharing All Good Things

Verse 6

Let him that is taught in the word communicate unto him that teacheth in all good things.

The word translated "communicate" is the Greek word *koinonia,* which is often used to indicate *fellowship* or *community.* It also has the connotation of communication between people or of distribution of something among them. It is in this sense Paul was using it in this verse. His meaning is brought out clearer in the New American Standard Bible: "And let the one who is taught the word share all good things with him who teaches."

As we proceed, we will see this idea of sharing "all good things" with those who "share the Word" establishes the theme of the next four verses. What Paul was introducing in this verse is the basic principle of sowing and reaping, which he developed further in verses 7 through 10.

The Galatians had been giving large sums of money and goods to the legalistic teachers. Now it was time they shared these blessings with those who taught "good things" from God's Word.

Why did Paul suddenly switch from the subject of restoring to fellowship those who have fallen into sin to this topic of sharing finances and blessings? This is actually not a switch from one theme to another; it is the continuation and development of the one central theme of chapter 6: *koinonia.*

Paul was teaching the Galatians about community, the shared life. He wanted them to understand that in Christ they were one with each other, that they shared together one common faith, one common heritage, one common commandment. That's why he spoke of lifting up the brother who has fallen into sin, of bearing the burden too heavy for one brother to carry alone, of "communicating" the good things of life with the brother who "communicates" the Word to all.

He wanted these people to realize they were not in this thing alone; it is all for one and one for all. He also wanted them to know nothing they gave to each other is ever really lost because God will make sure it is returned to them in multiplied abundance so there will be plenty for all.

Law or Principle?

Verses 7-8

Be not deceived; God is not mocked: for whatsoever a man soweth, that shall he also reap. For he that soweth to his flesh shall of the flesh reap corruption; but he that soweth to the Spirit shall of the Spirit reap life everlasting.

"Be not deceived" (v. 7). It is likely this issue of sharing arose because the legalistic Judaizers who came in behind Paul were draining the Galatians of their material goods, using them to finance the spread of their religion of the Law. In fact, it was probably strict adherence to the Old Testament law of tithing causing the problem. Paul was writing the Galatians to free them from the letter of the Law with its binding restrictions based on obligation and duty. He was writing to set them free through the principle of sowing and reaping, which releases from obligation but results in manifold blessings to the one who gives as well as to the one who receives.

The principle of tithing is far different from the law of tithing. Tithing was a part of the Old Testament law, but Paul was reminding the Galatians they were not under Law, but grace. He wanted them to understand giving was a definite part of the overall plan of God, but it was never intended to be an obligation or duty. Instead, it was to be the normal way of life for those whose spirits had been born anew by the Holy Spirit of God.

Like Abraham who instituted it, the principle of tithing existed long before the Law came into existence. The coming of the Holy Spirit freed those who are in Christ Jesus from the restrictions of the Law that they might live in the fullness of the Spirit. The primary fruit of that Spirit is love.

The reason you and I tithe today is not because we are demanded to do so by Law, but because we are moved to do so by love. The Law came by Moses, but love was shed abroad in our hearts by the Holy Spirit. The Law was carved in stone; it is external, cold, dead. The love of God is written on the heart; it is internal, warm, alive. The Law demands, but grace gives. That's the principle Paul wanted the Galatians to understand.

"God is not mocked: for whatsoever a man soweth, that shall he also reap" (v. 7). Traditionally this verse has been taught in connection to sin. For years it was used as a warning that we were not to delude ourselves into thinking we could "get away" with sinning. Because of such teaching we developed a kind of "Big Brother Is Watching" complex. Verses like this one were a constant reminder to us to beware because sooner or later our sin would find us out. That is true, to a degree, but it is only the negative side of the principle of sowing and reaping.

An evil harvest occurs only when bad seed has been planted. There is another side to this story, one that only recently has begun to be publicized. That side says good seed produces a harvest of good, both for the one who sows and the one who reaps.

Part of the reason for the traditional negative interpretation of this verse is an attitude of fear and mistrust. In the past, pastors were reluctant to preach the complete message of liberty in Christ because they were afraid if their people knew they were free there would be nothing to "keep them in line." Verses like this were dug up as a sort of warning.

Whether true or not, it was not really the heart of Paul's message to the Galatians. What he was stressing here is not fear, but freedom from fear. He was underscoring his message of the shared life by assuring the Galatian believers they should never be afraid to give because God has established a principle of life that guarantees no one can ever give himself poor. This verse is not so much a warning about reaping the wages of sin as much as it is a promise of reaping the fruit of the Spirit.

The principle of sowing and reaping runs throughout the Bible. In Mark 4 Jesus taught a parable about the sower and the seed. When His disciples showed they didn't understand it, the Lord told them in essence, "If you don't understand this parable, you won't understand any of them" (v. 11). He was saying all teaching in the Word of God revolves around the sowing and reaping principle.

This principle is very simple: Whatever a person sows, he will reap. That's why Jesus taught the people of His day to be givers because what they gave would be returned to them, "good measure, pressed down, and shaken together" (Luke 6:38). He did not mean by this teaching, they were to give in order to receive; that would be self-centered rather than other-centered. Jesus' message was the same as Paul's. "Don't be afraid to give to those in need; you won't come up short. I can assure you there's plenty more where that came from!"

The "seed faith" principle works to the degree we understand it is an assurance that sets us free to give, not an enticement to get us to give. That concept is as false as the teaching we give because the Law requires us to. One is legalistic; the other is materialistic. The true principle of giving is love. The first is Law-motivated, the second is profit-motivated, but the third is love-motivated. Paul wanted these people to know which of these three motivations God rewards.

"For he that soweth to his flesh shall of the flesh reap corruption but he that soweth to the Spirit shall of the Spirit reap life everlasting" (Galatians 6:8). Paul was telling the Galatians if they sowed to the lusts and passions of their flesh, they would reap lust and passion. Giving in obedience to Law and giving simply to get are both means of sowing to the flesh. The nature of flesh is like that of the ground: it will produce whatever is sown in it.

Since the flesh is destined for corruption, all it can produce is corruption; but the Spirit (or the spirit) is different. It is eternal, incorruptible. It, too, will reap whatever is sown in it. Therefore, we want to sow to our spirits because the product will remain throughout eternity. We will reap a bumper crop of good that will never see corruption. That's a crop worth investing in.

If We Faint Not

Verse 9

And let us not be weary in well doing: for in due season we shall reap, if we faint not.

There are two ways to guarantee a crop failure when sowing spiritual seed. The first is to sow it unto the flesh. Since the flesh is carnal, it cannot reproduce spiritual seed. The second is to neglect the seed sown in spiritual ground. Once the seed is sown, it must be carefully tended. The ground must be cultivated, the seed watered, and the grass and weeds removed. All this is hard work, as any farmer can tell you. Living by the principle of sowing and reaping requires diligence, but it is well worth it when harvest time comes.

The seed sown in good ground will never produce a harvest if the sower "faints" because of the trials and frustrations brought on by the enemy who comes in to sow tares (weeds) among the wheat (good seed). The writer of Hebrews understood this truth when he warned "lest ye be wearied and faint in your minds" (Hebrews 12:3).

It is not in the spirit we are tempted to give up; it's always in our minds. It is there the battle takes place as the devil attacks in an effort to cause us to give up. We must remember we are never beaten until we decide we are beaten. As long as our minds are firmly set, the devil and his demons are powerless to prevent our seed from producing a harvest of fruit. The time to rejoice in that harvest is not when it is finally brought in, but while the seed is still in the ground. That's faith in action, faith that keeps us from digging up the seed before it has had a chance to reproduce.

Do Good unto All Men

Verse 10

As we have therefore opportunity, let us do good unto all men, especially unto them who are of the household of faith.

Paul taught that as Christians we are to do good to everyone, but most of all to other believers. We are to love the world, even our enemy, but not like we love our brothers and sisters in Christ.

Paul wanted the Law put away along with all its fruit. When believers become legalistic, they become judges of one another instead of those who love and care. Now that the Galatians had heard Paul's message, they needed to treat each other as the Lord treats them. God loves the sinner but not like He loves His own children. We need to do the same. We love the sinner and want him to be born again, but we do not fellowship with him as we do with other believers.

241

How Large a Letter

Verse 11

Ye see how large a letter I have written unto you with mine own hand.

From here to the end of the book, Paul was concluding his remarks so he jumped quickly from one thought to another. This particular verse has been the subject of great debate in Christian theological circles for many years. Those who hold to the theory that healing is not part of the Atonement cite it to prove Paul himself was sick throughout his life and ministry. They point out here he admits to having to write in large letters, probably because he suffered from some serious eye disease. Others say the Greek word translated "letter" refers to the epistle itself not to the individual letters of it. Therefore, they say this verse indicates Paul had no such vision impairment.

The truth is, in Greek as in English, this word "letter" is used for both an alphabetical letter and an epistle, so it could be taken either way. However, it does seem more likely Paul was referring to the epistle than to the alphabetical letter because the word is in the singular: "See what a large letter I have written," not, "See what large letters I have written."

It is possible, however, there is an even more logical explanation of Paul's meaning, especially when we note Galatians is not a large epistle compared to others such as Romans or 1 and 2 Corinthians. Could it be Paul had more to say than is recorded here in this one rather short letter? In many ancient manuscripts, the letter to the Galatians is followed by the letter to the Hebrews. Just as there has been a long debate about the meaning of this word "letter," there has also been a lengthy and inconclusive debate about whether Paul was the author of the book of Hebrews. Some hold it was written about the same time as Galatians. The reason Paul's authorship of Hebrews is questioned is because in all his other books he begins by identifying himself right off (as in Galatians 1:1: "Paul, an apostle."). Hebrews begins immediately with teaching.

Yet the two books are parallel in many ways. Both speak to the same theme of the Law in contrast to grace. In reading both epistles, I am led to wonder if perhaps Paul wrote them both at the same time, Galatians serving as the introduction to the book of Hebrews that followed. This would make the "large letter" Paul referred to. In this case, the first part of the letter would have been sent to the Gentile converts in Galatia who would have received it with enthusiasm and interest. The second part would have been sent out to converted Jews in Jerusalem among whom a letter from Paul might have met with much less enthusiastic acceptance. If so, this would explain Paul's not identifying its authorship. If these hypotheses are correct, they would lend support to the theory that what Paul was saying here in Galatians 6:11 was, "See what a long letter I have written to you people there in Galatia."

In any case, the claim that this verse "proves" Paul suffered a chronic eye disease is unfounded, as is the assertion that healing in the Atonement is "disproven" by such isolated references. It is amazing to me how some will hang on to such vague Scriptures to disprove something so plainly brought out in important passages of the Word of God. Physical healing is one of the major works of Jesus on the cross. (See Psalm 103:3; Isaiah 53:3-5, 10; Matthew 8:17.)

Glory only in the Cross

Verses 12-14

As many as desire to make a fair show in the flesh, they constrain you to be circumcised; only lest they should suffer persecution for the cross of Christ. For neither they

243

*themselves who are circumcised keep the law; but desire
to have you circumcised, that they may glory in your
flesh. But God forbid that I should glory, save in the cross
of our Lord Jesus Christ, by whom the world is crucified
unto me, and I unto the world.*

"As many as desire to make a fair show in the flesh,
they constrain you to be circumcised; only lest they
should suffer persecution for the cross of Christ" (v. 12).

The meaning of this verse is made clearer in the New
International Version, which reads, "Those who want to
make a good impression outwardly are trying to compel
you to be circumcised. The only reason they do this is
to avoid being persecuted for the cross of Christ." This
reminds us of Paul's statement in Galatians 5:11: "And I,
brethren, if I yet preach circumcision, why do I yet suffer
persecution? then is the offence of the cross ceased."

Paul was arguing that those preaching circumcision
to the Galatians were doing so because they wanted to
gain glory for themselves and avoid being persecuted for
preaching the true Gospel of the cross.

"For neither they themselves who are circumcised keep
the law; but desire to have you circumcised, that they may
glory in your flesh" (Galatians 6:13). Paul pointed out the
contradiction in the message these Jews were preaching. If
the Galatians were required to be circumcised to keep the
Law, why didn't their teachers keep the Law themselves?
In Acts 15 Peter made the statement to the church counsel
in Jerusalem: "Now therefore why tempt ye God, to put
a yoke upon the neck of the [Gentile] disciples, which
neither our fathers nor we were able to bear?" (v. 10).

In other words, Paul was asking the Galatians, "Why
do these Jews demand you Gentiles be circumcised and
keep a law they themselves cannot keep?" Then he gave
the answer: "that they may glory in your flesh." "They are
just doing it because it makes them appear more zealous

for God. It takes away attention from their own failings and calls attention to yours. They can't keep the Law, but they can make themselves look righteous by subjecting other people to it. It's all for show. They just want to bring glory to themselves."

"But God forbid that I should glory, save in the cross of our Lord Jesus Christ" (v. 14). Paul knew better than to try to bring glory upon himself. Instead he placed the glory where it rightfully belongs, on the One who gave His life that we might live. We should not glory in our faith, but only in the Author and Finisher of our faith. Nor should we glory in our salvation, but in the One who purchased that salvation for us with His own precious blood. David reminded us: "Salvation belongeth unto the LORD" (Psalm 3:8). After his sin with Bathsheba, David prayed to God: "Restore unto me the joy of thy salvation" (Psalm 51:12). We have been given His salvation.

Glorying in our prosperity or our health or our success is also wrong because none of these things was originally ours. We have simply received them as a free gift in the Great Exchange. Jesus gave us His riches and healing and righteousness in exchange for our poverty, sickness, and sin. We should say with Paul, "God forbid that I should glory in anything other than the cross of Jesus Christ!"

Dead to the World

"By whom the world is crucified unto me, and I unto the world" (Galatians 6:14). Notice, there is a double crucifixion here. Paul said that the world was crucified to him, and he was crucified to it. As far as the world is concerned, you and I are dead. That's fine, as long as we remember that, like the flesh, the world with its lusts and affections is dead to us. The life we now live in the world we live to the glory of the One who loved us and gave Himself for us.

245

A New Rule

Verses 15–16

For in Christ Jesus neither circumcision availeth any thing, nor uncircumcision, but a new creature. And as many as walk according to this rule, peace be on them, and mercy, and upon the Israel of God.

"For in Christ Jesus neither circumcision availeth any thing, nor uncircumcision, but a new creature" (v. 15). Notice, it is only "in Christ Jesus" that circumcision avails nothing. There is a natural, physical benefit to be gained from circumcision of the flesh. But in Christ Jesus, in the spiritual realm, that outward physical change is of no consequence at all because God looks not at the flesh of a person but at the heart.

The Living Bible paraphrases this verse like this: "It doesn't make any difference now whether we have been circumcised or not; what counts is whether we really have been changed into new and different people." The thing that matters to God is the inside of a person, not the outside. The New Birth, the receiving of a new spirit within, becoming a new spiritual creature, walking in the Spirit (or spirit), is what really counts with God, not what is done in the flesh.

If no one is justified by acts of the flesh but by becoming a new creature in Christ, then it makes sense that no one is condemned by acts of the flesh. That's what Paul meant when he said now that we are new creatures in Christ, now that we walk not after the flesh but after the Spirit, there is no condemnation to us (Romans 8:1). Once a person is born again, once he becomes a new spiritual creature, then he is no longer under condemnation because he is no longer a subject of the kingdom of flesh but has become a citizen of the kingdom of the Spirit.

Thus his new spiritual life has nothing to do with acts of the flesh. This explains what Paul was talking about when he said he was dead to the world and it to him. The world is carnal; the believer is spirit. The two have no connection: "For what fellowship hath righteousness with unrighteousness? and what communion hath light with darkness?" (2 Corinthians 6:14).

"And as many as walk according to this rule, peace be on them, and mercy" (v. 16). So then we are "under Law," not the Mosaic Law, the Law written in stone, but the "Law" (the rule) of love, written in our hearts. When we live by this rule of the new life in Christ Jesus, we have peace and mercy ruling in our lives.

"Peace be on them, and mercy, and upon the Israel of God" (v. 16). This expression the "Israel of God" refers to the born-again Jews. Even though Paul was the apostle to the Gentiles, he never lost his burden and love for his fellow Jews, many of whom were born again, but who had no real understanding of who and what they now were in Christ Jesus. Wouldn't this blessing pronounced upon them by Paul serve as a marvelous introduction to the book of Hebrews, which does go into great detail to explain to Jew and Gentile alike who and what we all are in Him whom God has "appointed heir of all things" (Hebrews 1:2)?

No More Trouble

Verse 17

From henceforth let no man trouble me: for I bear in my body the marks of the Lord Jesus.

Who had been troubling Paul? The legalistic Judaizers. Religious people. They had persecuted him for years because he preached the liberating Gospel of Jesus Christ, the message you have been reading in these pages.

Paul was saying, "If you want to know what these religious Jews are really like, look at my body. I carry the marks of their persecution. I have been beaten, stoned, and persecuted for my stand of liberty. But I do not consider these marks of persecution, but marks for the Lord Jesus."

As strange as it may seem, religious people still oppose Paul's message. They just can't believe God would set people totally free to live by their own spirits. The reason they can't accept this truth is because they have no confidence in people. The reason they have no confidence in people is because they have none in themselves.

TNeither did Paul, the author of this epistle: "For we are the circumcision, which worship God in the spirit, and rejoice in Christ Jesus, and have no confidence in the flesh" (Philippians 3:3.) Yet in chapter 1 of that same epistle he told the Philippians, "And having this confidence, I know that I shall abide and continue with you all for your furtherance and joy of faith" (v. 25). What confidence was it Paul had in these people? The answer is found in verse 6 of chapter 1: "Being confident of this very thing, that he which hath begun a good work in you will perform it until the day of Jesus Christ."

Now we see where our confidence lies, not in our flesh or our abilities. Our confidence to live free of outward rules and regulations lies solely and totally in Him who began the good work in us. It is He who will perform it — not us. That's why we can be liberated to live by the Spirit and why we can set others free to live by the Spirit. The reason we can live free is because we are crucified with Christ; nevertheless, we live; yet not we, but Christ lives in us: and the lives we now live in the flesh we live by the faith of the Son of God, who loved us, and gave Himself for us (Colossians 2:20). When we live that way, we do not frustrate the grace of God.

To live like this will bring upon us persecution. Religion will not stand idly by and allow us to live free or to set others at liberty so they can live free. Paul knew that. That's why he told the Galatians to stand fast in the liberty wherein Christ had made them free (Galatians 5:1). He knew what we have learned: religion is the worst persecutor of the church that has ever existed. It has been the cause of more martyred saints than any other force in history. Yet it goes virtually unchallenged, even in our day, because it passes itself off as spiritual fervor.

Religion is not confined to the established orthodoxy; it can be found in every level of society, both within the church of Jesus Christ and without. Like sin, religion is not a physical action but a spiritual attitude. It is the attitude of the Pharisee who prayed, "Thank You, Lord, that I'm not like this poor sinner." It's also the attitude of James and John, Jesus' closest disciples, who wanted to call down fire and brimstone on those Samaritans who did not receive them as they thought they ought to be received. Religion is not the exclusive privilege of the theologians in their stained-glass cathedrals; it can be just as prevalent among revivalists in their traveling tents. A haughty spirit is not a restricted quality; anyone can have one. That's why we who oppose it the strongest must be the most careful of it, "lest [we] also be tempted" (Galatians 6:1).

Benediction

Verse 18

Brethren, the grace of our Lord Jesus Christ be with your spirit. Amen.

Meet Bob Yandian

Since 1980, Bob Yandian has been pastor of Grace Church, with a vibrant and growing congregation in his hometown of Tulsa, Oklahoma. He has a weekly teaching radio broadcast called *Precepts with Bob Yandian*. He is founder of *Grace School of Ministry*, a two-year ministerial training school.

Bob is widely acknowledged as one of the most knowledgeable Bible teachers of this generation. His practical insight and wisdom into the Word of God has helped countless people around the world live successfully in every arena of the daily Christian life.

In addition to the sale of over 200,000 books, CDs, and tapes world-wide, more than 22,000 books, CDs, and tapes have been donated to Bible schools, missionaries, prisoners, and people in need throughout the United States and around the world through *Bob Yandian Ministries*.

Bob attended *Southwestern College* and is also a graduate of *Trinity Bible College*. He has served as both instructor and Dean of Instructors at *Rhema Bible Training Center* in Broken Arrow, Oklahoma.

Bob has traveled extensively throughout the United States and internationally, taking his powerful and easy to apply teachings that bring stability and hope to hungry hearts everywhere. He has authored over thirty books and has been called "a pastor to pastors."

Bob and his wife, Loretta, have been married for over thirty years, are the parents of two grown married children, and have four grandchildren. Bob and Loretta Yandian reside in Tulsa, Oklahoma

Books by Bob Yandian

Decently & In Order

Proverbs

Ephesians

Resurrection

Faith's Destination

Righteousness: God's Gift to You

Family Defined

Spirit Controlled Life

Forever Changed

The Fullness of the Spirit

From Just Enough to Overflowing

Understanding the End Times

Grace: From Here to Eternity

Unlimited Partnership

How Deep are the Stripes?

Joel

Leadership Secrets of David the King

One Flesh

One Nation Under God

BIBLE NOTES

Acts Notes Pt 1

Acts Notes Pt 2

Colossians Notes

James Notes

Philippians Notes

To Contact Bob Yandian Ministries

Email:
bym@gracetulsa.com

Phone:
1-800-284-0595
Local: (918) 250-2207

Fax:
(918) 317-5025

Mailing Address:
Bob Yandian Ministries
9610 S. Garnett Rd.
Broken Arrow, OK 74012

bobyandian.com